THE ECONOMY OF EUROPE IN AN AGE OF CRISIS

The Economy of Europe
in an Age of Crisis

1600-1750

JAN DE VRIES

Associate Professor of History, University of California at Berkeley

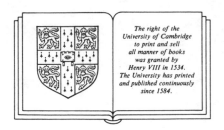

*The right of the
University of Cambridge
to print and sell
all manner of books
was granted by
Henry VIII in 1534.
The University has printed
and published continuously
since 1584.*

CAMBRIDGE UNIVERSITY PRESS

CAMBRIDGE

LONDON   NEW YORK   NEW ROCHELLE

MELBOURNE   SYDNEY

Published by the Press Syndicate of the University of Cambridge
The Pitt Building, Trumpington Street, Cambridge CB2 1RP
32 East 57th Street, New York, NY 10022 USA
10 Stamford Road, Oakleigh, Melbourne 3166, Australia

First published 1976
Reprinted 1978, 1980, 1981, 1982, 1984, 1986, 1987

Printed in the United States of America

Library of Congress Cataloging in Publication Data
De Vries, Jan, 1943-
Economy of Europe in an age of crisis.
1. Europe-Economic conditions. 2. Europe-History.
I. Title
HC240.D48   330.9'4'055   75-30438
ISBN 0 521 21123 9 hardcovers
ISBN 0 521 29050 3 paperback

Contents

Tables, figures, and maps

To Jeannie

Preface

My chief defense against the charge of attempting a work that requires a wiser and more widely-read author than myself is that very few other scholars have, in fact, written general economic histories of early modern Europe. Although the last twenty years have witnessed an enormous advance in our knowledge of the European economy of this period, a persistent gap remains between the several good general histories of the medieval period and the crowd of works that treat the Industrial Revolution. One reason for this is probably the difficulty of summarizing and generalizing from the most recent scholarship on the early modern economy. That scholarship, centered in France, has taken the form of local and regional studies, and has focused its attention on the delineation of social and economic structures. In contrast, the economic history of later periods, and North American economic history in general, has been fascinated with the measurement and analysis of growth and development.

Integrating the wealth of detailed information now available about the structure of the European economy into a study that focuses on dynamic elements - on development in a broad sense - is the task of this volume. I have attempted a presentation that will be useful to both undergraduate and graduate students. For the latter, in particular, a relatively extensive set of references has been included at the back of the book directing the reader to the supporting literature.

Although this book proclaims itself to be an economic history of Europe, the reader will quickly notice that not all parts of Europe are equally represented. The author's limitations have combined with the character of the existing literature to slight the economic history of Slavic Europe. For this I have only apologies to offer.

The reader will also note that monetary values are occasionally cited, mostly in pounds sterling, Dutch guilders, or French livres tournois. What were these monetary units worth relative to modern currencies and relative to each other? The first question has no brief answer. I hope that in the context of this book the reader can get some sense of what 100,000 pounds sterling or 2 million guilders meant in the seventeenth century. One helpful clue is to remember that the daily wage of skilled manual labor in Holland, where wages may well have been the highest in Europe, were usually near 1 guilder per day throughout most of the seventeenth and eighteenth centuries. The second question is easier to answer. Exchange rates remained relatively stable in the century after about 1650, with 11 guilders or 16 livres tournois equal to 1 pound sterling and, thus, 1.5 livres tournois about equal to 1 guilder.

To the extent that this book is successful in its efforts to merge two approaches to European economic history and to address two types of reader, much credit must go to the many colleagues who have helped me in this project. The footnotes provide (inadequate) acknowledgement of my indebtedness to hundreds of scholars on whose works I have relied. In addition I wish to mention several colleagues who have provided more direct assistance. For a decade, Harry Miskimin, the editor of this series, has given me much needed encouragement in this and other endeavors. Innumerable improvements in style and content are the result of William Parker's careful criticism. Discussions with him always seem to have a clarifying effect on my thought. Other colleagues who have notably assisted in various parts of this work are

Stanley Brandes, Carlo Cipolla, Nicholas Crafts, Paul David, Thomas Laqueur, Franklin Mendels, A.M. van der Woude, and Gavin Wright.

Wassenaar, The Netherlands   J. de Vries
April 1976

1
The age of crisis

Introduction

The subject of this book is the economic life of the five generations of Europeans who lived in the last great epoch before the onset of industrialization. This epoch, variously labeled as traditional or classic Europe, or the *ancien régime,* stands between two periods of notable economic expansion. It begins as the long sixteenth-century expansion - which includes the organization of a world-wide network of trade links - sputters fitfully to its end. Around the mid-eighteenth century it is dissolved by a quickening of demographic and economic life that inaugurates a long secular expansion. Fundamentally shaped by the Industrial Revolution, this new expansion altered the most enduring structural characteristics of economic life to usher in the Brave New World that we inhabit today.

The economic history of the seventeenth and early eighteenth centuries has long attracted attention for what light it could shed on the periods that preceded and followed it: here one could perhaps find the causes of the exhaustion of the vast empires and early capitalism of the sixteenth century as well as the preconditions of modern industrialization. While this period forms an identifiable unit in economic history, it does not readily offer unifying themes for the historian. Perhaps for this reason many historians have focused their attention on the structure - the immutable features - of economic and social life in this period. Such work has uncovered much that we shall make use of, but the emphasis of this volume is placed on identifying patterns of crisis and change and analyzing the processes by which the economy of traditional Europe was transformed.

The unfolding of economic life, even in the absence of dramatic new inventions or conquests, is shaped by irreversible processes. Modern economic theory relies heavily on the concept of stable equilibria toward which economic life tends to converge even though nudged away by some impulse. But, in fact, the varied impulses that affect an economy more often move it, however slightly, to new positions from which it is impossible to recapture precisely the former position. Of course, the existence of this historical dimension in all economic phenomena does not mean that economies are propelled irresistibly forward. On the contrary, the forces that gave momentum to the economic life of this period generated cleavages and had a pronounced differentiating impact. The period was seen by some nations as a golden age, or at least the precursor to one, while it was for others an era of decadence and collapse. For all, the heavy impress of the past unavoidably limited the possible responses to new opportunities and pressures. One of those pressures was created by the drive of several social groups - each in its own way - to grasp control of a new, more usable economic power.

The seventeenth century has sometimes been labeled an age of power, in reference to the bureaucratic and military muscle of the absolutist states. The label is also appropriate in describing an economy in which the energy of hundreds of thousands of east European serfs was needed to produce enough surplus grain to feed a handful of west European cities, tens of thousands of Spanish muleteers were kept occupied in supplying a single city, Madrid, with necessities, millions of slaves were shackled to the Brazilian and

Caribbean plantations to supply Europe with sugar, and untold thousands of horses were doomed to a life of endless circling while harnessed to grain mills and industrial machines.

Resources such as these - cumbersome and difficult to control - were the foremost requirement for economic growth, and they did not come easily. Increasing their supply could not be accomplished without altering the very structure of the society, for they were hidden in an economy of households, villages, and economically autonomous market towns and small administrative cities. Primarily labor, but also foodstuffs, raw materials, and capital had to be liberated from this bound, localized economy to be marshaled for use in the larger-scale regional and international economies.

The merchants of Amsterdam and London, the administrators of Louis XIV's France, Gustavus Adolphus' Sweden, and Frederick William's Prussia, the military recruiters of the new standing armies all in their ways were working to open up the bound, local economy. There were, of course, powerful interests to defend the status quo, and the atmosphere of tension that necessarily arose was exacerbated by the crude tools used to increase the larger economy's claims on the local economy. Consequently the seventeenth century is marked by an unusual number of civil disturbances: aristocratic protests against the growth of the bureaucratic state and peasant revolts against new taxes, changed land tenure conditions, and food distribution measures that offended a sense of economic justice.

The tension and suspicion that accompany most assaults on settled practice were magnified in this period by the fact that the long sixteenth-century expansion of the European economy came to an end in the beginning decades of the century and a half under consideration in this volume. Thereafter political and social innovations in most of Europe had to accommodate to a new, more hostile economic environment.

The task of this chapter is to outline the characteristics of the economic crisis that settled in during the first half of the seventeenth century.

Population

The European population, which had grown remarkably from the late fifteenth century and had in many areas far surpassed the levels attained in the early fourteenth century, gradually ceased growing in the seventeenth century. This new era of population stagnation differed from its fourteenth-century predecessor in the great variation of its timing and severity among the regions of Europe. In some areas of the Mediterranean the cessation of growth began in the 1570s while in some northern regions the growth trends did not break until the 1660s. Similarly, some areas suffered major reversals while others noticed only a check in the rate of growth. In any case, by the 1630s the rapid expansion of the labor force, which had been the chief instrument of increased output and relative price changes, was no more.

The most destructive demographic reversal hit central Europe. Around the numerous battlegrounds of the Thirty Years' War, economic dislocation and military operations combined with plague epidemics, particularly in 1628, 1635, and 1638, to decimate populations. In Hither Pomerania and Mecklenburg the population fell by 40 percent. Although certain principalities, particularly along the North Sea and in the Alpine regions, suffered much less, the population of the Holy Roman Empire as a whole probably declined by well over a quarter in the 1630s and 40s. The mid-seventeenth century brought destruction on a similar scale to Poland, while the Danish-Swedish war of 1658-60 occasioned a sudden 20 percent decline in the Danish population.[1]

The Mediterranean formed the other major region of declining population. Here, too, the pattern showed great variation. During the first half of the seventeenth century,

Italy as a whole declined from 13 to 11 million inhabitants, while northern Italy, the industrial heartland of Europe, lost a quarter of its population. In Castile the great plague of 1599-1600 was only the first of a series of reversals (both man-made and God-inflicted) that wiped out a quarter of the population by 1650. The peripheral territories of the Iberian peninsula were less hard hit, but in the early eighteenth century Spain's population still stood a full million below the 8.5 million it had attained in the 1590s.[2]

The population did not decline in northwestern Europe. Although the Southern Netherlands endured loss from both war and emigration in the 1570s and 80s, thereafter a recovery set in that lasted until the 1660s. In the Dutch Republic and in England a substantial population growth was continuous until the 1660s.[3]

In viewing these population patterns, we can carve western and central Europe into three zones (see Table 1). A Mediterranean zone, encompassing Iberia and Italy, recovered its early seventeenth-century losses only toward 1750. A central zone, encompassing France, Switzerland, and Germany, showed a modest growth over the 150-year period, most of it

Table 1. *Population of Europe (in millions)*

Zone	1600	1700	1750	1800
I. Mediterranean [a]	23.6	22.7	27.0	32.7
Index	100	96	114	139
II. Central [b]	35.0	36.2	41.3	53.2
Index	100	103	118	152
III. North and West [c]	12.0	16.1	18.3	25.9
Index	100	134	153	216
Total	70.6	75.0	86.6	111.8
Index	100	106	123	158

[a] Spain, Portugal, Italy. [b] France, Switzerland, Germany.
[c] England, Scotland, Ireland, Low Countries, Scandinavia.

coming, as in the Mediterranean, toward 1750. The third zone comprises the Low Countries, the British Isles, and Scandinavia. Here the mid-eighteenth-century population exceeded by half the 1600 levels. While nearly half of that growth had occurred by 1650, the century after 1650 was one of a distinctly diminished rate of growth, but not of utter stagnation. Were our data sufficient, a fourth zone could be distinguished in eastern Europe. The populations of Poland and Hungary almost certainly sustained a great decrease in the seventeenth century, but the timing and extent of the recovery are not known.

During the century and a half under review here, the European population grew by less than a quarter, at a long-term annual rate of only 0.14 percent, far below either the preceding or the following century. If this growth rate is unimpressive, what is impressive, and what profoundly affected economic life, was the redistribution of population. As Table 1 demonstrates, the northern and western zones gained relative to the rest of Europe. The decisive shift came in the fifty years after 1600, when the population of northern and western Europe rose from 50 to over 70 percent of that of the Mediterranean zone. Later in this volume more data will show that there also occurred a significant redistribution within the zones as types of cities and agrarian regions experienced quite varied fortunes.

Why did the long-term demographic expansion of the sixteenth century come to an end? Was the new trend a response to changed economic conditions or did it provoke such changes? The first step in answering these questions is to examine the birth and death rates, the immediate variables that determine population growth or decline. The classic connection between economic conditions and death rates, linked to the name of Thomas Malthus, predicts that a growing population is likely to outstrip the economy's ability to support it. The population's health is thereby endangered by famine and malnutrition. Could Europe have reached an economic ceiling in the early seventeenth century in which a precarious balance between population and food supply was constantly threatened by inadequate harvests? Fernand Braudel, the historian of the Mediterranean basin, believes such a ceiling was attained in the 1580s, and E. Le Roy Ladurie, writing of the southern French province of Languedoc, explains the cessation of growth thereby invoking Malthusian crises. Indeed, detailed studies of individual villages and districts have identified demographic crises in this most densely populated of large nations. During the span of a few months or a year the death rate rose to a level several times higher than normal. The mortality struck suddenly although, in retrospect, it might have been predicted, for low grain reserves and a poor harvest combining to force prices upward often preceded the crisis. During this period the survivors, witnesses to the disaster, postponed their marriages, failed to conceive children, and, if they could, took to the road to flee the scene of tragedy. When the high mortality had passed social and economic life took steps to adjust: a spate of marriages and conceptions followed, and within a few years much - perhaps all - of the human loss had been made good.

Everyone could count on confronting this sort of experience in his lifetime, and many met their ends in them. However, these crises were not everywhere of equal severity. In grain-growing villages where social cleavages were pronounced and transport facilities primitive, demographic crises caused by harvest failure were most destructive. (This does not necessarily mean that they faced a true Malthusian situation; rather, they were particularly vulnerable to climatic accidents.) Many villages in northern France were of this type. But many more were able to cushion the blow through the existence of more varied economies and cheap transportation. In England (where the Poor Law of 1597 imposed on each community the obligation to support its poor) and the Low Countries (with ready access to the international grain market), the death rate and the price of grain did not move together sufficiently to generate true crises of subsistence. This does not mean that they were not visited periodically by appalling mortality.[4]

Another factor forcing up the death rate is now accorded more importance: epidemic diseases - most notably bubonic plague, smallpox, typhus, and influenza. The general nutritional level of a population affects its ability to resist diseases, but epidemics struck all types of communities in good years and bad. The French province of Anjou suffered severe plague epidemics in 1583, 1605, and 1625, and dysentery in 1639 and 1707. Seville, the focal point of Spain's imperial economy, was struck in 1599-1600, 1616, and 1648-49. From the last of these epidemics it never recovered. In northern Italy the plagues of 1576-77 and 1630 created labor shortages and caused the flight of the well-to-do from the cities, thus compounding the problems of Italy's already vulnerable industries. On the other hand, the plagues that hit London and Amsterdam (those of 1623-25, 1635-36, 1655, and 1664 each killed over one-tenth of Amsterdam's population) appear to have been nothing more than temporary setbacks.

These plague epidemics, the most severe since the fourteenth century, cannot be tied directly to the state of the European economy. They had a life of their own and the affected communities were quite helpless in controlling them.[5] Yet before we conclude that an outside force intervened to stop Europe's population growth, we must account for the fact that plague-inflicted losses in central Europe and the Mediterranean took generations to be recovered while in northwestern Europe they only briefly interrupted the growth of population. Moreover, the stagnation of population that set in after the 1660s occurred when plagues were disappearing from the European scene. The last great European plague epidemic, which struck Marseilles in 1720, was an isolated event. The other epidemic diseases continued to rage, but their impact, in contrast to plague, was normally confined to restricted areas and restricted classes and age groups.

The other variable, the birth rate, was long regarded by demographers as standing at a physiological maximum before urbanized, industrialized societies arose in the nineteenth century. This view of unchecked fertility must be rejected for European populations in the seventeenth century. Fertility is now thought to have been quite sensitive to economic conditions. Detailed demographic studies have uncovered behavior consistent with the practice of conscious family limitation as far back as the early seventeenth century. Contraception was never a general practice in this period and, thus far, we are confident of its existence only in Geneva and several French and English villages.[6] But fertility could also be reduced by delaying the age at marriage for women and by celibacy. Such a trend can be identified in many areas (see Table 2). As the marriage age rose from an average in the low twenties to one in the high twenties in the course of the seventeenth century, the number of children per marriage necessarily fell. For example, in three French villages women marrying between the ages of 20 and 24 gave birth to an average of 8.2 children during their lifetimes while those marrying between 25 and 29 had only 6.5 children. In another French village, as the marriage age rose the births per marriage fell from 5.7 in 1600-39 to 4.6 in 1720-59.[7]

These adjustments in marriage customs and family size are not yet fully understood, but they seem highly significant. After all, the society that requires perhaps a tenth of the population never to marry and that requires of the rest the postponement of marriage until the late twenties - and at the same time withholds the recognition of full adulthood from all but married couples - is imposing a great emotional and physical burden. Nowhere else in the world do we see such a set of customs; no evidence exists for it in ancient or medieval Europe, and modern industrial societies have also aban-

Table 2. *Average age at first marriage for women*

Colyton, England		Ducal Families, England		Elversele, Flanders		Amsterdam, Holland	
1560-1646	27.0	1330-1479	17.1	1608-49	24.8	1626-27	24.5
1647-1719	30.0	1680-1729	22.2	1650-99	26.9	1676-77	26.5
1720-1769	27.0	1730-1779	24.0	1700-49	28.0	1726-27	27.2
						1776-77	27.8

Geneva, Switzerland (Bourgeoisie)		Amiens, France (Poor; bourgeoisie)			Altopascio, Tuscany	
1550-1599	22.0	1674-1678	24.0	25.2	1625-1649	18.6
1600-1649	24.9	1692-1697	24.9	26.3	1650-1699	20.4
1650-1699	25.2	1721-1725	24.1	27.1	1700-1749	21.9
1700-1749	27.0				1750-1784	25.5

Sources: E. A. Wrigley, "Family Limitation in Pre-industrial England," *Ec. H. R.* 19 (1966), 82-109; T. H. Hollingsworth, "A Demographic Study of the British Ducal Families," *Population Studies* 11 (1957), 4-26; Paul Deprez, "The Demographic Development of Flanders in the Eighteenth Century," in D. V. Glass and D. E. C. Eversley, eds., *Population in History* (London, 1965), 608-30; S. Hart, "Historisch-demografische notities betreffende huwelijken en migratie te Amsterdam in de 17ᵉ en 18ᵉ eeuw," *Maandblad Amstelodamum* 55 (1968), 63-69; L. Henry, *Anciennes familles genevoises* (Paris, 1956); Pierre Deyon, *Amiens, capitale provinciale* (Paris, 1967); Francis B. McArdle, *Altopascio, 1587-1784: A Study in Tuscan Rural Society,* (Cambridge, forthcoming).

doned this European marriage pattern. What sustained the European peoples in the observance of these customs?

Were the delayed marriage age and consequent smaller families a reaction to reduced employment opportunities in the seventeenth century? To the extent that marriages depended on the acquisition of land or a place in a trade, postponement would seem to be a fitting response to economic contraction or stagnation. But it seems unreasonable to use short-term changes in economic prosperity to explain what was plainly a long-term, relatively stable pattern of marriage behavior. Moreover, simple economic motives are an unlikely explanation for the marriage behavior of the aristocracy, among whom late marriage and celibacy are known to have spread.

The English peerage, because of its high fertility, grew in number in the early seventeenth century. One necessary result was a downward social mobility among nonheirs which caused intense competitiveness and divisiveness among the British upper class. Among peers born between 1625 and 1675 fertility was much reduced, and among those born between 1675 and 1749 celibacy, later marriage, and reduced fertility, together with higher mortality, caused their numbers to fall absolutely. The political and social consequences proved beneficial (to the peers, at any rate). Upward mobility and reduced competitiveness among these aristocratic families contributed to the stability of English society during the Augustan Age of Aristocracy, while the more frequent dying out of male lines contributed to the concentration of large estates (via inheritance through heiresses). Much the same demographic trend has been observed among such disparate upper income groups as the bourgeoisie of Geneva, the gentry landowners of Friesland, and the Venetian nobility: a tendency to die out appears to have been general among aristocratic families all over Europe in the century after 1650.[8]

Just as small families among aristocrats could preserve and concentrate wealth ownership, delayed marriage among peasants not only relieved pressure on the land but also permitted single young men and women working as servants and apprentices to amass a bit of wealth before forming households of their own. The motives for late marriage remain less than clear, but it is very possible that this remarkable trend expresses a desire for a higher standard of living at least as often as a scarcity of employment opportunities.

The cessation of population growth in seventeenth-century Europe differs from the demographic reversal of the fourteenth century in this essential respect: it was in part the result of efforts of several social groups to control their demographic and economic destinies, perhaps even to bring family size into accord with new concepts of well-being.

"In part" should be stressed in the last statement because Europeans did not yet have the means to control their population through a comprehensive population control mechanism. The seventeenth and eighteenth centuries claim our attention because crude forms of fertility control can be identified in many areas, but, as we have seen, no comparable control could be exercised over mortality. The fragile foundations of the economy rendered society vulnerable to elemental forces such as bacterial and rodent ecology and climate which could impose sudden shifts in the mortality level. These shifts might be temporary - an epidemic or subsistence crisis - but they could also be more enduring.[9]

Climate change is sometimes invoked to explain such long-term shifts in mortality. It appears that, besides yearly fluctuations in rainfall and average temperature, there existed (and exist) climatic cycles of longer duration (see Figure 1). Thus, the entire seventeenth century seems to have experienced a "little ice age" in which severe winters occurred with unusual frequency. The last decade of the seventeenth century stands out in northwestern Europe as an era of unusually wet summers and cold winters. In this area excessive moisture was the chief threat to harvests; perhaps, then, we should not be surprised to find that French tithe receipts fell abruptly in the 1680s and that severe harvest failures occurred in 1693-94 and 1709. In the course of the eighteenth century moderate weather conditions appeared with much greater frequency. Indeed, the good harvests of the 1720s and 30s in England have been called a "bounty of God" which, by depressing food prices, stimulated consumer demand for manufactures. But in this case the bounty of God did not extend to mortality: death rates rose in every decade from 1710 to 1740.[10]

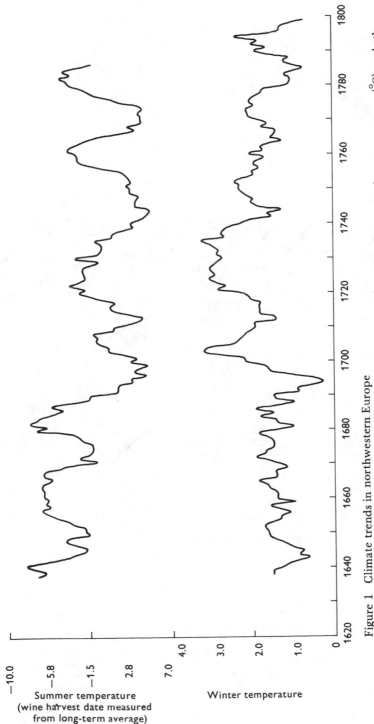

Figure 1 Climate trends in northwestern Europe

French average summer temperature (estimated from wine-harvest dates) and Dutch average winter temperatures (°C) are both expressed in nine-year moving averages. (Vendage after Le Roy Ladurie, *Times of Feast, Times of Famine*.)

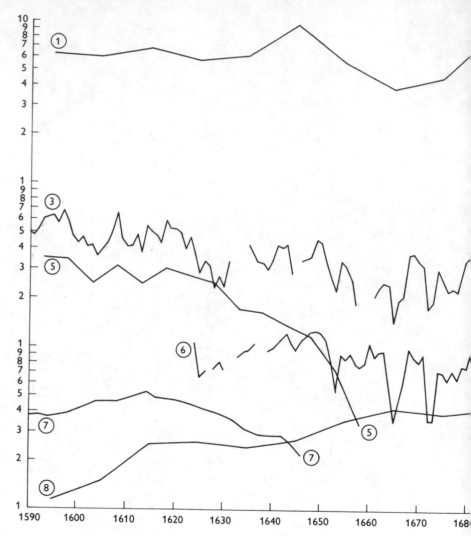

Figure 2   European trade indicators
1   Grain shipped westbound through the Danish Sound expressed in ten-year averages. *Scale:* 10,000s of lasts of grain; 1 last equals approximately 2 tons.
2   Grain exported from England expressed in ten-year averages. *Scale:* same as above.
3   Ships passing through the Danish Sound, both westbound and eastbound, annual data. *Scale:* 1000s of ships.
4   English domestic exports expressed in official values, annual data. *Scale:* millions of pounds sterling, by official value. Early eighteenth-century prices were used to aggregate values of the various exported commodities. Consequently, the trend reflects changes in the volume of exports more accurately than it reflects changes in actual value.

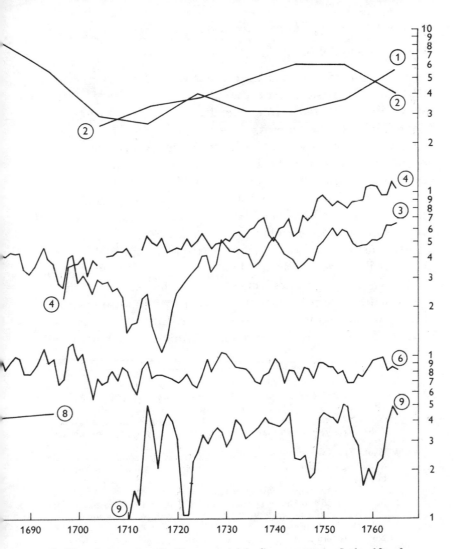

5 Silver imported at Seville expressed in five-year totals. *Scale:* 10s of millions of pesos (of 450 maravedis).

6 Revenue of "convooien" levied upon ships entering and departing Amsterdam, annual data. *Scale:* 100,000s of guilders.

7 Tonnage of New World shipping entering and departing Seville expressed in thirteen-year moving averages. *Scale:* 10,000s of tons of shipping volume.

8 Ships departing Europe for Asia expressed in ten-year totals. *Scale:* 100s of ships.

9 Ships entering Marseilles (except grain ships), annual data. *Scale:* 100s of ships.

Sources for the above data will be found at the foot of the following page. For data on yet another trade indicator, the average annual number of slaves shipped to the New World, see Table 3, p. 140.

Economic trends

Population trends were not alone in entering a new phase in the first half of the seventeenth century. Price, trade, and industrial output trends, to the extent they are known, display the same movement (see Figure 2). The spectacular inflation of prices in the sixteenth century leveled off in the early seventeenth century and began to decline - as early as 1637 in Milan and as late as 1663 in Danzig. These trends refer to averages, of course; prices for individual commodities showed considerable variation, the importance of which will be considered later.

Often associated with the price trend is the volume of Spanish silver imports from Mexico and Peru. If it were true, as many contemporaries believed, that the inflow of silver stood behind the price inflation, then the diminution of that inflow would dampen prices. Thus, great importance has long been attached to the decline of silver imports which began in 1625.

Sources of data in Figure 2 (pp. 14-15)

1 Nina Z. Bang, *Tabeller over Skibsfart og Varetransport gennem Øresund, 1497-1660,* 3 vols. (Copenhagen, 1906-22) and Nina Z. Bang and K. Korst, *Tabeller over Skibsfart og Varentransport gennem Øresund 1661-1783 og gennem Storebaelt 1701-1748,* 3 vols. (Copenhagen, 1930-45).

2 David Ormrod, "Anglo-Dutch Commerce, 1700-1760," Ph. D. diss., Cambridge University, 1973, p. 406. These figures include wheat, rye, barley, and malt.

3 Bang, *Tabeller over Skibsfart.*

4 B. R. Mitchell and Phyllis Deane, *Abstract of British Historical Statistics* (Cambridge, 1962), pp. 279-80. These figures are for domestic exports only; they exclude re-exports.

5 Earl J. Hamilton, *American Treasure and the Price Revolution in Spain 1501-1650* (Cambridge, Mass., 1934), p. 34.

6 J. C. Westermann, "Statistische gegevens over den handel van Amsterdam in de zeventiende eeuw," *Tijdschrift voor Geschiedenis* 61 (1948), 3-15; Johan de Vries, *De economische achteruitgang der Republiek in de achttiende eeuw* (Amsterdam, 1959), pp. 188-90.

7 Huguette and Pierre Chaunu, *Séville et l'Atlantique* (Paris, 1955-60).

8 Niels Steengaard, "European Shipping to Asia, 1497-1700," *Scan. Ec. H. R.* 18 (1970), 9.

9 Charles Carrière, *Négociants Marseillais au XVIIIe siècle* (Marseilles, 1973), pp. 1046-47.

Whatever its impact on prices (which will be considered in more detail later), the inflow of silver was undoubtedly closely connected to the volume of Spain's trade with the New World. Various factors, including the exhaustion of mines, the tragic decline of the Indian population, and the growing self-sufficiency of the New World economy, caused both the New World demand for European goods and the European supply of silver to fall. The Seville-Atlantic trade peaked in 1608-10 and began a steady descent after 1622.[11]

This was not the only trade route to suffer. The crisis of the colonial economy brought stagnation to the slave trade. The quarter century after 1625 was the only one between 1500 and 1750 in which slave shipments from Africa to the New World did not grow. The East India trade, after a generation of spectacular growth, made no further gains in volume between 1620 and 1650. Within Europe the Baltic trade turned sharply downward after 1624, as did the overland cattle trade from Denmark to the Low Countries and the Rhineland.[12]

The crisis in international trade could not fail to be reflected in the industrial sector of the European economy. Beginning at the turn of the century, northern Italy, for centuries a major textile producer, saw its industries sink into insignificance. In Flanders, the output of the Lille woolens industry fell by half in the decade after 1635 while the worsted center of Hondschoote, after making a recovery from the ravages of the war with Spain, inaugurated a definitive and lasting retreat into bucolic obscurity in 1638. The nearby French textile centers of Beauvais, Amiens, and Reims began to decline in the decade after 1625, while across the channel in England woolen cloth exports, which accounted for nearly all English exports, declined sharply in the late teens and twenties (see Figure 3).

The great European expansion of the sixteenth century was coming to an end. Even university enrollments, which had grown explosively in nearly every part of Europe, began a

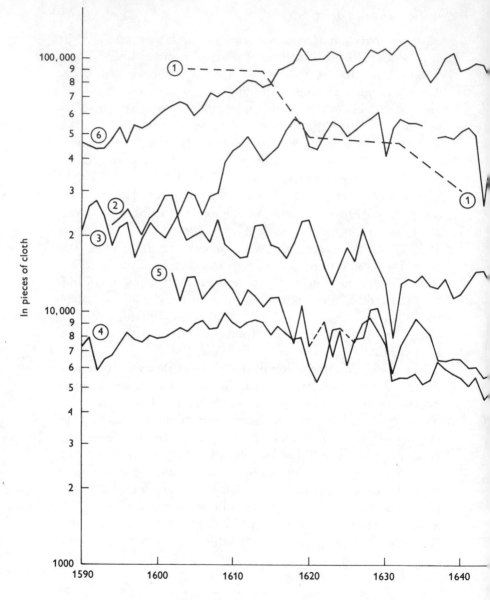

Figure 3   Trends in textile production

1   Export of undressed shortcloth from London in five isolated years.
2   Woolen cloth production in Hondschoote.
3   Woolen cloth production in Venice.

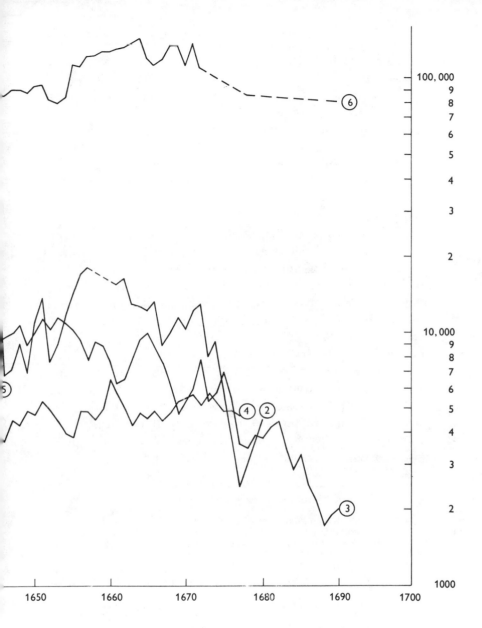

4 Woolen cloth production in Lille.
5 Woolen cloth production in Florence.
6 Woolen cloth production in Leiden.
Sources for data will be found at the foot of the following page.

permanent decline after 1620. Could it be that in these more somber times people took to heart the oft-repeated complaint that schools flooded society with unemployed *literati* full of subversive notions?

While there was no single event that ushered in this new phase of European economic history, a good candidate for the title of turning point is the trade crisis of 1619-22. Its immediate cause seems to have been an inventory crisis. That is, large unsold stocks of goods tied up the capital of merchants and forced reductions in orders for industrial production. This problem was compounded, particularly in central Europe, by large-scale currency manipulations. Thereafter, the worsening situation created by the Thirty Years' War, weak colonial markets, and persistent currency experimentation - including debasements, changed gold-silver price ratios, and supplemental copper coins - all conspired to prevent full recovery.[13] In the years that followed, one after another of the indicators described above turned downward. Most stayed depressed until at least the mid-century point. Thereafter, the colonial trades in both east and west revived while industrial output in England showed clear signs of renewed growth. Toward the end of the century Brazilian gold imports were again augmenting Europe's money supply, and a few more signs of trade revival could be found.

Sources of data in Figure 3 (p. 18-19)

1　Barry Supple, *Commercial Crisis and Change in England 1600-1642* (Cambridge, 1959), p. 137.
2　E. Coornaert, *La draperie-sayetterie d'Hondschoote* (Paris, 1930), pp. 494-95.
3　Domenico Sella, "The Rise and Fall of the Venetian Woollen Industry," in Brian Pullan, *Crisis and Change in the Venetian Economy* (London, 1968), pp. 109-10.
4　Pierre Deyon and Alain Lottin, "Evolution de la production textile à Lille aux XVIe et XVIIe siècle," *Revue du Nord* 49 (1967), 30-3.
5　Ruggiero Romano, "A Florence au XVIIe siècle, Industries textiles et conjoncture," *Annales* 7 (1952), 32.
6　N. W. Posthumus, *De geschiedenis van de Leidsche lakenindustrie* (The Hague, 1939), pp. 129, 930-31.

While these broad trends affected nearly every part of Europe, they were not universal. One economy defied the trends as if it thrived on the adversity that afflicted others. The economy of the Dutch Republic (plus that of Sweden whose development up to 1662 occurred to a large extent under Dutch auspices) grew rapidly throughout the first two-thirds of the seventeenth century. Its foreign trade, textile industry, and population all grew while those of other states stagnated.

The character of the seventeenth-century economic crisis exhibits complexities that do not yield to simple explanations. It was of long duration although the timing varied among countries. It affected countries unequally; some never recovered while others were set back only briefly and even gained competitive advantages. As the crisis continued the economies of southern and central Europe lost much of their international orientation. The importance of both the Baltic and the Mediterranean seas receded as the Atlantic seaboard became increasingly the fulcrum of European trade. How can we explain this multifaceted economic crisis?

Explanations

One explanation, which takes its lead from the cessation of population growth, argues that a Malthusian crisis of population pressing upon a fixed ceiling of agricultural output was primarily responsible for the observed trends. At first glance this approach seems attractive. By 1600 population growth had been rapid for over a century; in most places population densities had surpassed considerably the peak levels of medieval Europe on the eve of the Black Death. In this period agricultural prices rose more rapidly than almost any other prices and most classes suffered a drastic reduction of purchasing power. An excessive man-land ratio undoubtedly inflicted chronic hardship on some regions, notably in the Mediterranean area, but one can doubt whether a true

Malthusian crisis dominated seventeenth-century Europe. From what has already been noted about demographic trends it is clear that the behavior of vital rates is not generally consistent with such an explanation. The marked regional diversity of overall population trends casts further doubt on this view. The economic base of European society was undependable and the population stood defenseless against ravaging epidemics. However, this state of affairs was not new in the seventeenth century and does not constitute a Malthusian crisis.

An explanation that has the virtue of integrating economic with political history assigns the major blame for economic decline to the bellicosity of the age of power and absolutism. The incessant wars, notably the Thirty Years' War, the mid-century civil disturbances in England, France, and Spain, the general European wars between 1683 and 1721, and the War of the Austrian Succession cannot fail to have destroyed important economic assets. Later in this volume we will discuss the explosive growth of the size of armies and navies and the improvements in their equipment. The destructive capacity of military forces took a quantum leap in the seventeenth century, but we must nevertheless discount warfare as a general cause of the economic crisis. Aside from the fact that the timing of military destruction and economic stagnation does not lend unqualified support to this view, the major weakness of the argument is that the destruction and dislocation of warfare was local and that a compensating economic stimulus of orders for equipment and payments for services very likely made up for these losses. Thus, the incessant wars stimulated some sectors of the European economy while it wrought havoc with other sectors; the taxes imposed by the wars overburdened some regions and acted as a leaven in the economic life of others. The changing structure and location of economic activity cannot be understood without including the impact of war, but it is hard to prove that military action checked the growth of the European economy's aggregate output.

A third view focuses on the money supply. The historian of the Seville-Atlantic trade, Pierre Chaunu, asserts that the crisis of the 1620s and its aftermath was ultimately caused by a failure to finance a growing volume of trade. His argument runs as follows: the frequent debasements of coinage of nearly all European states in the sixteenth and seventeenth centuries were symptomatic of a chronic shortage of circulating currency. Debasement, a recoinage in which coins of a given face value reappear with a reduced silver or gold content, had the effect of increasing the stock of money. To the extent that prices rose to restore the previous silver or gold price equivalent, devaluation was self-defeating; at best it provided only a temporary increase in the effective stock of money. Spain's silver imports eased this shortage and, by providing trading capital as well as fueling inflation, actually encouraged investment in trade and shipping. A European economy whose expansion was driven by growing disbursements of silver from Seville came to a standstill once these injections of silver began to diminish in strength. The expedient of copper coinage and devaluations that spread through Europe in the 1620s exacerbated the problem by creating monetary chaos.

This monetary explanation requires the acceptance of several assumptions. First, we must know that Spanish silver imports rapidly found their way into the circulating medium of a large part of Europe. Second, we must be convinced that the use of credit instruments such as bills of exchange did not become sufficiently widespread to reduce the need for the precious metals in international trade. Finally, we must believe that the drain of gold and silver from circulation through hoarding or export to the Orient did not compensate for rising and falling silver imports. Regarding the last point, analyses of Indian coins show that they arrived on the subcontinent very shortly after being minted in Europe. Moreover, the minting dates were often long after the silver had been mined and, presumably, shipped to Europe. Thus, there is reason to be suspicious of the view that the official records of silver imports to Seville correspond with additions to the stock of money in Europe. There also is reason to believe that the silver import statistics themselves are faulty. Both the records of mercury production (mercury was required to extract silver from its ore) and recent studies of seventeenth-century smuggling practices indicate that silver production and shipments to Europe after the 1620s did not decline as rapidly as has long been supposed. Monetary instability played an undisputable role in the short-term cycles of the European economy - notably in the crisis of 1619-22 - but we cannot rely much on the view that the economy rose and fell with the flow of precious metals from the New World.[14]

A final approach to the problem argues that institutional and social conditions within Europe erected obstacles to further growth at least as important as the technical limitations of production. A society of peasants and landowners provided quite limited markets even as their incomes rose, and traders who accommodated themselves to such markets were, for all their capitalist spirit, unable to revolutionize the economy. Economic growth caused by expanding to new areas and by serving larger populations had definite limits, as the collapse of the extractive colonial economy of Spain demonstrated. As merchants accumulated profits there were few investment alternatives to buying land, government offices, palaces, even works of art. This portrait of an economy in which capital is misinvested out of frustration is what Eric Hobsbawm calls capitalism within a feudal framework.

However, this approach to the seventeenth-century economy is not able to explain the specific events that brought earlier expansion to a halt, and it suffers from reliance on vaguely defined "obstacles" and "forces." Indeed, any theory about the seventeenth century that makes use of the abused terms "feudalism" and "capitalism" deserves a sceptical reception. But this theory of general crisis has some virtues: it directs attention away from explanations that rely on outside forces such as population pressure, bullion imports, and warfare, and directs it toward the economy itself. It supplements the economic historian's typical preoccupation with measures that affect output with an analysis of the sources of demand for goods and services in the preindustrial economy. Finally, it focuses on the social structure that supports a given economic system and draws attention to the fact that changes in investment, production, and consumption do not occur in isolation from the social structure.[15]

Economies in decline

As outlined above, the new economic climate left hardly any area of Europe untouched. But treating it as a European-wide phenomenon does not permit us to investigate its most significant consequence: the stark redistribution of economic strength and the heightened differentiation observable among regions and states. What needs to be emphasized is the fact that an era of economic setbacks was not simply the opposite of an era of economic expansion. The crisis should not be thought of as a return to older and more backward forms of economic and social organization, an era in which society slides down the slope that had been scaled laboriously in the preceding period. The irreversibilities inherent in economic life which were mentioned earlier in this chapter require that the decline take essentially new forms - and it is on this point that its significance rests. The European economies displayed varying capacities to turn the manifold problems that faced them to their advantage - or to succumb to them.

Oddly, while theories of growth abound, the process of retrenchment and decline has rarely been considered in a systematic way. It happens that the seventeenth century was particularly rich in declining economies. There were also a few economies that rose to positions of leadership for the first time and these will be accorded considerable attention in later chapters, where the processes of change and adaptation will be emphasized. But before proceeding we should examine the general features of those economies that quite suddenly and irrevocably toppled from their positions of leadership.

Around 1600 Venetian economic leadership in the Mediterranean area came to a definitive end. Although Venice had faced stiff new challenges throughout the sixteenth century, it seemed to contemporaries in the closing decade of that century that she had regained the position enjoyed for so many centuries previous. But beginning in 1602 a rapid succession of new problems overwhelmed this maritime empire. The spice trade was lost for good to the Dutch and English who had now begun their penetration of the Indian Ocean; the textile industry suffered from high costs and withered away in the following half century; the city's position as an international center of book publishing became untenable because of the rejuvenated Catholic Church; the Thirty Years' War deprived Venice of her most important market while the debasement of the Turkish currency sharply increased the cost of cotton and silk to the Venetians. Only a resilient, innovative commercial population could have overcome such setbacks. It was the widely-held view of contemporary Venetians that they no longer possessed such qualities. Nicolo Contarini, in his history of Venice written in 1623, declared that "the Republic was at that time [the sixteenth century] in the apparent confidence of all princes . . . there was an abundance of everything. Mercantile commerce flowed from all sides. But . . . luxury and idleness accompanied prosperity." People had changed and now the response to economic problems was defensive and restrictive. Indeed, many of the richest nobles withdrew their capital from commerce altogether. They preferred the security of landowning and the comfortable life of country gentlemen. Thus we see in the seventeenth and eighteenth centuries the combined spectacle of the Venetian economy contracting to a regional distribution function while the city is adorned with splendid palaces along the Grand Canal, cafes, gambling houses, prelenten celebrations that last for months, operas, the comedies of Goldoni. Venice became a tourist center as its wealth holders diverted their capital from commerce to agriculture and a life of leisure. Was this the result of a moral change in the Venetian nobility or the reflection of a frank recognition that competition in the new international economy was hopeless?[16]

The inability to compete affected not only the Venetians. As we shall see in Chapter 3, the woolens, silk, and metallurgical industries of all the north Italian cities declined as they lost their foreign markets. In 1650 a Milanese official thought he had put his finger on the cause of this loss when he observed that "Men's wits have of late sharpened everywhere." But that does not go far enough. Industrial costs - of raw materials, labor, and transportation - were high in Italy and no one seemed capable of making the changes in techniques and institutions needed to remain competitive.[17] This rigidity seems to be a common characteristic of declining economies. It can be observed in many parts of seventeenth-century Europe. As a consequence, an enormous advantage was given to those few regions where institutions and opportunities encouraged cost-reducing innovations. Vast international markets quickly fell into their laps and the long-established locational pattern of industrial and commercial activities underwent dramatic revision.

Nowhere was the rigidity of declining economies more apparent than in Spain. The weakness of Spain's economy became obvious at the peak of her international power under Philip II. The costs of his foreign policy as measured in tax revenues and manpower combined with a pattern of controls and privileges in the domestic economy to hobble the productive sectors while bloating such consuming interests as the nobility, the church, and the bureaucracy. When the government defaulted on its payments and declared bankruptcy (for what proved to be far from the last time) in 1596, when the inflow of silver ceased to grow shortly thereafter, and when depopulation spread through central Castile as its economy lost its vitality, a despairing, disillusionment spread through Spanish society. The literature of the period, *Don Quixote* most obviously, reflects what the historian Jaime Vicens Vives described as the "subterfuges of a society sunk in destitution and at the same time eager to hide its difficulties." [18]

But this was not a society unaware of what was happening. A whole school of economic reformers, the *arbitristas,* wrote mountains of tracts pleading for new measures. Nothing escaped their attention: the reforms they advocated ranged from measures to revive industry by banning the export of raw materials and the import of manufactures to limitations on the number of days the extravagantly expensive royal court could be in session. Indeed, in 1623 a *Junta de Reformación* recommended to the new king, Philip IV, a series of measures including taxes to encourage earlier marriage (and, hence, population growth), limitations on the number of servants, the establishment of a bank, prohibitions on the import of luxuries, the closing of brothels, and the prohibition of the teaching of Latin in small towns (to reduce the flight from agriculture of peasants who had acquired a smattering of education). But no willpower could be found to follow through on these recommendations. A few months after the *Junta* filed its report the English Prince of Wales arrived for a state visit; the king, his court, and the great nobles all abandoned their ostentatiously assumed austerity. It is said that the only accomplishment of the reform movement was the abolition of the ruff collar, a fashion which had imposed ruinous laundry bills on the aristocracy.

As country folk abandoned their unprofitable farms to seek work as servants in the aristocratic cities, as the *Moriscos* (nominally converted Moors who formed the backbone of certain industries) were expelled from the country in 1609-14, as people sought a veneer of education so they might acquire economic security in the ever-expanding bureaucracy and, particularly, in the Church, as anyone with a bit of money bought a patent of nobility to avoid the onerous tax levies, the economy collapsed. One observer remarking on the frustration of every reform proposal lamented that "those who can, will not, and those who will, cannot."

If the combination of privileged classes raising greater and greater obstacles to reform and desperate government cannibalizing the economy to squeeze an extra drop of tax revenue is most apparent in Spain, it was not absent elsewhere - and it was a combination of evils most difficult to inhibit when the overall economy was stagnant or declining.

The age of crisis is not an idle label. It is not uniformly applicable but it cast an unmistakable gloom over much of Europe. It set in motion the pens of reformers, schemers, and crackpots, and it activated governments to initiate measures, chiefly defensive, that we today call mercantilism. It produced a desire for stability and order that helped along the construction of absolutist governments.

Still, in this economy, hemmed in by restrictive measures and vested interests as it was, opportunities existed. The discoveries of earlier times lent advantages to new locations; the needs of absolutist governments were unprecedented; the markets available to producers who could reduce costs were impressive. Describing the process by which these opportunities were realized and portions of the European economy were gradually unbound from their restrictive posture is the task of the following chapters.

2
The agrarian economies on divergent paths

Peasant agriculture

Seventeenth-century Europe was a peasant society. It is easy to lose sight of this fact when contemplating the imperial power of its monarchs and the capitalistic development of its bourgeoisie. The strivings of Europe's privileged and urban classes were supported by the often fragile scaffolding of a peasant economy. The ambitious plans of the kings, aristocrats, clerics, merchants, scientists, and scholars depended on the peasant economy with an immediacy that made it impossible for these persons to forget it for any length of time.

We may be faulted for overdramatization in asserting that the potential for the development of the European economy was locked up in its peasant villages and hamlets. Yet it could hardly have existed elsewhere - here the great majority of the European population lived and worked. It is customary today to identify in underdeveloped countries a modern, urban sector and a backward, rural sector, and to attach one's hopes for economic progress on the ability of the urban sector to reach into and transform the lethargic agrarian economy. Such an identification of "modern" and "backward" would be inappropriate in application to preindustrial Europe. The urban sector, in contrast to the cities of present-day peasant economies, was not linked to and supported by a modern, urban world elsewhere. As a consequence the peasant econo-

Map 1 Europe, showing regions mentioned in the text

my of Europe had to develop through its own efforts; it could not be stimulated by inputs, technology, or subsidies from an advanced society as transmitted by nearby cities. Urban and overseas markets were, of course, not without influence on the development of agricultural output, but this was more in the form of providing a challenge than of controlling a response.

Here, in the peasant economy, was the labor, much of the capital, and the agricultural output - or, one should say, the potential output. The European peasantry had long been harnessed in varying ways to provide resources in support of local powerholders and local cities. If the basic economic unit of early medieval Europe had been the manor, and the peasants' surplus channeled to uphold a warrior caste of noblemen, it had long since been superseded in economic importance by the local market town and its hinterland. One can view the European economy of the late sixteenth century as consisting of hundreds of towns with hinterlands of 50 to 100 square miles. The great bulk of all agricultural output that left the farms was disposed of within these units. That which flowed beyond these little regions was but a tiny portion of total output, but it was of strategic importance. On it depended the grand designs of monarchs and merchants alike. The task that confronted the burgeoning state and commercial interests during the long economic expansion that stretched into the seventeenth century was to tap the resources of the peasant economy for the benefit of new and more distant institutions. The problem to be overcome was, of course, not simply logistical - transport and distribution; it was also technical and political - to increase the peasant surplus and to legitimize new relationships between the peasants and their superiors.

This account makes the agenda before those who controlled or wished to control the European economy rather clearer and simpler than it was perceived to be, but it does remind us that in the agrarian economy more than elsewhere economic, political, and social aims were inextricably mingled. The reorganization of agriculture, the augmentation of state power, and the revamping of class relationships went hand in hand all over Europe.[1]

Here we might pause briefly to consider the actual pattern of agricultural intensity and specialization with which the long sixteenth-century economic boom endowed Europe. The flow of goods proceeding beyond the local marketplace was in most regions still small, but in certain regions, where these trade flows converged, their importance was much more than superficial. Everywhere it is remarkable how the small percentages of output that entered interregional trade encouraged differentiations in land use which in later decades would be intensified and which have had enduring effects on the landscape and economic geography of Europe into the twentieth century.

By the 1620s, at the crest of the sixteenth-century boom, one could readily distinguish several large agricultural zones. Grain, the staple of the European diet, was grown almost everywhere, but several areas had gained the reputation of frequent exporters. Those in the Mediterranean, Sicily and Andalusia, had proven themselves inadequate to satisfy the growing demand of that region, but in the north, the vast granaries of eastern Germany and Poland, connected to the Baltic by navigable river systems, such as the Vistula, had grown rapidly in the course of the sixteenth century. By the first half of the seventeenth century, an annual average of 140,000 tons of grain, chiefly rye, flowed westward through the Danish Sound to fulfill the demand of urbanized north-western Europe (as well as the Mediterranean).

Areas more remote from navigable water and urban markets were tending to specialize in livestock raising. In southern Italy and Castile this took the form of sheep raising in a system of transhumance. Shepherds led flocks to high mountain pastures during the summer months and brought them back to lowland zones in the winter. Cattle breeding occupied the peasants of the eastern and northern reaches of Europe - Hungary, Lithuania, the Jutland peninsula of Denmark, and the highland zones of the British Isles. Each year drovers led the oxen over the long overland routes connecting these breeding grounds with the fattening pastures near the cities of the Atlantic seaboard. By the 1620s 60,000 head of Danish oxen annually passed the tolls at Rendsburg, in Schleswig, en route to Holland and the Rhineland.

At the focal points of the trade routes from these broad belts of grain and livestock specialization stood the great urban markets of London and Paris, the cities of the Low Countries and the Po valley, and smaller markets in the Rhineland and on the Mediterranean coast. In the hinterlands of these cities intensive garden farming outside the town walls had gradually expanded and made its influence felt over broader areas. Horticulture, various forms of arboriculture, and vineyards covered the small fields tended by lavish amounts of labor; fodder crops and special industrial crops such as dyestuffs and hops could be found in these pockets of intense agriculture rightly called by German geographers *intensitätinseln.*

Because of the capital invested by urban landowners and the commercial facilities available in the nearby cities, agriculture in the favored districts was quite specialized and market oriented. In most of Europe, however, the market-bound produce consisted of irregular surpluses, highly vulnerable to a long list of variables and which formed the residual of the harvest after tithes, feudal dues, and rents had been paid to the rural elites, and family needs had been satisfied.[2]

We can gain an impression of the vulnerability of the surpluses on which so much of the elaborate civilization of seventeenth-century Europe rested by examining the harvest yield ratios. Today yields are commonly expressed in bushels per acre or in the decimal equivalent. When yields are so meager that the seed which must be saved out of the harvest for the next year's crop is a significant portion of the total, a ratio of the yield harvested to the seed sown is the most informative expression of the land's productivity. Consider a family of five members farming 8 hectares (20 acres) of arable land in a three-course rotation in which each year a third of the arable is devoted to bread grains. The per capita grain consumption can be set at 250 liters - enough for about a pound of bread per day. If each hectare is sown with 200 liters of seed and the yield ratio at the harvest is 4:1, the peasant household will have produced enough grain to feed itself and 1.4 other persons. If the yield ratio should fall to 3:1, the surplus would vanish and the household would fall short in its own needs by nearly a fifth. On the other hand, if the yield ratio could be doubled to 8:1, the output could feed the peasant household plus 10 others as well. That is, when the yield doubles, the persons fed nearly triples, and the nonagricultural population that could then be supported increases sevenfold.

We cannot be certain of the per capita grain consumption or of the average size of farms for Europe as a whole; these details varied from place to place. But the general consequences of fluctuations in the yield ratios were as this little exercise describes them. So, what in fact were the yield ratios? The peasants of the seventeenth and eighteenth centuries have not been so kind as to keep records of such matters, but some estate managers and landowners did so. From their scattered records the Dutch historian B. H. Slicher van Bath has attempted to produce average yield ratios for fifty-year periods. On the estates of Poland, the ratios stood at about 4:1 in the early seventeenth century, and by the eighteenth century they had if anything, declined. In Germany the yield ratios also stood at about 4:1 in the early seventeenth century and in the second half of the eighteenth century they were closer to 5:1, but much of this advance was accounted for by northwestern Germany (in particular, East Friesland and Schleswig-Holstein) where they rose to over 6:1. In the Low Countries and England, on the

other hand, the miserable yield ratios of 4:1 had been surpassed in the Middle Ages; in the early seventeenth century
they stood at 6:1 and by the second half of the eighteenth
century were nearly 10:1. For France and the Mediterranean
countries, several studies have provided figures showing that
yield ratios did not rise in the period we are investigating. [3]
Now, in agrarian history, each field has its own history and
broad averages hide as much as they reveal. But what *is* re-
vealed by these imperfect figures deserves emphasis. First, in
broad stretches of Europe a miserly yield ratio of about 4:1
was common - a yield that could support very few nonfarm
persons in the best of years and which guaranteed, in the
inevitable poor harvests, desperate famine and intense struggle among the claimants to the harvest. Second, while most
of Europe remained thus poised on the edge of scarcity, some
regions were increasing agricultural productivity, and thereby
laying the foundation for a more secure and diverse economy.

Increasing output

The great task that confronted the European economy was to increase agricultural output. The well-being of a
population swollen by the demographic advance of the sixteenth century depended on a more varied and reliable food
supply which, by reducing malnutrition, could improve the
population's economic effectiveness. But in an era of little
aggregate population growth this did not act as the primary
force pressing for increased output. The ambitions of the
social elites, and particularly of governments, also required a
more abundant supply of agricultural products. Their ambitions required raw materials, foodstuffs, and also labor that
could be liberated from local peasant economies only with
the achievement of a more elastic supply of agricultural products, but the obstacles to increased output in an economy of
preindustrial technology and peasant social organization were
formidable.

Augmenting the cultivable land through clearing and reclamation - the simple accumulation of productive factors - is the most straightforward way to increase output. It had, of course, been widespread in the medieval expansion, what Marc Bloch called the great age of clearing. The expansion of the sixteenth century owed much to the renewed use of lands abandoned in the aftermath of the Black Death. In most of Europe, however, there was little opportunity for such a simple extension of cultivable land. With the exceptions of the northern frontiers of Scandinavia and the Christian-Turkish frontier zones of eastern Europe, most unused lands could be productive only after the investment of large amounts of capital. Most such activity centered on the river and coastal marshes and lakes. Venetian landowners were pushing forward with the drainage of large tracts along the River Adige before the softening of grain prices in the last decades of the sixteenth century robbed the enterprise of its profit potential. In northern Europe, where the downturn of prices was delayed for many decades, the first half of the seventeenth century proved to be a golden age of drainage. In the Dutch Republic, where men had long been occupied with the drainage of coastal marshes, the rising value of land and the growing mass of mercantile profit combined to encourage many of the leading capitalists of Amsterdam to invest in projects of lake drainage. These schemes were highly speculative, depending for their success on the daring application of new advances in windmill technology. The success in 1612 of the large Beemster lake drainage (one of the investors being Johan van Oldenbarneveld, the ill-starred Grand Pensionary of Holland) inaugurated a flood of investment capital in similar projects. By mid-century urban investors had sunk an amount in excess of the combined capitalization of the Dutch East India and West India companies and had drained some 36,000 hectares in the northern peninsula of Holland alone to increase the cultivable land area by more than a quarter.

The hydraulics engineers and construction teams trained on these projects found many foreign assignments to supplement their domestic activities. The early Stuarts' hiring of Cornelius Vermuyden to drain the English fens - a project that ultimately improved the quality of nearly 160,000 hectares - is well known. However, at this same time drainage projects were being carried out on the marshy banks of the Vistula in Poland, along the shallow North Sea coasts of northwestern Germany, in the Atlantic tidal flats of Poitou around LaRochelle in France, and, under the patronage of Pope Urban VII, in the Pontine marshes south of Rome.[4]

This capital-intensive form of land acquisition was highly sensitive to the economic climate. With the downturn of agricultural prices after the mid-seventeenth century drainage activity diminished rapidly. In certain regions, most notably the Dutch Republic, the new land directly affected the supply of agricultural products, but in Europe as a whole it can be said that land augmentation of all types was no longer the chief avenue to increased supply. If the land area cannot be increased without undergoing great expense, there is but one alternative: increasing the productivity of the land, which chiefly takes the form of adopting more intensive crop rotation systems.

Long before the seventeenth century most of England and the North European Plain stretching eastward from the English channel had adopted the three-course rotation. In the first year of such a rotation a field is sown in the late fall with a winter grain such as wheat or rye. This is harvested the following summer, whereupon the land rests until the next spring, when a summer grain - barley or oats, perhaps - is sown and harvested in the fall. Then in a final year the field is allowed to recover its fertility and remain fallow before beginning the cycle over again. The farmer would, of course, need at least three fields so in any given year he would have one field in each stage of the rotation. In the Mediterranean basin and Scandinavia, however, climatic conditions did not generally permit this system and the less intensive two-course rotation, with half the land lying fallow in any given year, continued to prevail. Of course, many variants of these rotations could be found and there were areas, particularly in the East, where a primitive system of several years of temporary cultivation followed by decades of abandoned fallow persisted in use. //

When one considers that one-half to one-third of the arable land of Europe lay fallow each year and that the fields under crops in many areas yielded harvests no more bountiful than four times the seed sown, one can see that the scope for intensification was very great. If the amount of fallow could be reduced and/or the fertility of the soil increased, agricultural output would grow significantly. The interdependence of these two goals posed a considerable technical obstacle. The purpose of fallow was, of course, to maintain soil fertility so that a reduction of fallow would undermine the other goal. This could be compensated for by increasing the supply of manure, another important source of soil fertility. But this would require a larger livestock herd and larger pastures, and how could pastures be enlarged except by reducing the size of the arable fields? The peasant or estate owner contemplating intensification had to confront this vicious circle of manure supply and arable land. It rarely could be overcome by purchasing fertilizers. The sale of manure was typically forbidden in farm leases, and transport costs in most areas would have been prohibitive in any case. Only in the environs of large cities, the *intensitätinseln,* was it possible to solve the problem by purchasing night soil - human wastes and city garbage. In most of Europe the problem had to be overcome on the farm itself.

The basic methods for creating a more intensive agriculture were not unknown. In the early seventeenth century books offering agricultural advice were published in large numbers as were the published observations of travelers to the centers of advanced agricultural techniques in Flanders and

Lombardy. Indeed, the basic facts could be found in the agricultural handbooks of Imperial Rome.

The arable fields, previously devoted primarily to grains, needed to be planted with a wider variety of crops. Pulses, such as peas and beans, and legumes, such as clover, when interspersed with grain crops had nitrogen-fixing qualities that improved soil fertility even in the absence of fallow. Moreover, pulses and legumes, as well as root crops, the most important being turnips, produced a fodder supply that supported a larger herd of livestock, particularly during the fodder-scarce winter months. A larger herd, of course, produced a larger manure supply for the arable fields. Fitting these new crops into the rotation required the abandonment of the two- or three-course rotations and the reduction or abandonment of the fallow year. A common rotation incorporating these improvements, publicized by Richard Weston, an English traveler in Flanders in 1652, consisted of alternating years of grain with turnips and clover. Known as alternate husbandry, it suppressed the fallow altogether. A more radical system, called convertible husbandry, consisted of abandoning the distinction between arable and pasture land and adopting a rotation cycle of from seven to perhaps eleven years. The cycle provided for growing grains, pulses, and roots for several years in succession after which the land was sown with clover or another grass and was then converted to an artificial pasture for several years before it was again plowed up.

The farmer interested in increasing yields had other options. He could increase the amount of manure available for spreading on the arable by keeping his livestock penned up and stall feeding them; he could sow his fields in rows rather than broadcast, he could weed more thoroughly, plow and harrow more frequently, and, although this does not exhaust the possibilities, he could construct water meadows - artificial ponds - which would flood his hay lands in the early spring thereby forcing an early crop of lush grass.

All of these practices affected harvest by either reducing
fallow, increasing fertilizer supply, or improving soil quality.
All of these practices, moreover, were generally known,
although they were not everywhere equally applicable.[5] Why
then, was agricultural development so slow and uneven? If
the technical solutions to the problem of low land productivity were no great mystery, what *were* the obstacles to increasing the food supply?

Institutional inflexibility is perhaps the most obvious obstacle. It is certainly the most frequently cited obstacle. The
introduction of new methods always meets with resistance
and this problem is compounded when novelty threatens certain groups or requires the concerted actions of several persons. Noble, clerical, and bourgeois landowners who leased so
much of the land to peasants were eager to protect their land
from tenants who might deplete the soil by overcropping.
Their leases frequently stipulated conservative practices and
frequent fallows. Moreover, tithe rights and even rents were
often expressed as a portion of the grain crops. The growing
of novel crops was often, rightly, considered an effort to
evade the full payment of one's obligations. A more general
and more serious problem, however, was the inflexibility
engendered by the common-field system. Over the centuries
large parts of Europe, particularly on the North European
Plain, came to adopt this system. In it, the arable is divided
into strips, each cultivator using a number of strips scattered
about the unfenced fields. The pasture lands are held and
used in common by the peasants, each enjoying the right to
graze livestock in some proportion to the size of his arable
holdings in the open fields. The same is true of woodlands
and wastes where the peasants can gather timber, stone, and
other commodities. A final characteristic of this system is the
regulation of the use of arable and pasture by an assembly of
the village cultivators. Its functions included such matters as
the appointment of shepherds to tend the village livestock
and setting quotas for each villager's grazing rights, but by far

its most important function was the coordination of planting and harvesting. The practice of throwing open the harvested arable fields to stubble grazing by the livestock required that each peasant sow the same crop and harvest it by the same date. This evidence of cooperative farming was not an expression of an ancient communal bond; rather it resulted from sometimes quite recent efforts to increase output (by augmenting the fodder supply) within the context of the two- or three-course rotation system.

The common-field system did not pose an insuperable obstacle to agricultural innovation. There often existed enclosed fields on the edges of the great common fields not subject to these communal constraints. Moreover, agreements among the cultivators could alter the rotation system. But achieving such agreement was difficult and time consuming. Meanwhile, the ability of any single peasant to introduce new crops, let alone change rotations, was severely limited.

The system discouraged innovation in other ways as well: the division of the arable into small scattered strips intensified the problem of neighborhood effects. That is, such fragmented holdings exposed the crops of a diligent farmer to the slovenly practices (such as poor weeding or drainage) of a neighbor. Similarly, the mingling of all the village livestock on the common pasture frustrated any individual's efforts to breed stock of a higher than average quality. Finally, the existence of such fragmented holdings increased the time consumed in gaining access to one's strips; this too discouraged more labor-intensive practices.

Thus, the new, more complex rotations, and innovations of all sorts, could be introduced within the common-field system only with great difficulty. In most instances, the enclosure of the land into consolidated farms was necessary for the full application of the new methods. But such a transformation of land use met with persistent and often successful resistance. The common-field system offered peasant farmers, particularly small farmers, security and, perhaps ironically, independence. The commonly-held pasture, woodland, and waste gave guaranteed access to strategic commodities; the common-field system's typical overcommitment to grain farming seemed to assure adequate local food supplies; the custom of permitting the village landless to graze a few beasts on the common pasture was crucial to their well-being. The scattered arable strips, spread over the different types of soil found in a village, reduced the risk of crop failure faced by the individual peasant. (Obviously, they did nothing to reduce the risk faced by the village as a whole.) More importantly, scattering offered the peasant a loosening of the time constraint faced in the performance of each farming operation. Weather conditions dictate an optimal time for each task. When a peasant's land is consolidated and all of one soil-type, he is likely to find that the performance of each task in its brief, optimal period demands more labor than he and his family can provide. If he is in a position to hire laborers this problem is easy enough to solve; if not, he can reduce the greatest peaks of demand for his labor by holding scattered strips whose varying qualities would each have their own optimal times - with luck, each different from the others.

There existed, then, a considerable village constituency in opposition to the carving up of the land into enclosed, consolidated holdings, however necessary this might have been for technical change in agriculture. The transformation of common-field into enclosed villages proved to be a long drawn-out process; around 1700 half of England's agricultural land remained to be enclosed. Even more remained on the North European Plain; on the other hand, there were many areas where the common-field system had never existed.[6]

Another obstacle to increased supply revolved around the investment of capital. Water meadows, enclosure, orchards and vineyards, larger livestock herds, new buildings and equipment - all these requirements of more productive agriculture demanded capital. The problem was not so much the inadequacy of agricultural income as it was the diversion of agricultural income by landlords to unproductive investments and consumption, and the inadequacy of tenancy conditions that caused many projects to founder on the shoals of tenant-owner mistrust.

More important than any of these obstacles was peasant resistance to greater intensification. We must be careful not to mistake this for peasant ignorance or a slothful disregard for material advancement. All of the measures outlined above that could increase output per unit of land required significant additions of labor input. This was far more important than capital input in producing the higher yields. The reader familiar with the law of diminishing returns will not be shocked to find that the marginal productivity of labor tended to decline as more and more of the peasant household's labor was lavished on a fixed amount of land. The extra plowing and harrowing, the careful weeding, the hauling of more manure, the pulling of turnips, the feeding of livestock - all these new tasks required a percentage increase of labor that was likely to exceed the increase of output. If there were no competing claims on the peasant household's labor, these tasks may have been assumed anyway - an expression of the self-exploitation characteristic of family enterprises where the individual workers are unpaid. But peasants were not only cultivators; they performed many other tasks to provide themselves with clothing, tools, housing, and transportation. Consequently, peasants, when left to themselves, assumed more labor-intensive forms of agriculture only when population pressure and land shortage forced it upon them as the only solution to the food problem.

"When left to themselves" is, of course, the crucial proviso. Peasants are, by definition,[7] never left to themselves. They must pay rents, tithes, taxes, and feudal dues, and the marketplace frequently exerts some influence on their production decisions.

The financial obligations with which European peasants were burdened need a word of explanation. There were a few places where private property in the modern sense of the word was already well established. Here a tenant paid a commercial rent for his land and whatever land taxes the government might impose. But much the largest part of Europe remained subject to ambiguous property laws, a legacy of medieval feudalism. Here no one could claim an exclusive ownership of the land; instead, the land was encumbered with obligations to several powerful claimants. The specific form of the obligation and the relative importance of each of these claimants could vary exceedingly but a general idea of the situation can be presented using France as an example.

Unless a parcel of land was allodial - never having been subject to feudal controls - it was subject to the payment of seigneurial dues. These were, first of all, the *cens,* an annual recognition payment, which served to recognize the rights of the holder of the seigneurial authority in the area. When the land passed into the hands of another peasant through inheritance, exchange, or sale, the seigneur would collect the fees of *lods* or *ventes,* and in some cases he would even demand the forfeiture of the land to himself. Whether these rights were paid in kind or money, and were trivial or real burdens, all hinged on local custom.

The seigneur also enjoyed *banalités,* the right to levy tolls; to require villagers to use seigneurial mills, wine presses, or ovens; to monopolize the sale of wine produced in the seigneurie; to monopolize the keeping of pigeons and rabbits; to hunt and fish within the jurisdiction of the seigneurie. These rights might be forgotten, or they might have been commuted, suppressed in exchange for a lump-sum payment from the villagers. Conflicts over all these obligations were decided in seigneurial courts, where the seigneur himself administered justice.

These seigneurial dues, in their endless variety, are distinct from rent. The peasant who in other respects owned his land was nevertheless subject to seigneurial authority where it existed. If the peasant did not own his land, he paid in addition to these dues a commercial rent which could take many forms depending on the length and security of the lease and the legal status of the tenant. Labor services, an obligation of servile tenants, no longer existed in most of France or the rest of northwest Europe. But elsewhere, particularly in Europe east of the river Elbe, such obligations (*frondienst*) could require peasants to spend over half their time in uncompensated work on the estates of their landlords.

In addition to seigneurial dues and rent, land was subject to tithe payments. Protestant and Catholic countries alike preserved this obligation, although in the former the tithe was more likely to have been commuted by a lump-sum payment of the villagers. Where the tithe remained, payment was nearly always demanded in kind, although the crops subject to tithe and the portion of the harvest to be paid varied widely. In northern France it was often one-eleventh of the harvest; in the south it was much less. The tithe holders, incidentally, were rarely the local parish priests. By the seventeenth century the recipients were not even always ecclesiastical.

Finally we come to royal taxes. In nearly every state some type of land tax yielded the bulk of government revenue. In France this tax was called the *taille* (discussed further on pp. 200-1).[8]

What is remarkable about the agrarian history of the seventeenth and eighteenth centuries is the degree to which these varied economic pressures on peasant society were intensified. The levers of control available to the other social groups were worked with new energy and in novel ways. To meet these new obligations the peasant household *had* to become more open to market forces; to become more of a market producer, the household also had to become more of a market consumer. The precise measures varied from place to place, as did the results. We would attribute to the privileged classes more originality than they possessed to say they wished to destroy the peasantry. An alternative social structure would then have been hard to imagine. But in many areas peasant economic life was altered, and in one country, England, it lost many of its essential characteristics. Indeed, if we took literally the anthropologists' insistence that peasants cease to be peasants (and become "farmers") when their production is oriented primarily to the commercial market rather than to fulfilling directly family needs, we would have to say that a large portion of cultivators in many regions of Europe were ceasing to be peasants before the mid-eighteenth century. We might go even further and suggest that the widespread commercialization of European agriculture that preceded the rise of modern industry is a unique feature of both western economic and political development.[9]

In the accounts of agrarian change that follow, the suffering of peasants will be all too evident, but there was an achievement as well. In earlier ages increased output usually arose under the pressure of growing population and consequently high food prices; correspondingly, abundant production and low food prices typically arose only when a decline in population undermined aggregate demand. The century after 1650 saw food prices fall more than most other prices; it is usually referred to as an era of agricultural depression. But in this case the cause of the price decline was not so much population decline (which was confined to specific regions) as it was the continued growth of output. The ability of cultivators in certain regions of Europe, at least, to increase agricultural output in such an environment, without having the growth of population wipe out the gain, is of primary importance in understanding the broader economic growth of the European economy.

Diverging structures

The seventeenth-century economy placed new demands on agriculture. As population growth slowed in most areas, and declined precipitously in some, the aggregate demand for basic commodities weakened. Prices tended to decline and in many areas by the mid-century, rents were falling and cries of an agricultural crisis could be heard. However, the real incomes of food buyers tended to rise. Because basic foods such as bread became more plentiful and, hence, cheaper, the proportion of income left to purchase "luxuries" - such as livestock products, beverages, and manufactures - rose. Thus, the demand for selected agricultural goods - those characterized by income elastic demand - tended to grow. At the same time concentrations of demand in cities and armies of unprecedented size altered agricultural markets. In short, it was a time that demanded flexibility on the part of the landowner and peasant, who wished to benefit from these opportunities.

The political structure of many European states was also in flux in this age of crisis. That, too, invariably subjected the agrarian structure of society to new pressures because the monarchs, nobles, and even the bourgeoisie depended in varying ways on their control over land, peasants, and grain for their social and political power. The interplay between changing political structures and changing market pressures created the condition where divergent paths were being followed in the agrarian life of the various European states - some for better, some for worse.

Spain

To examine the bad news first, we can begin in the Mediterranean basin. Spanish agriculture had shown itself inadequate to meet the nation's needs by the last decades of the sixteenth century. The crown's control of grain prices, which dated from 1539, had the predictable result of discouraging peasants from producing this basic, but unprofitable, commodity. By the 1590s imports from as far as the Baltic became necessary to alleviate famine. The price con-

trols were kept until 1756. During this entire period the
Spanish grain supply was carefully regulated, but undependable. The two-course rotation persisted into the eighteenth
century while tithe records show a stagnant output at the
meager yield ratios of 3 or 4 to 1. As a consequence grain
imports averaged over a million bushels per year in the 1750s
and 60s. In many years Madrid, in the center of the Iberian
peninsula, had to be supplied by mule caravans carrying imported grain from the coasts.

When we delve into the underlying causes of Spain's - or
more accurately, Castile's - chronically inadequate arable agriculture, we quickly confront the fundamental political policies of Spain's Habsburg government. In grain as in many
other commodities the crown pursued policies that favored
the consumer over the producer. In part this can be accounted for by the crown's need, in earlier decades, for political support from the municipal governments. Still, it should
not surprise us that Spain was better at consuming than at
producing.

It is only partially right to say that the crown favored
consumers over producers. Certain producers were favored as
well, again at the expense of arable agriculture. Wool production had long formed a mainstay of the Castilian economy
and provided Spain's leading export. This industry was largely in the hands of the Castilian nobility, particularly the
twenty-five or so very largest landowning families, the
grandees. A political alliance between the crown and the
grandees was gradually fashioned beginning in the thirteenth
century on the basis of granting extensive privileges to the
aristocrats' sheep-raising interests in return for the royal right
to tax wool exports. The nobility enjoyed a chartered monopoly on sheep raising, called the *Mesta,* which was periodically strengthened by a protective crown. Many of these privileges harmed peasant agriculture, the most destructive being
the prohibition on the enclosure of arable lands, lest the
migratory routes and grazing privileges of the *Mesta's* herds

be infringed upon. The crown, in return for these privileges, had a source of tax revenue both large and easy to tap.[10]

In the seventeenth century this long-standing alliance plus the controls on grain prices precluded viable peasant farming. In the ensuing crisis the aristocrats and the Church came to own the vast majority of the land. Aristocratic holdings, protected from possible sale or alienation by entails known as *mayorazgos*, were typically operated, without active involvement by the owners, as extensive grazing operations employing little labor. The unprofitability of the more labor-intensive grain production relegated it to the peasant sector. Spain's peasants were generally not enserfed, but in this economic environment they found they could use their freedom for little besides selling their property and moving to the towns, enrolling in the army, or joining a religious order.

The *Mesta*, privileged though it was, found foreign markets for its high-quality wool declining as the international textile industry experienced profound change in organization and in consumer preferences. In the late seventeenth century the flocks declined to half their sixteenth-century peak while arable farming remained hobbled by restrictions, vagabondage became endemic, and vast areas of rural Castile suffered depopulation. As late as 1797, after several decades of rapid repopulation, the census listed 932 deserted villages, mainly in central Castile.

Along the Mediterranean coast of Spain were regions of more labor-intensive, market-oriented production. Particularly in Valencia this productive agriculture depended in large measure on the labor of the *Morisco* minority. These nominally Christianized Moors worked small, irrigated fields of vines, rice, sugar, and mulberries. The expulsion of this minority in 1609-14 disorganized Valencia's economy. The remaining Christians prospered for a time, but by the 1620s the chief markets for such specialized products collapsed as Seville suffered from the declining volume of transatlantic trade while Italy's cities shrivelled with the contraction of their textile industries. The agrarian depression that had struck Castile earlier now hit Valencia; the population, suffering from plagues, floods, and a sharp increase in taxes imposed by the Duke of Olivares to finance Spain's military intervention in Italy and Flanders, was too overburdened to respond effectively. One consequence was the abandonment of many irrigation facilities in Murcia and Valencia. Only in Catalonia did a permanent agricultural advance occur during this otherwise desperate era. The policies of Catalonia's powerful representative assembly plus the existence of an important urban market fostered the evolution of an agrarian structure of enclosed farms operated by tenants who enjoyed secure tenures and fixed rents. The commercial development of Catalonia, so different from the rest of Spain, was facilitated by the evolution of an agrarian structure which, while not immune from the general market weakness of the seventeenth century, provided an incentive for investment and technical innovation that permitted Catalonian peasants to pursue a varied production of grains, vines, and horticultural crops.

The new Bourbon monarchy installed after the War of the Spanish Succession took a new approach to agrarian policy in Castile, but it was to take many generations to overcome the effects of this legacy of mismanagement. Most of Spain entered the industrial era with an agrarian sector that not only was incapable of meeting the normal needs of the economy, but that also was dominated by a social and legal structure which misallocated agricultural resources and discouraged capital investment.[11]

Italy

The rapid growth of population in the sixteenth century and the consequently strong demand for grain had left its mark on Sicily, the western Mediterranean's chief granary. In this period the wheat monoculture using a simple two-course rotation which was practiced on much of the island was extended up the slopes of mountains and into forests. Olive orchards were sometimes burned to make room for more grain. In the seventeenth century the result - deforestation and soil erosion in the uplands, malarial marsh formation in the lowlands - reduced the island's peasantry to misery. A key factor in this development was the conduct of the nobility that owned most of the land and leased it for rents payable in kind. Their luxurious life in Palermo and their maladministration denied the island's interior both the capital needed to increase output without mining the soil and the physical security needed to permit cultivators to live near their fields. As the nobles confined themselves increasingly to Palermo, the peasants confined themselves increasingly to their hill towns. The fields became a kind of no man's land cultivated in an exceedingly primitive manner.

Many of the same problems affected the southern half of the Italian peninsula. In the Kingdom of Naples the sixteenth-century grain boom had produced a class of commercial grain farmers whose indebtedness - manageable while prices rose - put them in a precarious position when prices fell in the seventeenth century. Their exposed position was made worse by the wealth of the Church and noble landowners, whose superior capital resources in a time of growing peasant debt permitted them to throw together huge estates devoted to the relatively profitable sheep grazing. Banditry and political revolt became endemic in this polarized environment, further undermining the viability of peasant farming.[12]

Agriculture in the north Italian plain of Venetia, Lombardy, and Piedmont showed an entirely different face from that in the south. By the end of the sixteenth century this vast region enjoyed a European-wide reputation for its intensive agriculture. The region's dozens of important cities provided insatiable markets for a wide variety of industrial crops and foodstuffs. Rice was already an established crop of the irri-

gated lowlands, madder and woad provided dyestuffs, and
mulberry cultivation supplied Europe's largest silk industry.
Vines and fruits were widespread, and grain yields are said to
have been very high. This system found its support from the
twin pillars of a lavish application of labor and strong urban
demand. In contrast to the northern European rotation systems described earlier, Mediterranean agriculture was more
flexible. The collective restraints of common fields were
absent as was the strong link between livestock herd size,
manure supply, and arable land. Stock played a lesser role in
a region where good pasture was scarce (because of the climate) and heavy draft animals less numerous (because of the
use of lighter plows in the region's thinner soils). Mediterranean peasants compensated for the scarcity of livestock and
manure through greater application of labor and a reliance on
vines and various forms of arboriculture, notably the mulberry and olive trees. This gave them the ability to adjust
quickly to changes in the character of their markets.

Such flexibility had its drawbacks as well: the dangers of
overextending the arable and depleting the soil. There is some
difference of opinion about whether this in fact occurred in
northern Italy in the seventeenth century. Fernand Braudel,
writing of the entire Mediterranean basin, asserted that the
inelasticity of agricultural output stopped the sixteenth-
century expansion and that the result of this impasse was to
be the "refeudalization of the seventeenth century, an agricultural revolution in reverse." Writing specifically about the
mainland possessions of Venice, Daniele Beltrami claimed
that Italy's overpopulation dried up former sources of food
supply for Venice and forced the city to rely increasingly on
its hinterland. This stimulated an excessive extension of
arable land which, in turn, undermined fertility. Another observer, S. J. Woolf, has noted the introduction of maize in
the course of the seventeenth century and the ability of the
region to remain self-sufficient in foodstuffs as rural population grew in the eighteenth century. These events, he sus-

pected, cast some doubt on the somber picture sketched by Braudel and Beltrami.[13]

The existence of a Malthusian crisis in northern Italy is, thus, in doubt. The level of intensification achieved in earlier centuries was not much exceeded, however, and the social environment in which this precocious agriculture now found itself made technical advances unlikely.

The collapse of Italy's urban industries in the early seventeenth century reduced demand for many of the region's agricultural specialties at the same time that the contracting urban population provided a weakened demand for foodstuffs. The combination of declining prices, high taxes, and - after the 1630 plague - labor shortage, forced rents to decline by 50 percent on many Lombard estates. The nadir of this economic collapse came around 1650. Thereafter population growth resumed, but it was confined to the countryside. As a consequence, the revival of agriculture assumed forms quite different from earlier centuries.

The unprofitability of Italian industry and commerce caused the mercantile wealth of Venice, Lombardy, and Tuscany to pour into the land market. The Venetian nobility, for instance, had been acquiring mainland estates throughout the sixteenth century; by 1600 they owned some 11 percent of the *terraferma's* cultivated land. But in the seventeenth century, when agricultural prices declined, their purchases actually increased. By 1740 they held over 20 percent of the land and had transformed themselves from a commercial to a landed aristocracy. In Lombardy the old feudal landowning nobility was joined by a patrician nobility of mercantile origins as well as by a new nobility of bourgeois officeholders created by the Spanish overlords. By the end of the seventeenth century the patricians had been completely severed from their mercantile wealth.

The greatest of the Lombard landowners leased large estates to tenant managers who hired labor and ran impressive commercial operations. But most landowners found easier profits in a different sort of operation. The price collapse had saddled many peasants with crushing debt burdens, while the renewed growth of rural population once again generated a strong demand for land. In response landowners leased out their extensive holdings in very small plots (76 percent of the Venetian nobility's land was let out in units of under 5 hectares) on sharecropping tenures to the growing, land-hungry rural population. These small, undercapitalized farms became characteristic of Piedmont and Tuscany as well as Venetia.[14]

In summary, the intensive farming methods for which northern Italy was famous continued in use, but in a very much altered environment. The decline of the urban economy forced most peasant agriculture into a less market-oriented posture. This, together with the spread of share-cropping, made the social and political setting decidedly more "feudal" - to use that word in its nineteenth-century polemical sense - than it had been in the sixteenth century. Agriculture now bore directly much more of the burden of maintaining the privileged classes of Italian society in their accustomed style.

Eastern Europe

The agricultural structure of the lands that stretch eastward from the river Elbe differed in every way imaginable from that of northern Italy. But here, too, the age of crisis dealt unkindly with the peasant. A combination of circumstances had conspired to transform the peasants of these states from free colonists to enserfed laborers on huge grain estates. The political dominance of the nobilities over their princes, the sparse population that rendered the land value-less without a secure labor force, and a booming demand for grain in western Europe all contributed to the construction of sprawling, serf-operated demesne lands. The early years of the seventeenth century saw this system attain the heights of its prosperity. Westerners, chiefly Dutchmen, controlled the ports and the export trade, but production and sale were firmly in the hands of the estate owners. In Poland, interior cities withered as local merchants were bypassed - indeed, forbidden from transacting business abroad - by the estate owners who traded directly at the Baltic ports.

In the forty years after 1620 the estate owners' prosperity was seriously undermined. The western demand for grain slackened: partly because of slower population growth, mainly because of a significant increase in western grain output. Figure 2 (line 1) shows the trend clearly. While the export of Baltic grain averaged 68,500 lasts per year in 1600-49, it fell to less than half that in 1700-49.

This exogenous factor was not the only adverse influence on eastern Europe. In an economy that depended entirely on its ability to harness the labor of hundreds of thousands of peasants, a decline in population struck directly at the volume of output and the incomes of the landowners. The armies fighting the Thirty Years' War brought such disease and disorder to Pomerania, Brandenburg, and Mecklenburg that, as noted earlier, population fell by 40 percent by 1650. In Poland the Cossack Wars beginning in 1648, and the Swedish invasion and attendant disorders of 1655-60 had a similar impact. The population of Masovia, the region around Warsaw, fell by half between the surveys of 1578 and 1661.

Ironically, the landowners' response to these reversals of sixteenth-century conditions was to pursue with renewed energy the enserfing and estate-building policies of the past. The grain markets were weak but the economy offered few alternative sources of income for the Prussian Junkers and Polish magnates. Because labor costs were the only economic variable under their control, they pursued a policy of *bauernlegen* - peasant oppression - in earnest. The unfavorable times, moreover, undermined the small landowners and remaining free peasants more than the great nobles. We see, as a consequence, in a district of Poland, the percentage of farms owned by noblemen with fewer than 100 farms fell from 17 percent in the mid-seventeenth century to under 10 percent in the late eighteenth century. In the same period farms owned by noblemen with over 500 farms rose from 31 to 42 percent of the total. To the south, in Moravia, the great nobles' share of the land rose from 36 percent in 1610 to 60 percent in 1656. Areas where estate formation had not yet taken place now saw their peasant agriculture destroyed. On the Pomeranian island of Rügen the majority of the 2900 farms in 1574 were between 10 and 40 hectares in size. Only two holdings exceeded 100 hectares. The Swedish administration of the island after the Thirty Years' War, which had left many farms empty because of depopulation, supported estate building. By 1695, 111 *Adelshöfen* - noble estates - had absorbed over half the island's cultivated land.

The distribution of political power is fundamental to understanding the course of agricultural development in this region. Wherever the compulsory labor services of the peasants were greatest in the seventeenth and eighteenth centuries, one found not only the great estates on which they labored but also a political structure in which neither royal authority nor the self-interest of the bourgeoisie could succeed in checking the authority of the nobility. Poland, Swedish Pomerania, Mecklenberg, and the Baltic states of Estland, Livland, and Kurland were of this type. The rising power of the Hohenzollerns in Brandenburg-Prussia could be identified as a novel exception to this pattern. And, indeed, a noteworthy policy of both Frederick William I and Frederick II was the encouragement of immigration to settle the reclaimed lands of their underpopulated states. But on the existing estates they, too, made no effort to ameliorate Junker rule. The 1653 agreement that had established the authority of Frederick William, the Great Elector, explicitly reserved local affairs to the Junkers: royal power stopped at the estate gates.[15]

Denmark

The agrarian developments of both Italy and East-Elbian Germany, for all their differences, display a kind of involution by the privileged classes. In reaction to the economic contraction of the seventeenth century, they turned their attention inward upon the countryside, battening on the peasantry in ways that made agricultural progress difficult to achieve. Denmark provides another example of such involution, one with an interesting twist.

The Danish nobility, just as their eastern colleagues, took energetic steps to participate in the sixteenth-century grain boom. Their share of the cultivated land grew from 25 to 44 percent in the course of the century, and the burden of compulsory labor services on the peasantry grew commensurately. Much as the Poles, the Danish nobles sought to reduce the domestic bourgeoisie by favoring foreign - chiefly Lübeck and Hamburg - merchants in their export activities.

These parallel developments ended abruptly in 1660. In that year the wreckage of the state at the hands of Charles X of Sweden - the loss of Halland and Schonen, the plague epidemics that decimated the population, and the staggering debt imposed by the military campaigns - provided a setting in which the king, Frederick III, through adroit maneuvering and in alliance with the Copenhagen bourgeoisie, managed to dismantle the apparatus of aristocratic control and replace it with a new system of royal absolutism. The noble estates, legal exemptions, and landowning privileges all were abolished. The king gradually conferred titles upon his bourgeois supporters, and by generously distributing royal lands to them created a new nobility.

With the king now firmly in the saddle, agricultural organization was restructured to suit royal purposes. Two aims can be seen in the arrangements encouraged by successive royal enactments: the transformation of the nobility into a class of royal administrators, and the preservation of the peasantry in a form that would facilitate tax collection while it maximized tax revenue. By differentiating the nobility into two groups, by forbidding enclosure and demesne consolidation, and finally by making the nobles responsible for the taxes due from the peasants on their lands, the crown achieved the first of these aims. The second was accomplished by forbidding the destruction - through enclosure, or division - of peasant holdings. The crown was eager to preserve peasant holdings sufficiently large to generate a substantial taxable surplus.

Throughout this century of monarchial absolutism the crown's policy was conditioned by the economic contraction in which export markets for oxen and grain withered. It seemed sensible to develop the kingdom as a vast royal manor administered by the nobility. The taxes were generally collected in kind and dispatched to Copenhagen to support the growth of the royal capital. For the nobles, who continued to operate estates, an outlet was secured for their surplus grain in Norway (governed by Denmark until 1814). The imposition of onerous import levies on foreign grain prevented Norwegians from buying it elsewhere. In 1733, as a capstone to the system, the crown insured a cheap labor force for the indivisible farms by binding peasants aged 14 to 35 to the land (after many years of falling grain prices had provoked more and more peasants to default on their obligations and abandon their farms).

When export markets grew and prices rose in the second half of the eighteenth century, the crown decided to abandon this system and threw Danish agriculture open to free, individualist farming. The response was swift and dramatic. But in the seventeenth-century crisis a stagnant agriculture, overcommitted to grain cultivation, was preserved by being fastened to an absolutist state.[16]

Western Germany

Going from east to west across an invisible line that generally follows the river Elbe, we enter the Europe of more ancient settlement, denser population, greater urbanization, and more varied social structure. These features shaped the agrarian structure of the western states in such a manner that the response to the seventeenth-century crisis contrasted sharply with that of the eastern states.

First of all, the social diversity of the west German states had checked the spread of noble-dominated estate agriculture. The fragmentation of the area into small states did not prevent the princes from trying to imitate the Renaissance and absolutist monarchs of the west, and the Lutheran Reformation strengthened the hand of many by placing Church resources under their control. Moreover, the numerous cities of southern Germany and the Rhineland provided markets that stimulated intensive peasant farming and viticulture in many areas. Consequently, on the eve of the Thirty Years' War west German agriculture was based on peasant production units; the labor burdens on the peasants were light or, particularly in the north, almost nonexistent and, in many scattered areas, farming practices were highly labor-intensive.

The Thirty Years' War is the great central event around which the history of German agriculture - as of so many other things - revolves. While other areas of Europe experienced a slackening of population growth, Germany suffered the loss of perhaps a third of its population. The price and wage trends of Germany show in correspondingly exaggerated form the general European trends.

The immediate effect was, of course, a dramatic deterioration of agricultural practices. The effects on agriculture of marching armies, the forced quartering of troops, and general disorder can be seen in data compiled from Brunswick. The average herd size plummeted decade by decade, until the end of the war in 1648. Without draught animals and manure the peasants had no choice but to let more land lie fallow: before the war one-third lay fallow each year; by its end one-half did. Yield ratios did not decline much in this period (the land that remained under cultivation was no doubt the best), but the total harvests did fall as a result of this forced reversion to less-intensive methods. The same retrogression has been identified in other parts of northern Germany where complex crop rotations with infrequent fallow were given up in favor of the three-course rotation system.

In the postwar reconstruction of the German economy there was no lack of noble landowners who wished to follow the example of their eastern colleagues by converting large portions of the depopulated, capital-starved countryside into estates. Overcoming the problem of high labor costs (the result of acute labor scarcity) through the increase of compulsory labor services also appealed to them. In most areas, particularly in the north, this course was successfully resisted. The princes, their pretentions to sovereignty bolstered by the Peace of Westphalia, strove to fashion absolutist regimes. To this end they opposed estate formation and pursued a policy often labeled *bauernschutz* - peasant protection. The farm units, though they might lie abandoned, were not to be thrown together into estates (which would strengthen the landowners); their integrity was to be protected by the state so that peasant households would once again inhabit them. The *bauernschutz* program went on to prohibit the division of farms among heirs and the contraction of mortgage debt by peasants. All of these policies aimed to preserve peasant farms as permanent and fruitful units of taxation.

In some areas the potential tax revenue was further raised by legal rulings that tended to convert the prevailing form of tenancy, *meierpacht,* from a leasehold to a hereditary tenure. Rental payments became fixed and as German prices rose beginning in the late seventeenth century, rents tended to decline in real value. As a result, in Brunswick the total payment of rent and taxes paid by peasants between 1620 and 1760 was held to about one-third of farm revenue. But while rents claimed the bulk of this amount in 1620, by 1760 the bulk consisted of tax payments. A peasantry secure in its control of the land and absolutist governments secure in their control of tax revenue took shape in Hannover, Brunswick, and other small north and west German states.[17]

It cannot be said that the rural population as a whole benefitted from the *bauernschutz* policies of the princes. When we inquire into the impact of seventeenth-century political and economic trends on the peasants, we confront a phenomenon present not only in northwestern Germany, but also throughout France, the Low Countries, and England: the coalescing of a class of large, secure farmers. *Anerbenrecht*, the inheritance custom of passing on farms intact to a single heir, played a large role in this process. Electoral Saxony, as an example, had raised the prohibition of farm fragmentation to a constitutional principle. Consequently, when the rural population doubled between 1550 and 1750 the *bauern*, who cultivated the large farms, remained numerically constant while their percentage of the rural population fell from 70 to under 40 percent. The same situation has been observed in the Principality of Lippe, the County of Paderborn, and elsewhere. To make matters worse, the destruction wrought by the Thirty Years' War created the opportunity to throw together more large farms - and more large taxable units. In the central German Thuringian states wartime population loss was never made good as prewar hamlets disappeared to make way for large, consolidated farms.[18] Standing behind this process - and worsening the lot of those peasants not in possession of such a farm - was the market situation that encouraged livestock raising over grain production. The lower labor requirements of the former combined with the consolidation and protection of large, tenanted farms to create a significant change in rural social structure. The following chapter will attempt to describe the consequences of this development for industry. The social structure of many parts of western Europe was altered to favor the creation of a class of substantial peasants with secure leases together with a growing landless class. But in Germany the market conditions in the decades after the Thirty Years' War did not provide much opportunity for increased labor demand through intensified production. The century after 1648 was primarily a century of recovery.

France

Nowhere in Europe did the political and economic consequences of inelastic agricultural production force themselves on the consciousness of contemporaries as well as historians as in the grandest political entity of all, France. The land of classic absolutism was a society under great economic pressure. The sixteenth-century economic revival brought France's population up to about 20 million, making it the most densely populated large state in Europe. From then until at least 1720 French population and agricultural output behaved as though a stubbornly unyielding ceiling had been reached - a Malthusian situation in which the provision of subsistence became a constant preoccupation and subsistence crises erupted with almost predictable periodicity.

Added to the often unfulfillable demands for subsistence were the growing demands of a developing absolutism. If Henry IV, early in the seventeenth century, wished to see a chicken in the pot at the Sunday supper of every Frenchman, his finance minister, Sully, and those of succeeding Bourbon monarchs were much more interested in the well-being of the French treasury. We will later have occasion to examine the steady growth of the principal tax, the *taille*. This tax, levied primarily on peasant land, and the salt tax grew relentlessly and placed the peasantry in a frequently untenable position. As the royal bureaucracy, the military, and the subsidies of the French monarchs grew, so did the need to extract more from the peasantry. During the reigns of Henri IV and Louis XIII royal taxation grew four- or fivefold while the available money supply remained constant at best. Peasants were thereby driven into the market in a scramble for cash that was becoming increasingly scarce in rural France. Very little of the tax revenues sent to Paris returned in the form of central government expenditures; the consequent drainage of coin from the countryside hobbled commodity markets by increasing the difficulty of transforming farm surpluses into cash. It was this fiscal novelty and its consequences that provoked most of the peasant rebellions that occurred with increasing frequency in the first half of the seventeenth century.[19]

French agriculture, called upon to feed an enormous population as well as bankroll a monarchy of vast ambition, failed to increase its productivity.[20] The reasons for this are not simple to isolate but seem to lie in the special character of yet another obligation of the peasants: the maintenance of their social superiors through rents, tithes, and feudal dues.

By the sixteenth century at the latest the French nobles had disengaged themselves from direct control over the land; by monetizing peasant obligations they had disengaged themselves from marketing as well. Their demesne lands had been parcelled out to tenants who often enjoyed fixed rents and hereditary tenures. Nobles retained their seigneurial rights, however, and for many these now formed their most important source of income. However prudent such arrangements may have been for the aristocrats of earlier centuries, their seventeenth-century descendants found them inadequate, even dangerous. By the seventeenth century many decades of inflation had undermined the value of fixed rental property, and the reinvigorated crown showed itself capable of depriving the seigneurs of important and lucrative judicial powers. Indeed, many ancient noble families had been forced to sell their lands and feudal rights as well. The purchasers had frequently been bourgeois families eager to upgrade their social standing through land acquisition.

The greatest of the new landowners were in many ways creations of the crown. Royal service had brought many bourgeois families wealth, judicial appointments, and a new status as *noblesse de robe* (in contrast to the old feudal-military nobility, the *noblesse d'épée*). The prestige of the old noble way of life proved capable of diverting the loyalties of these new nobles of bourgeois origin. They spearheaded a new aristocratic counteroffensive bringing legal and commercial expertise to the mission of increasing landowners' incomes and reasserting the nobility's political leadership over rural society.

The options open to the disgruntled nobles and their new allies were not numerous. The reestablishment of estates would have allowed them to deal directly in the large-scale marketing of grain, a lucrative prospect. But the effort to enclose and expropriate village common lands and convert leased farms to demesnal use met stiff opposition not only from the peasants but also from the instruments of royal government, the intendants and courts. The fiscal interests of the absolutist state required that the traditional structure of authority that placed noble landowners and seigneurs directly above the peasantry be short-circuited. Thus crown agents were active in encouraging the creation of formal village assemblies (to administer local tax collection) and in using the courts to guarantee the heritability of customary tenures. Thus fortified, peasants frequently succeeded in defeating projects to revive direct agricultural production by large landowners. Too often stymied in this line of attack, the landowning classes acted to increase their incomes in a way still open to them. They rejuvenated old feudal dues, many of which were rediscovered by lawyers specializing in this practice. The old feudal right of *mortmain,* whereby the death of a peasant required the reversion of his land to the seigneurial lord, was revived with particular eagerness. This feudal reaction, which breathed new life into anachronistic practices, is probably best understood not as the result of the backward mental bent of French noblemen but as the result of the energetic pursuit of a "second-best strategy" to increase incomes: it was less desirable than the constructing of large enclosed farms, but it was also less risky, costly, and time consuming.

The spread of sharecropping tenures also fits this analysis.

In the early seventeenth century the growing attractiveness of marketing grain stimulated landlords' efforts to reassemble their demesne. The royal policy of *bauernschutz* frustrated them in this aim and they turned to *métayage*, a sharecropping tenure long popular among the bourgeois owners of small parcels of land, as an alternative means of gathering farm produce into their hands. Landowners found it possible to convert long-term tenures to *métayage* despite royal policy protecting peasant holdings. The increased burdens imposed upon the peasants by royal taxation and feudal reaction alike tended to undermine their economic position and force them into debt. The lesser peasantry in particular succumbed to indebtedness in their efforts to survive the periodic food crises that wracked France. Thus was the protective policy of the crown subverted to permit the spread of *métayage* tenures.

Holdings over which landlords formerly held little power to adjust rents could be transformed into small farms supplied with livestock and equipment and let out to indebted peasants on short-term leases, perhaps for no more than one year. The leases stipulated which crops were to be grown and reserved for the landlord at least half of the harvest. Because there were no incentives for either party to invest capital in such holdings, *métayage* was a form of rural reorganization that offered no long-term improvements to the French economy; its attraction was strictly short-term and confined to the landowner.[21]

The absolutist policy of diminishing the independent political power of the nobles strove to tie them to the crown. This required the maintenance of a splendid court offering lucrative patronage opportunities, a large officer corps (and occasional wars), and other devices to secure the loyalty of the nobility through economic dependence. For many *noblesse d'épée* this strategy worked smoothly. But for many others, and for the economically more aggressive *noblesse de robe* in particular, it spurred efforts to increase income. Both to keep up with the level of expenditure required by residence in Paris and Versailles and to secure a measure of independence from a fickle crown, noble landowners pressed their agents and lawyers to increase their incomes. With agricultural reorganization ruled out by the policies of absolutism, the next best method was to squeeze more income from the peasantry through sharecropping tenures and the revival of feudal obligations. Correspondingly, there seemed no better way to invest money in agriculture than simply to extend one's holdings at the expense of others. Most tenures gave neither the landowner nor the tenant the incentive to invest in increasing farm productivity.

Sectors of French agriculture existed to which this somber picture of social conflict immobilizing agricultural progress does not apply with full force. Besides grain, the great commercial crop of France was wine, and viticulture proved capable of responding positively to the steady growth of demand. The rising real incomes of Europeans, particularly after 1650, affected their drinking habits. Northern Europeans, among whom wine drinking had been confined to the well-to-do, were eager to drink wine more regularly, and merchants, particularly the Dutch, were eager to be their suppliers. A dynamic export market together with growing domestic demand caused vineyards to spread with such speed that by 1715 officials claimed it threatened the grain supply. Indeed, in 1731 the government forbade new plantings of vineyards. As the American historian Barrington Moore remarked, "it is pleasant to contemplate wine drinking as at least a partial cure of economic backwardness."[22] Unfortunately for France, the rapid growth of the wine industry did not seriously affect the structure of the agrarian society. Viticulture is highly labor-intensive; this militates against its being conducted on large, well-capitalized farms. Landowners eager to profit from the wine market simply let out tiny parcels on which the poorer peasants lavished their labor to produce a crop that the landowner could extract as he extracted grain -

through seigneurial rights and sharecropping tenures.

Wine production provided no lever to effect a major change of the agrarian structure, but grain production did have this potential. And if powerful forces strove to shore up the peasant social order, there were capitalist elements at work to undermine it as well. The diversity of peasant social structure observable among the various regions of so large a nation does not encourage generalization. Still, a distinction can often be made, particularly in the common field zones of northern France, between the *manouvrier,* the humble cultivator of a few acres who lacked sufficient resources to muster a plow team or avoid periodically entering the labor market, and the *laboureur,* a peasant farmer with a plow team and land sufficient to support his household and provide for his needs.

One must not exaggerate the cleavage between these two categories. In reality, the one faded into the other, and they often made common cause against seigneurs and tax collectors. But they were also linked by a debtor-creditor relationship that developed into something approaching class distinctions under the pressure of the periodic subsistence crises of the seventeenth century. For the *laboureur* stood prepared regularly to market a grain surplus. In the years of grain shortage and during the long secular upturn in grain prices beginning in France around 1730, the *laboureur* was in a position to prosper. The *manouvrier,* on the other hand, often entered the market as a consumer rather than as a producer. Thus, in the Beauvais region north of Paris, the severe crisis of 1647-51 has been identified as the opportunity that permitted many *laboureurs* to buy land from smallholders ruined by famine-level prices. In this region a relative handful of these large tenants and owners, each with perhaps 100 hectares of land, a dozen horses, and a large livestock herd, stood at the apex of village society, extended credit to the lesser peasants, hired many *manouvriers,* and produced a large part of the marketed grain. These *laboureurs* further strengthened their hold over their village economies after the 1730s when rising grain prices enabled them to attract credit with which they actively bought up more land and equipment.

Even more conspicuous was the emergence from among the *laboureurs* of a veritable caste of very prosperous *fermiers,* usually large tenants of consolidated farms owned by nobles or the Church. But here a contrary tendency was at work. Many *fermiers* were not farmers at all: that is, they did not supervise the exploitation of their holdings. Instead, they collected rents on behalf of their landlord from sharecoppers among whom their holdings had been divided. The *fermiers généraux,* as they were known, became a kind of rural bourgeoisie participating in the peasant-squeezing conduct that the social and political climate of absolutist France had made the only avenue for advancement.[23]

These *fermiers* should be viewed as a social type peculiar to a half-capitalist society; they existed and prospered as the intermediaries between the seigneurial, cash-starved rural economy and the monetized market and governmental economy. The relative strength of social classes imposed a "second-best" solution to the problems of landlords' incomes which succeeded in increasing the flow of payments to the recipients of tax, rental, and seigneurial revenue in a way that offered little scope for either organizational or technological progress in French agriculture. As a result the problems of grain supply and tax revenue, both of which stemmed from the undercapitalized, exploited peasantry, remained as the dominant political and economic issues to the end of the *ancien régime.*

The Low Countries

The interregional flows of grain, wine, cattle, wool, and other products were sufficient to tax the transportation capacity of many areas, but they rarely affected the bulk of the rural population in more than a marginal way. That is, they did not preempt local markets and the peasant household itself as the primary destinations of agricultural output. In the Low Countries, which since the 1580s had been divided into the Dutch Republic and the Southern, or Spanish Netherlands, many of these trade flows found their focal point: here the most profound and far-reaching specialization process operated to reorganize the agrarian structure and raise up the most thoroughly commercialized agriculture of Europe.

Commercialized agriculture was no recent innovation here, of course. Highly urbanized Flanders and neighboring Brabant had supported labor-intensive, market-oriented farming in the fourteenth century. In the seventeenth century this commercialization both spread and deepened. It embraced the entire maritime fringe of northwestern Europe and altered in function from the provisionment of the numerous towns to the production of special crops for international markets. Thus, agriculture in the Low Countries did not simply respond to the growth of urban markets; it reoriented itself to take advantage of the new opportunities for trade and specialized production. The limitations of the soils in this low-lying region and the accessibility it enjoyed because of the ocean and river routes that converged here contributed to this specialization. But most important, and most interesting, was the responsiveness to opportunity that characterized the region's agrarian structure.

The Dutch Republic's agrarian structure exhibited novel features whose origins stretched back many centuries. The process of land reclamation established a set of drainage institutions that gave peasants some voice in local affairs and a vehicle to secure cooperation in improvement schemes. The dominance of livestock farming had induced commercial relations and lightened the control of noblemen over rural society. These conditions could have been found long before the seventeenth century, but by then the revolt against Spain further reduced the role of the nobility while a waxing merchant class began to invest heavily in land reclamation. Moreover, price trends now favored dairy and livestock production. The stage was set for the transformation of unproductive peasant holdings into large, commercial enterprises. Despite the dense and growing population of the Republic, the farms remained relatively large and capital, rather than labor-intensive. In a region where feudalism had never played a large role few obstacles stood in the way of establishing a capitalist land market and short-term leases payable in money. Because social advancement in this urbanized state did not depend on the grandeur of one's country seat, landownership remained primarily a commercial venture. As a consequence the peasant economy of Holland and the other maritime provinces rapidly came undone. No royal protection or community resistance could prevent the move toward commercialization. Those with access to capital became large tenants or peasant proprietors; the others sought employment in crafts and shipping or moved to the cities. In this way agriculture came to account for a minor part of the labor force in much of the Republic; in the rural province of Friesland in 1749 farmers, their servants, and hired laborers composed about a third of the labor force.[24]

Where agriculture devoted itself to butter and cheese making and cattle raising, the best suited farm structure, large farms and a large nonfarm population providing goods and supporting services arose without hindrance. Elsewhere, near the cities and where soils were well suited, extremely labor-intensive small farms proliferated to provide horticultural crops, tobacco, bulbs, and industrial crops such as madder, hemp, and hops. These specializations could assume their importance not simply because of the size of nearby urban markets but also because of the commercial facilities available for export and for the importation of grains.[25]

The importance of the Republic's ability to import grain requires special emphasis. The rise of Amsterdam as Europe's grain entrepôt served many regions in occasional years of harvest failure, but it served the Republic *every* year; by far the largest portion of Baltic grain exports were consumed in the Low Countries. Not only did the correlation between Amsterdam and Baltic grain prices become stronger, but the absolute gap between grain price levels in the two regions narrowed: Holland benefitted from a decline in her grain prices relative to the European "average." The economic interdependence of the Dutch Republic and the East-Elbian States is striking given the distance separating them. Is there also an interdependence between the specialized free labor force that arose in the former and the enserfed peasantry of the latter? Do we have here an early example of Marx's claim that the "veiled slavery of the wage worker in Europe needed for its pedestal, slavery pure and simple in the New World"?[26] The "colonial" character of the Baltic economy is obvious, with its port cities controlled by western merchants and its dependence on the exchange of raw materials for manufactures. But one might question whether the mode of production used in eastern Europe arose inevitably from its market role as the supplier of grain to the Dutch cities. Apart from the fact that the enserfment process began before western grain markets began to attract Baltic producers, those producers lost a large part of the Dutch market in the late seventeenth and eighteenth centuries to a supplier that used free labor, England. Once again, we see that the key factor in controlling international markets was low cost. The social structure of the eastern European lands identified labor costs as the variable that could be controlled; England's success in the eighteenth-century grain trade demonstrates that there was another viable approach - increasing productivity.[27] The Dutch were not indifferent to which states supplied the international grain market. They exercised a much greater control over Baltic trade than English trade and consequently garnered shipping and trading profits from the former. But the

Republic's specialized domestic economy benefitted from cheap grain no matter where it was from or how it was produced.

In the Republic the agricultural depression of the seventeenth century was delayed until late in the century as price and demand changes that threatened agriculture elsewhere were capitalized upon by a responsive agrarian structure which developed a strongly marked differentiation in land-use and even social structure. However, the Republic was by no means immune to the agricultural depression. The success of its agriculture rested in no small measure on capital investment in livestock, drainage, transportation, and farm equipment. In the decades after 1680 falling prices combined with the stubbornly irreducible burden of drainage costs, taxes, and wages to create a price-cost squeeze that forced rents to decline while their payment fell into arrears. Bourgeois landowners disinvested, reclamation works came to a standstill, and many farmers abandoned such expensive practices as the heavy manuring of pastures. Compounding these problems were the cattle plagues which, beginning in 1714, periodically wiped out a major portion of the Dutch herds.[28] The commercial character of the Republic's agriculture remained (that was now irreversible), but further advances, dependent as they were on capital investment, had to await a more favorable economic climate.

In the Southern Netherlands (modern Belgium), we find the classic land of small, labor-intensive farms. Here, in contrast to the Republic, noble landowners were numerous and powerful and a feudal past affected the character of land tenure. The needs of the large textile cities of medieval Flanders had stimulated peasants to cultivate intensively their small parcels of land not attached to the large grain-producing holdings of the nobility. In the fourteenth and fifteenth centuries the weakness of grain markets increased the willingness of landlords to permit new crops to be cultivated and more intensive rotation systems to be employed, but intensive farming in Flanders and Brabant remained the specialty of the small peasant.

On the large grain farms that hired labor the intensification of land-use, which caused the marginal productivity of labor to decline, became unprofitable as soon as the marginal productivity of labor dipped below the market wage rate. But on peasant farms, family members shared in the output in such a way that an economist would say they were "paid" their average product, rather than their marginal product.[29] Such workers would put down their tools and rest only when the utility, or enjoyment, derived from the product of their exertions to intensify further their agricultural practices was exceeded by the utility or pleasure, gained from replacing those exertions with leisure. In the Southern Netherlands the peasant self-exploitation that was needed for highly intensive agriculture could flourish because of a combination of extreme population pressure and growing markets for the products of intensive peasant holdings, such as flax, dyestuffs, plus spun and woven linen. The trend was also forwarded by the presence of urban landowners willing to fragment their property to accommodate the growing peasant population in return for rents that exceeded those available in capitalist agriculture - that is, large farms hiring wage labor.

Another factor encouraging the spread of tiny holdings was the gradual substitution of potatoes for bread in the Flemish peasant's diet. The potato offered handsome yields to labor-intensive cultivation and permitted a somewhat larger population to be fed per acre of arable land. Its introduction into Flanders has been dated from the first decade of the eighteenth century which is also when it begins to influence Irish agriculture. In most of northern Europe it did not begin to play a significant role until after 1740, when it began its rapid spread, altering basic food consumption habits. By 1800 potatoes covered 15 percent of the arable land in the province of East Flanders.

Among the other methods used by Flemish peasants to increase output were the stall feeding of livestock to ensure the capture of all manure for application on the arable fields, careful shifting of the rows of field crops to spread soil depletion evenly, and the using of every manner of substance - industrial by-products in particular - as fertilizer. All of these measures caused Flemish yields to attain very high levels. In fact, by the mid-eighteenth century this densely populated land had actually become a net exporter of grain.[30]

These accomplishments, however much they impressed contemporaries, did not gain high living standards for the Flemings. On the contrary, they were low, and, if anything, declining. It remained for another nation's agriculture to combine the intensive farming techniques of the Low Countries with large-scale farming which could apply more capital and secure higher incomes.

England

A unique agrarian structure evolved in England: its origins stretch back to the fifteenth century, and its culmination must be placed in the mid-nineteenth century. By then much of the English countryside was dominated by great landed estates, divided into large tenanted farms, and worked by wage laborers. The elaboration of an agrarian structure over such a long time period makes the historian's task of finding turning points and crucial events in this process, let alone explaining its causes, very difficult. Still, one event stands out as uniquely important - the English Civil War.

During the sixteenth century English noble landowners tried to lay hands on the lands long ago disbursed in long-term, often hereditary tenures. Their efforts were comparable to the strivings of their continental counterparts, with the exception that the Englishmen had rather more success in appropriating village wastelands and enclosing former demesne lands. The profitability of large enclosed fields for sheep raising in that era escaped no one. Aristocrats could profit from the fact that there existed among the more prosperous peasants men willing to push in the same direction for a clarification of the muddle which was feudal land law and a rationalization of land-use practices. Still, in England as on the Continent, the crown looked on the drive toward agricultural rationalization with suspicion and apprehension. It was in the English Civil War that the crown lost forever its ability to resist the imposition of capitalist relations on the land. Feudal tenures had been enforced by the Court of Wards. This was abolished. Enclosure schemes had been blocked by the Prerogative Courts. These were abolished. Royal courts had generally struck down entails, legal devices to insure that an aristocratic family's lands would never be alienated. Henceforth court rulings would support these devices.[31]

Before the Civil War the great aristocratic families and the numerous gentry landowners had been increasing their share of English landownership. But this trend was obscured in the unprecedented volatility of the land market. Landowning families rose and fell with great frequency, and this, indeed, directly contributed to an atmosphere in which English society could fall into warring camps.

By the time of the Restoration, however, both the great peers and the regional gentry could put all this behind them. From then until the nineteenth century they settled down to a steady aggrandizement of land, the ownership of which was now shorn of its feudal ambiguities. The largest landowning families gained the most. Their extra-agricultural incomes from state service, royal subsidies, urban land speculation, and mining gave them an advantage in a market where high land prices reflected the social return as much as the economic return that purchasers expected to reap.

The process by which rural England came to be blanketed by large estates is a long, slow-moving one with origins far before the seventeenth century. But in the decades after

1640 the obstacles to its triumph were removed. Even the internal disequilibrating factor of a growing number of peers and a rising gentry population vanished after the Civil Wars as the aristocratic population failed to reproduce itself, thereby contributing to a further concentration of landownership.

Few of these estates possessed significant home farms. The great landowners of both England and eastern Europe exercised enormous political power in their respective societies, but the conduct of English landowners differed from that of the eastern European estate owners in their eschewal of direct exploitation of a controlled labor force. One historian speculates that this was out of a fear of the (often absentee) owners that they would be hoodwinked and cheated by a mass of supervisors and employees whom they could not control. It is simpler to explain their preference for leasing their lands in large, tenant-operated farms by pointing to the lower per acre labor requirements of Britain's more livestock-oriented agriculture and the competitive, multisector labor market in which the landowners would have had to compete.

The political triumph of the English aristocracy destroyed the institutions that might have preserved an entrenched peasantry on its small holdings as in France. On the other hand, because of the economic atmosphere of the Atlantic region and the less labor-intensive character of English agriculture, the aristocracy did not pursue the peasant-enserfing policy of their east European counterparts. In England a third agrarian structure arose of estates as units of ownership, large tenant farms as units of production, and an agricultural labor force drawn from a free labor market.[32]

Small independent farmers and cottagers continued to exist. In the more remote and less fertile areas in particular they were numerous; but each economic crisis saw some of these small men sell out to those with more ample resources. The future did not belong to them.

How did England's unique agrarian structure contribute to its success in increasing output sufficiently to warrant the century after 1650 being given the label of "agricultural revolution"? The answer to this question used to focus on the landowner himself. The improving landlord of England (in contrast to the absentee rent recipient of France) was thought to have stimulated improvements by using his broader intellectual horizons to inform his tenants of new practices and by using his ample financial resources to underwrite the capital improvements on his property. This idealized view of the English landlord cannot be sustained. The London season kept him from his estates enough to make him an absentee much of the year and, when in residence, the pressure to build country houses and entertain forced him to order his stewards to squeeze more rental income from his holdings just as surely as the court life of Versailles generated such pressure in France. The late seventeenth and eighteenth centuries in particular saw a boom in country house building of unprecedented proportions and a refinement of tastes that generated unheard-of expense.

What is left of the improving landlord explanation is the undeniable growth in efficiency in estate administration which ensured that tenants would be spurred to diligence or be replaced. Also remaining is the stabilizing influence exerted by moneyed landowning families during times of low agricultural prices. In such times, which recurred with frequency in the century after 1650, the absorption of rental arrears and the shouldering of tax and maintenance costs by the landowner were common among the largest of them because they could draw upon funds from nonagricultural sources and could borrow with greater ease than could lesser men.[33] Here was a source of investment unavailable to Dutch agriculture, where agricultural investment collapsed at the end of the seventeenth century. But, for all that, the agricultural revolution is chiefly the product of working farmers.

Until the mid-seventeenth century England's agriculture divided into three large zones. The heavy-soiled valleys of the south and east were covered with open-field villages in which grain growing predominated. The uplands of the north and west were characterized by stock breeding, and on the light-soiled zones of the south that were interspersed with the grain growing valleys, sheep grazing and mixed husbandry spread on the large, often enclosed farms that had been the chief innovation of the previous century.

The boom in wool prices came to an end in the early seventeenth century, the product of a changing textile industry as well as government laws prohibiting raw wool exports to ensure low raw materials prices for England's basic industry. The enclosure process slowed noticeably thereafter until enclosure by parliamentary act finished off the remaining open fields after 1750. Besides the many enclosed fields there were other improvements in English agriculture observable at the crest of the long economic expansion of the sixteenth century. The growth of the London market together with the arrival of Flemish refugees from the war-torn Low Countries stimulated the growth of a large horticultural sector in the vicinity of the capital. Flemings were also instrumental in introducing or expanding the cultivation of hops, dyestuffs, and clover.

Another enterprise of this period, also dependent on Low Countries' expertise, was the drainage of the Fens. Royal patronage pushed through this transformation of tens of thousands of acres of peasant-used grazing, fishing, and fowling land into more intensively cultivated large tenant farms.

Improvements such as these, for all their importance, could be found in many parts of Europe. It was in the succeeding period, when an agricultural depression gripped all of Europe, that the greatest technical changes were introduced to English agriculture. Herein lies an important reason for the significance of English agricultural expansion. Intensified farming induced by population pressure is unlikely to increase significantly the marketable surplus. When a major increase in output is achieved during a period of population stability, and when the farm labor force is, if anything, decreasing, the impact on real income and the structure of the economy can be profound. It was the good fortune of English agriculture, or, more correctly, certain sectors of English agriculture, to be in a position to respond to the challenge that was created by falling prices of grain and wool after the 1660s. Livestock and dairy prices held up in the last decades of the seventeenth century encouraging farmers to shift a portion of their operations from arable to pasture. As we noted earlier, such adjustments were not easy given the physical and communal constraints that affected open-field farmers in particular.

The best-placed farmers were those on the light-soiled scarps of southern England. Their soils were too weak for specialization in grain farming and had long been converted to large sheepwalks. These sizeable, enclosed farms profited from their structural ability to innovate and from the fact that the legumes and fodder crops used in highly-intensive Flemish agriculture - clover, and turnips in particular - were well suited to their light, well-drained soils. These crops, when introduced in crop rotations such as the alternate and convertible husbandry, improved soil fertility and structure and made possible the maintenance of larger livestock herds. Roots such as turnips augmented the fodder supply, thus permitting herds to expand, while it was possible in crop rotations including legumes such as clover and sainfoin to reduce and even eliminate the traditional fallow years. These cropping innovations could occur in infinite variations (see p. 40 for more detailed discussion), and, together with the construction of water meadows to relieve early spring fodder shortages, they permitted the farmer to increase his livestock business at a time when meat, hide, and dairy prices held up better than most others. But of more far-reaching importance, these innovations also lowered the costs of grain production at a time when grain prices were weak and declining.

The development of the light-soiled zones as low cost grain producers raised a challenge to the heavy clay vale farmers whose incomes had long depended chiefly on grain sales. Unable to introduce the innovations outlined above for reasons of soil limitations and institutional rigidity, many smaller farmers were forced to liquidate. Larger farmers restricted their arable in favor of expanded pastures. This shift undermined employment opportunities in the densely populated open-field villages; rural industry came to play a larger role in these hard hit areas.[34]

The agricultural depression forced a sharper differentiation of economic structures among the various zones of England. Greater specialization tended to squeeze small farmers out of grain production but such modest countrymen continued to find a place in forest and upland zones. In these areas, lightly populated until the seventeenth century, smallholders could piece together a living from dairying and industrial by-employments. A considerable redistribution of rural population occurred in the seventeenth and eighteenth centuries as agriculture was reorganized under the pressure of falling prices. The Act of Settlement of 1662, an effort to halt this redistribution by restricting migration, had only local success.[35]

If this process of reorganization was painful, it was also successful. An island roughly self-sufficient in grain in the early seventeenth century became a major exporter in the eighteenth century, exporting more than all Baltic exporters combined during the first six decades of the century. An annual average of 72,000 tons of wheat and rye, plus 60,000 tons of barley and malt left English ports in the two decades following 1735.[36]

When identifying those responsible for the agricultural revolution the government cannot be ignored. In 1670, to compensate for low wool prices, a product of the prohibition on raw wool exports and the simultaneous encouragement of Irish wool imports, the government ended its longstanding protection of the consumer interest in the grain trade. In the following decade the famous Corn Laws were elaborated which encouraged grain exports with bounties that grew in generosity as the domestic grain market weakened. The subsidies on barley and malt exports were particularly attractive.

Credit must also go to the landowners. If the usefulness of the large farm structure they were creating was not their primary motive for creating it, their willingness to plow a portion of their profits back into the land, and the amateur interest of some of them in breeding and in travelling abroad and publicizing new agricultural practices are characteristics not found everywhere in Europe.

Ultimately, credit must go to the estate stewards and tenants. It was among them that a remarkable energy - sometimes a rapaciousness - seems to have reigned. Falling prices culminating in a profound depression in the 1730s and 40s, when prices stood below the level of the 1660s by a third, imposed a severe profit squeeze on farmers. The ability of the larger farmers to increase output in this setting increased their total revenue but insured that low prices would continue to prevail. If this was a disappointment for them, and a catastrophe for small grain farmers, it gave to the growing nonagricultural sector of the English population a higher real income that buoyed aggregate demand for industrial products, colonial goods, and housing.

The peasantry: disappearing or consolidating?

Seventeenth-century peasant society faced economic pressures that threatened to destroy an ancient and venerable way of life. In England, where many historians speak of enclosures destroying the peasantry, "removing them from the historical stage," this process is well known. But the threat was not simply one emanating from enclosure-minded capitalist landowners. It also came from within the peasantry and often predated actual enclosures. Thus, W. G. Hoskins in his classic study, *The Midland Peasant*, laments that "in a way, the peasant community was breeding its own downfall, by producing a class of successful landowners, both native and strangers, whose interests and whole way of thinking gradually became estranged from the peasant system under which their ancestors had lived and prospered in earlier times."[37] Cleavages arose in the course of the seventeenth century, long before the village Hoskins studied was enclosed. And England was not alone in this process. Under different political institutions and different landownership patterns much the same differentiation of the rural population was underway in Germany, Holland, and France. Under princely protection a class of large hereditary tenants consolidated its hold on the land in northwestern Germany. A combination of subsistence crises and noble landowners' leasing policies let the richer *laboureurs* of northern France become a caste of labor-hiring, money-lending grain speculators. Even in Tuscany, the classic land of the small sharecropping peasant, a rural bourgeoisie emerged from the ranks of the peasantry to run commercial enterprises reliant on the labor of an expanding rural proletariat.

In Holland agriculture by the mid-seventeenth century had become the province of a minority of rural dwellers. In the following century this minority consolidated its position even more and developed a way of life with a rich material culture that set the farmers apart as a kind of aristocracy from the laborers, boatmen, craftsmen, and traders who populated the countryside.

In all these regions, the "farmers" acquired a mental outlook characterized by an interest in material comforts, status, and even urban influences plus a familiarity with the written word as it was used to formalize contractual and market relations. The gap between these relatively secure cultivators and the supporting cast of rural dwellers was now such that the village and parish ties linking peasants together ceased to hold the moral authority they once had. And as industrial employment rose to become the chief support of many of this supporting cast, or caste, the poor, too, elaborated a way of life foreign to the peasant culture of earlier generations.

3
Restructuring Industry

Industry and the agricultural depression

The seventeenth and eighteenth centuries witnessed
major changes in European industry. These were not primarily technological changes. Rather, industrial organization experienced profound though gradual changes while industrial
location was dramatically altered. Also affected was the composition of output. Although there is controversy about
whether or not total output rose significantly in this era of
stable population, there can be no doubt that certain key
industries grew enormously.

To understand how the industrial sector of a basically agricultural economy was restructured we cannot avoid considering it in the context of the agricultural depression that
gripped Europe during the century after 1650. Industrial production could not fail to be affected by falling farm prices
and declining rents. We will outline the nature of that impact
in a generalized model that is meant to serve as background
for the more detailed account of industrial change that follows it.

The demand for basic foodstuffs eased off after about 1650
as population growth slowed or was reversed while output
remained stable. The resulting decline of grain prices, by lib-
erating income from expenditure on basic necessities, stimulated the demand for such relative luxuries as meat, beverages, horticultural crops, and manufactures. As described in

the preceding chapter, the improvement of the ratio of livestock to grain prices stimulated cost-reducing innovation in
some areas which, by increasing output, further dampened
agricultural prices.

The general situation became one in which the prices of the
greatest necessities - bread grains - fell the most. The effects
of this price decline can be separated into two component
parts. On the one hand, an income effect appeared which
increased the demand for manufactures. This in turn encouraged labor to enter the expanding industrial sector. The declining agricultural incomes of farmers and cotters who were
unable to adapt their crop mix or lower production costs
combined with the strength of industrial prices to induce a
substitution of industrial for agricultural employment.

This substitution effect encouraging the movement of bad-
ly placed farmers into industrial employment had important
ramifications of two sorts. First, it fostered the removal of
industry to the countryside. The attractiveness of rural labor
to entrepreneurs had long been known. To the extent that
industrial by-employment utilized the dead time between the
seasonal peaks of agricultural labor demand, its opportunity
cost (the value of the time in available alternative employment) was very low indeed. Now the supply of such cheap
labor was growing at a time when labor costs in urban industry were being held up by rising excise taxes and competition for labor from the tertiary sector. As a consequence, the
transferral of industry from city to countryside became increasingly advantageous. A side consequence of this trend
was to reduce and in many cases to put an end to urban
population growth. This obviously discouraged rural to urban
migration.

The second ramification of the price-induced reallocation
of labor derives from the behavioral characteristics of households which ceased living chiefly from agriculture and came
to depend for the bulk of their livelihood on wage labor and
industry. Among such households the demographic character-

istics of peasant society tended to lose their force. A prole-
tarian pattern of early marriage and frequent childbearing
supplanted the late marriage pattern of land-bound peasants.
This gradual process of "proletarianization" together with
the cessation of urban population growth in many areas tended to dissolve the characteristic marginal market involvement
of the classic peasant economy. Both the large farmers and
the small cottagers were less able to strive for self-sufficiency
than their ancestors. This state of affairs further increased the
demand for manufactured goods.

In summary, the demand for manufactured goods was increased by a direct income effect and by an indirect process
of social differentiation. The supply of industrial labor was
increased by a direct substitution effect as well as by its
demographic and social by-products.

Industrial location and the diffusion of skills

The economic trends generated by the agricultural
depression played a large role in the restructuring of European industry, but they did not act unaided. Government policies of industrial protection, colonial development, and
industrial subsidy also contributed to these changes.

Europe's industrial heartlands at the end of the sixteenth
century could boast of a considerable antiquity. Ever since
the thirteenth and fourteenth centuries the cities of northern
Italy and Flanders had been preeminent as producers of textiles and luxury furnishings. While metallurgical trades were,
by their nature, widely scattered, Liège and Milan stood out
as suppliers of armaments. Of course, many smaller centers
had arisen to provide for regional needs, but a remarkable
number of such centers could be found in the Rhenish, Swiss,
and eastern French areas that connected Flanders with northern Italy. And within this area the location of industrial activity, although present in many rural districts, remained
dominated by such cities as Venice, Milan, Augsburg, Liège,
Amiens, and Ghent.

The old industrial centers persisted partly because of the difficulties inherent in transmitting industrial technology to new places. Capital scarcity, to which economists today sometimes attribute the slow diffusion of techniques to backward areas, was not the main problem because few industrial processes required a large fixed-capital investment. Human skill played a much larger role than capital in an age of hand production processes, and the diffusion of new methods required, first of all, the diffusion of persons skilled in advanced techniques.

It happened that the political and religious turmoil of the late sixteenth and early seventeenth centuries set in motion groups of refugees whose skills were particularly advanced. The Spanish efforts to suppress the Dutch revolt plunged the Flemish economy into ruin. In the years after 1580 Flemish gardeners removed to the vicinity of London, laid the basis of English horticulture, and introduced hops cultivation - and, hence, beer brewed with hops, a product better able than nonhopped beer to withstand transportation to distant markets. Flemish textile workers, particularly those from the important center of Hondschoote, fled to Leiden, in Holland, and to the vicinity of Norwich, in England. The specialty of Hondschoote - light, inexpensive woolen cloth - took root in these new locations and rose to transform the textile industry of western Europe.

The political unrest of the early seventeenth century, by disrupting normal trade channels, also stimulated the development of new production centers. Notable among them were copper and iron mining and smelting and the armaments manufacturing activities begun in Sweden under the leadership of metallurgical workers from Liège and the Meuse valley.

The French Huguenots, fleeing France after Louis XIV revoked the Edict of Nantes in 1685, spread industry throughout Europe. In England, the glass and paper industries owed their technical development to Huguenot immigrants but even in agrarian Prussia many industries benefitted from the

Hohenzollern policy of encouraging Huguenots to settle there.

The diffusion of innovation did not always depend on large-scale migration. Often the movement of a few strategic individuals sufficed, and in the seventeenth century governments eager to develop certain industries sought to attract foreign craftsmen with special talents. Louis XIV could not abide the Huguenots in his midst; still he supported colonies of Dutch protestant shipbuilders at the new naval depots he was intent on developing. Peter the Great returned to Russia from his European tour with 640 Dutch and other western craftsmen to found a variety of strategic industries. In the absence of emigrant Italians skilled in silk making, John Lombe, an Englishman, spent two years in Italy as an industrial spy in 1716-17. His mission was to master the intricacies of the Bolognese silk-throwing mill. The construction of such mills was no secret since the plans had been published a century earlier, but the technology was useless without hands experienced in operating the complex contraptions. With this experience, Lombe was able to make a success of silk making in England; his factory soon employed 300 workers.

When the English government wished to encourage the linen industry in Ireland, it paid the Huguenot Louis Commelen to move to Ulster and teach the more sophisticated continental methods there. By 1711 a Linen Board had been established to encourage expansion and teach improved techniques. Here we have an early example of an organized effort to spread skills in the absence of immigrants. The British were sensitive to the need for such efforts, perhaps, because of the fiasco of the Cokayne project of 1614-17. Until then most English cloth had been sent to Holland for dyeing and finishing. Requiring considerable skill, these processes accounted for a large portion - as much as 47 percent - of the final price of woolen cloth. Cokayne proposed to reserve for England a larger part of the total value-added in its cloth. Just as an earlier ban on the export of raw wool spurred the growth of English cloth making, so his ban aimed to spur the growth of the dyeing and finishing trades in England. Co-kayne's proposal also included transferring to others - primarily himself and his friends - the cloth export business from the Merchant Adventurers, a trading monopoly. The scheme failed, owing to Cokayne's disingenuousness and the impossibility of increasing the number of skilled dyers and finishers simply through protective legislation.[1]

This is not to say that the intervention of governments contributed nothing to industrial relocation. The strictures of mercantilist writers directed the attention of seventeenth-century officials to the balance of trade as a key indicator of economic health. The reduction of imports by what we would today call a policy of import substitution seemed to be an obviously desirable objective. To that end England strove, through tariffs and the Navigation Acts, to replace imported ships, sail cloth, paper, and glass with domestically produced counterparts. Because other factors in the late seventeenth century were gradually making English industry more efficient, these protective measures generally speeded the maturation of the affected industries. By themselves, however, such measures frequently disappointed their backers.

In France, Louis XIV's finance minister, Colbert, pursued a many-sided policy of industrial support. Because he believed (erroneously) that France had been Europe's greatest industrial power during the reign of Henry IV, he saw his task as restoring that appropriate state of affairs. With the tariffs of 1667 he all but prohibited the importation of a wide variety of manufactures. He established dozens of "factories," privileged with royal charters and subsidies, to produce tapestries (formerly imported from the Southern Netherlands), glass (formerly from Venice), porcelain, and other luxury products. He issued endless regulations, most notably in a wide-ranging ordinance of commerce of 1673, defining the correct production methods, business practices, and quality standards of French industry. He established schools to train women in lace making, to replace the Flemish article. To bolster the precarious domestic sugar refining industry he initiated the energetic, and costly, enforcement of restrictions on the trade of France's sugar producing West India islands.[2]

Colbert succeeded chiefly in endowing his country with uncompetitive, high-cost industries, many of which did not survive the end of his patronage. In time, however, a process of learning-by-doing transformed some of these hothouse ventures - notably sugar refining, the mirror factory of St. Gobain, and the tapestry factories - into efficient, profitable enterprises. While in the politicians' eyes such long-term success justifies the short-run cost, the economist is inclined to point to the accumulated losses in the early years and ask whether such a sum, invested in other sectors of the economy, might not have produced an even greater long-run return.

But let us sidestep such speculations and simply accept that the rulers of most seventeenth-century states were not content to let an invisible hand distribute economic assets among them. They faced the economic crisis by seeking, through legislation and open warfare, the redivision of the volume of European economic activity in their favor. Attention should be called to the fact that the impact of the military and administrative initiatives, often combined under the heading of mercantilism, went far beyond this immediate objective. In my view their unintended and indirect impact surpasses the intended in importance. This new economic activism, combined with the powerful economic forces of price trends and labor supply, so altered industrial cost conditions as to endow Europe with a new industrial structure.

Technological change

The changing economic environment of Europe in an agricultural depression together with the activity of governments in the fields of colonial expansion and military expenditure acted to stimulate the industrial sector. The mere existence of a stimulus does not guarantee a response, of course, and in industrial production this warning is particularly true of traditional economies. Most industrial processes were characterized by constant returns to scale: that is, the growth of output required a proportional growth of the inputs of labor and raw materials. This characteristic made expansion cumbersome, and, as the required quantities of labor and raw materials grew, production at any given location became increasingly expensive.

There can be no question that the decisive breakthrough in making industrial output more elastic in response to growing demand occurred in the Industrial Revolution beginning in the late eighteenth century. But the preceding phase, sometimes called "proto-industrialization," laid the groundwork for the great transformation by achieving a significant lowering of costs and increase of supply within the confines of "Renaissance technology." This was achieved primarily in the sphere of organization, but incremental technological improvements also played a role, and these we will consider first.

Several well-known devices increased labor productivity in branches of the textile industry. None affected the basic spinning and weaving processes, but they are often looked upon as precocious forerunners to eighteenth-century textile mechanization. William Lee's knitting frame, invented in 1598, was slow to gain acceptance in the face of guild hostility, but found a place for itself in England by the mid-seventeenth century. Then the hosiery industry was centered in London which had 400 of the country's 650 frames. In the decades thereafter the lower labor costs of the Midland counties, where marginal farm labor was becoming increasingly abundant, attracted the industry away from the metropolis. By 1727 over 7000 frames were in operation, mainly in the east Midlands.

The ribbon frame, permitting one person to make 12 ribbons at a time, was patented in 1604 by the Dutchman, William Dircxz. van Sonnevelt. The device, sometimes called the Dutch loom, spread to many parts of Europe. In the course of the seventeenth century the silk throwing mill, an exceedingly complex and costly installation spread from its Bolognese place of invention to the north Italian countryside, Lyons, and ultimately, England.

In the metals sector wire-drawing machines and slitting mills, used to convert iron bars to sheets and rods for the nail-making industry, spread from Germany and Liège to England in the course of the seventeenth century. The slitting mills, established in profusion along the banks of the Wear and Stour rivers in the vicinity of Birmingham, did much to establish that area as the center of metal fabrication for all of England and its colonial markets.[3]

One could go on with this list, pointing to horse-powered and wind-powered fulling mills, oil presses, and butter churns, to show that a great deal of attention was focused on increasing labor productivity in this era. But one must admit that in most areas these devices could only nibble at the edges of the problem.

One economy, that of the Dutch Republic, owed much of its rise as an industrial power to a series of technological advances. A description of them should convey both the power and the limitations of technology before the Industrial Revolution. The Dutch Republic's industries before the seventeenth century consisted primarily of urban textile production for local markets, brick making, and herring packing - itself based on a pickling process invented in the fifteenth century. In the compass of a few decades after 1580, industry attained an entirely new level of importance. The textile industry felt the new impulses just when refugee Flemings introduced to the old textile city of Leiden the new light woolen cloth. Next came the shipbuilding industry, which came to dominate European markets on the strength of three major innovations. First, a new wind-powered lumber sawing mill, invented in 1596, replaced hand sawing wherever the guilds did not forbid it. Second, the newly designed *fluitschip* provided a bulk cargo vessel of such efficiency that it established a standard unattained by the ships of other nations until well into the eighteenth century. Third, shipyards equipped with cranes and stockpiled with precut timbers reduced construction costs far below those of competing nations. The Dutch shipbuilding industry, which had been scattered among many seaports, now focused on a few centers to take advantage of the economies of large-scale production (and to escape guild regulations forbidding mechanized lumber sawing). The villages strung along the river Zaan, near Amsterdam, rose with these new methods to form by far the largest shipbuilding center in all of Europe. At its peak in the late seventeenth century it is possible that some 500 new ocean going vessels were built yearly in the Dutch shipyards.

The windmill, a power source of considerable antiquity, was harnessed by the Dutch to permit mechanization of a wide range of industrial processes. Besides lumber sawing, the windmill provided power in paper making, oil pressing, paint making, and starch making. These by no means exhaust the list. In the Zaan villages alone some 600 industrial windmills operated in 1725, each employing perhaps a half-dozen men. The forty-five paper mills each employed forty to fifty.[4]

Finally, Dutch industry benefitted from improved transportation which permitted an expanded use of peat, a cheap but bulky fuel. As the transport costs of peat fell, it could be applied to a whole range of fuel-intensive industries: brick making, ceramics, linen bleaching, brewing, distilling, salt boiling, and sugar refining. By the second half of the seventeenth century the Republic achieved a position of international importance in each of these industries.

The Republic's industrial advance is an anomaly in seventeenth-century Europe. While elsewhere industrial costs were reduced by shifting to low cost rural labor, the Republic's industrial locations remained predominantly urban and its labor was relatively well paid. But the technological advances on which these achievements were based could not be continued. Peat, unlike coal, could not generate the intense heat needed in metallurgy and steam power; windmills, unlike steam engines, reached the upper limit of their power-generating capacity very quickly; canals, unlike railways, suffered from severe geographical limitations. The technical refinements of Dutch industry are properly understood as the ultimate refinements of a centuries-old technical tradition rather than as a stepping-stone to the technology of the Industrial Revolution. The stark fact that the scale of output had been measurably increased was, however, of international significance. By raising the standards of material culture and increasing the volume of trade, Dutch industry, perhaps a *curiosum* in the broad sweep of industrial development, prepared the ground for industries in other regions. Indeed, by the 1670s these were already driving many Dutch industries into retreat.

Organizational change

Long before the seventeenth century the form of industrial organization characteristic of medieval municipalities had been forced from its dominant position. Handicraft production by guild artisans for direct sale to consumers continued to exist in small cities everywhere, and the struggle to preserve them had by no means been abandoned. Most cities still sought to preserve guild organization, and their convenience as a source of tax revenue and vehicle for economic regulation persuaded the French monarchs and many German princes to protect them.

But wherever artisans supplied regional or distant markets, merchants had inserted themselves between producer and consumer to adapt output to market demand and to finance the longer delay that arose between the purchase of raw materials and the sale of the finished product. The merchant's efforts to expand or change industrial production to suit market requirements and to increase profits constituted a challenge to the very existence of guilds. Such conduct undermined the regulatory and stabilizing function of these essentially precapitalist institutions. At varying rates of speed the guilds gradually ceased to be important. Where they persisted, in such old cities as Cologne and Aachen, for example, export industries simply fled to unregulated areas in the countryside.[5]

Enterprises of a capitalist character employing a sizeable number of wage laborers became more numerous in this setting, and the concentrated demand of absolutist governments occasionally encouraged the establishment of large firms. The linen-bleaching firms of Haarlem, for instance, employed forty to fifty laborers each; the glass-making firms of the Birmingham area commonly gave employment to a similar number. The fishing industry of Holland, which had consisted of hundreds of boat-owning captains who hired on crews of a dozen or so men, was transformed in the early seventeenth century. Thereafter the industry was controlled by firms owning several boats which hired both captains and crews. This transformation had been compelled by the war-induced concentration of the industry into two large ports, the growing complexity of marketing the catches, and the sharply rising costs of an outfitted fishing vessel.

More startling than any of these firms surely were the great state enterprises that arose in the seventeenth century: the naval shipyards and arsenals, the wharves of the joint stock companies (the Dutch East India Company employed directly 12,000 men toward the end of the seventeenth century), the processing works of the French Tobacco Monopoly, and the chartered industries of Colbertian France.

When all of these firms are added together, one cannot deny that a considerable wage labor force arose in the course of the century. Still, capitalist development is not necessarily a straightforward process, and the most significant development in industrial organization had little to do with these large firms, whose existence usually depended on state support or the use of unusually expensive and indivisible capital equipment.

Low-cost production and elastic supply were more commonly sought via a much more homely route: employing rural labor in a putting-out system. Rural labor had long been used, particularly in the spinning of linen and wool, to act as a reserve labor force for urban industry, while metallurgy, by its nature, utilized rural locations. What happened in the seventeenth and eighteenth centuries was a wholesale shift of industry, including rather sophisticated sectors, from city to countryside, and the elaboration of extensive networks, or circuits, to connect rural workmen with each other in successive stages of production and with regional, even international, markets.

The price trends and agricultural developments described earlier acted as powerful inducements to this movement. In those areas where lowered agricultural prices drove peasants to seek industrial by-employments, where slack local administration attracted small peasants to acquire squatter holdings, where agricultural prices encouraged a shift from labor-intensive grain production to more extensive grazing, and where partible inheritance created population pressures, a growing low-cost labor force became available to the industrial sector. As industry moved from urban to rural areas, urban employment fell, reducing to a trickle the flow of rural workers migrating to the old industrial cities. And as rural industry spread, the traditional habits of many highland communities - to send sons to serve most of their lives in mercenary armies - lost its rationale.[6]

The merchant who organized this growing labor force was an essential element in converting peasants from casual producers of cloth or nails for the village market into increasingly specialized cogs in an extensive network of rural households producing for distant markets. As these networks became denser, the competitive potential of rural industry undermined the viability of every sort of urban industry producing for outside markets; it even affected industries that served only their own cities. By the 1730s London shoemaking, despite the protection offered by the guilds, left the metropolis for Nottingham, where costs were much lower.

The linen industry of Haarlem provides a clear illustration of the progress of rural industry. At the beginning of the seventeenth century the city's linen weavers wove yarn produced by female labor in an extensive rural hinterland. By mid-century, Westphalian and Southern Netherlands' peasant households had taken over the weaving. Haarlem now acted as the focal point for a network of cloth factors who sent linen there for bleaching and final sale. By the early eighteenth century peasant-capitalists in the Wuppertal and Brabant had established rural bleaching works that left in ruins the costly Haarlem operations, which were now far from the producing areas.[7]

The active role of merchants in this process is well illustrated in Switzerland. Through their activity in the seventeenth century, the cotton and woolen industries of Zurich shifted to the nearby Alpine districts. When cotton production needed further expansion, Swiss merchants penetrated the Black Forest in search of low-cost labor. Their presence also affected clockmaking, which had been a by-employment already for many years. In the eighteenth century, it rose to a full-time trade as merchants connected the isolated producers to larger markets.

Iron production, because of its dependence on heavy raw materials and abundant local fuel supplies, had always been a rural industry. Metals fabrication had long been located in such places as Liège and Milan, but in the seventeenth century, it too spread to rural areas. Apart from labor costs, this relocation was affected by the need to enlarge the volume of production, particularly to satisfy the growing demand for simple objects such as buttons, nails, axes, plowshares, and small firearms. In northern Mark, around the fortress town of Charleroi and elsewhere in the Meuse River valley of Belgium, and, most spectacularly, in the Birmingham region of England, farm villages became overgrown with nailers and smiths, forming the nuclei of the industrial cities of later centuries.[8]

The textile industry

The industry in which the influence of merchants proved to be most significant was also the largest and most widespread industry of the traditional economy, the woolen textile industry. Because of its importance we should accord a special emphasis to its development.

The fortunes of an industry so large and diverse as the woolen textile industry cannot be described simply. A multitude of grades and styles existed, each with its own economic potential. However, the task of the successful producer was in large measure to switch to cloth with expanding markets and to reduce the costs of producing it.

In the early seventeenth century three basic types of woolen cloth can be distinguished. The most important type was broadcloth, a fine rather expensive cloth made from a carded, short staple wool. Of lesser importance were cheaper cloths such as worsteds and says made of a lower quality, combed, long staple wool. Combinations of these types and mixtures of wool and other fibers produced what the English called "stuffs" such as bays and serges.

As the sixteenth century came to a close, northern Italy probably continued to be the largest production center of the luxurious broadcloths. Here an industrial tradition of many centuries lived on in such cities as Milan, Cremona, Pavia, and Florence. Venice, which had earlier devoted itself to trade, became an important woolens producer in the course of the sixteenth century. Fifty years later very little remained of this ancient urban industry. The causes of this collapse were numerous. Political disturbances dried up the supply of Spanish wool on which the industry depended; northern competitors introduced new, cheaper cloths which quickly dominated Levantine markets; French trade policy and warfare in Germany closed important markets. The reaction of urban guilds to these challenges was to become even more devoted to the regulations that prohibited innovation. Labor supply problems were compounded by violent plague epidemics which caused wages to rise at a time when the industry suffered acutely from high costs. Taxation levels and, in Venice, government regulations requiring exported cloth to be carried in expensive Venetian ships only exacerbated the cost problems. The decline came swiftly. Venetian cloth output, at its peak in 1602, fell by half by the 1630s and dwindled to insignificance by the 1670s. The sketchier statistics of other cities support the well-documented Venetian trend. The textile industries of Como and Milan all but disappeared in 1650; in Florence, woolens production declined after the 1580s with the international crisis of 1619-22 being particularly severe.

A measure of relief from this catastrophic situation can be sought in the Italian countryside where some merchants fled to organize production away from the high-cost cities. The record of raw wool imports through the port of Venice indicates that its hinterland produced more woolen cloth in the late seventeenth century than a century earlier. Similarly, in the uplands of Lombardy the output of fustians (a mixture of cotton and linen) and silk yarn grew vigorously after 1650. But these new production centers could not compensate for the collapse of urban production; the disappearance of Italian cloth from export markets demonstrates the reduction of aggregate output.[9]

There seems to have been something more than unfavorable developments in the supply of inputs and the size of markets driving the Italian textile industry into oblivion. Surely such a long established, multi-centered industry would not almost disappear in .less than two generations unless there existed some deep-seated institutional and even attitudinal inflexibility that immobilized those who confronted the new industrial system and the changing character of markets coming into being during the seventeenth century. This conclusion appears particularly compelling when the fate of the Italian woolens industry is compared to that of England.

England's woolen textile industry was also old and large by the end of the sixteenth century. The country exported almost nothing else. The industry differed from that of Italy chiefly in its greater reliance on rural labor and on a domestic wool supply. The English, too, ran into problems in the early seventeenth century. Changes in agricultural practices adversely affected the quality of wool. (Improved grazing land helped sheep produce better mutton, but caused their wool to become longer and coarser.) The export of English cloth was entrusted to a monopoly trading company, the Merchant Adventurers, whose traditional sales connections in the Low Countries were in a state of disarray because of the political and commercial upheavals there. Most seriously, the principal markets for English cloth, in the Baltic, declined under the impact of reduced export earnings, monetary instability, and the Thirty Years' War.

The export slump of 1619-22 dramatically illuminated the crisis of England's traditional industry and stimulated much discussion of legislative relief. But the problems were not transitory. The Merchant Adventurers' exports of woolen cloth, which totalled 120,000 pieces in 1606, had permanently fallen to 45,000 by 1640.

The foremost problem of the English industry was its commitment to broadcloths at a time when production costs were rising and foreign markets declining. Flemish refugees had introduced to England - principally in East Anglia - the "new draperies," lighter cloth using the increasingly abundant long staple wool. This cloth promised to improve export volume by its lower price and its marketability in warm climates. But before the crisis of the English textile industry could be overcome, the practices of a large, old industry had to be altered. English merchants had to compete against entrenched foreigners in markets new to them, and, most importantly, an established producer of the new draperies had to be confronted.

The Dutch Republic dominated the production of the new draperies in the early seventeenth century. During the Dutch revolt refugees from the Flemish textile town of Hondschoote introduced the new fabrics there as well as in England. They took root rapidly in Holland because the old industry was moribund and, in any event, the Spanish wool on which it had depended was then unavailable to the Dutch heretics. The immigrant textile workers most profoundly affected the textile city of Leiden. From a population of 12,000 in 1582 the city experienced a remarkable growth, rising to become one of the largest industrial cities of Europe. By the 1660s it housed some 70,000 persons and attained an annual production of all types of cloth in excess of 130,000 pieces. The high costs of urban production were at least partly overcome by an abundant labor supply of refugees, a diligent attention to the advantages of specialization (over 125 separate textile trades came to be identified), and technological inventiveness as evidenced by the wind-powered fulling mill and the ribbon loom.

The Leiden industry, well led by merchant-manufacturers, captured many export markets with its attractive, inexpensive worsteds and fustians. The most significant new markets were in the Mediterranean where the losers were the Italians. It appeared for a time that the Dutch would supplant English suppliers in Spain as well.

The trough of the English woolens industry can be dated in the 1620s. The international trade depression of 1619-22, brought on in large part by monetary fluctuations, made English cloth virtually unsaleable abroad only a few years after the Cokayne project, described earlier, had weakened the traditional export mechanism for unfinished broadcloths. No sooner had the depression ended when in 1625 a severe plague struck London. The consequent flight of merchants brought commerce to a standstill in this unavoidable funnel for British exports.

Trade stoppages such as these had a severe impact on industries such as textiles in which production depended primarily on the volume of the circulating capital invested by merchants rather than on the fixed capital invested in machinery and other facilities. Circulating capital could be withdrawn from a depressed industry quickly causing a painful contraction of employment.

The fear that merchants would withdraw from the textile industry altogether proved unfounded. The years after 1630 witnessed a determined effort to rebuild foreign markets on the basis of a restructured woolens industry that produced the new draperies. These cheaper cloths gained ground quickly in the southwestern producing areas while the industry of the West Riding of Yorkshire, long a producer of cheap, coarse cloth, expanded greatly.

The successful transformation of such a diffuse, small-scale industry was clearly the work of many men. Too, the government helped by continuing its long-standing ban on the export of raw wool while at the same time forbidding the export of cattle and woolen cloth from Ireland. This all but compelled Irish agriculture to export raw wool to England. Consequently, England became a kind of catchment area for wool. Wool prices fell far below international price levels, giving the English textile industry an important cost advantage over its competitors, particularly the Dutch, who relied on the international market for the bulk of their raw wool.

It is tempting to assign the success of England's export drive to the wars it waged against its chief commercial rival, the Dutch Republic, in 1652-54, 1665-67, and 1672-74. In the first of these Anglo-Dutch wars the capture of the

Spanish textile market from the Dutch was a stated objective. But the basis of English success in building its new draperies must be traced to its lower costs. With low prices for raw materials, low-cost rural labor, and an increasingly efficient and energetic marketing network in the Mediterranean and in colonial areas, the English industry pressed prices downward to where Holland and most other continental producers could no longer compete.

The French woolen textile industry, for instance, recovered from the 1630-40 collapse of output in old urban centers such as Beauvais, Amiens, Lille, and Reims only by protecting its domestic market with prohibitive tariffs and offering subsidies to cloth exports. These incentives, inaugurated by Colbert, offered some stimulation to the spread of rural production most notably in the southern province of Languedoc. There woolen production rose in the 1680s and, with subsidies paid by the Provincial Estates, actually competed with England for Levantine and North African markets. Woolen cloth exports from Marseilles, the compulsory port for Languedoc cloth exports, rose fivefold in the first half of the eighteenth century. (But here, as in northern centers, rapid recovery occurs only after the 1720s.)

In the face of English competition the Leiden industry shifted increasingly to a specialization in *lakens,* a high quality broadcloth made of Spanish short staple wool. Only in such expensive cloth could the Dutch industry, with its high urban labor costs, remain competitive (because labor costs made up a smaller percentage of the total price). This specialization gave the Dutch industry several decades of further life, but markets in the high quality end of the textile market were static. England, by the 1660s and 70s, had captured the dynamic new draperies market.[10]

Highly significant for England's industrial future was the fortunate fact that the new draperies were not the only type of cloth whose expanding markets endowed English industry with a leading sector. The demand, particularly colonial and industrial demand, for linen (as slave clothing, coffee and indigo sacks, mattress covers) grew vigorously through the eighteenth century. Because the skills needed in linen spinning and weaving were not great and because flax production was well suited to the labor-intensive little farms of poor cottagers, the linen industry spread with ease through the countryside. On the strength of the continuously increasing demand, part-time linen production was taken up by ever larger numbers of cottagers in such areas as Brittany, Silesia, Westphalia, Flanders (which exported - mainly to Spain and her colonies - an estimated 200,000 pieces of linen cloth by 1766), Scotland and Ireland. The combined output of the last two countries rose from 3.2 million yards in 1710 to about 20 million yards in 1750.[11]

Another light, cheap cloth - cotton - gained a toehold in Europe as imported Indian calicoes increased in popularity. Actually, the European product was usually the mixture of cotton and linen called fustians. The inability of European producers to master the techniques of the more delicate Indian article required this compromise. Fustians was certainly a minor cloth, but despite this the rural workers active in its production were more caught up in capitalist relations than were linen producers, or even woolen producers. This was so because the raw material supply and finished product marketing problems of the industry were particularly complex, therefore inviting systematic merchant intervention. Rural fustians production could be found already in the seventeenth century in such places as Catalonia, the Callarate district of Lombardy, the Lake Constance district of Switzerland, and Normandy, the Vosges, and around Orléans in France. The strong demand for cotton allowed its production to flourish in all these regions. For instance, raw cotton imports to France grew at an annual rate of nearly 4 percent throughout the eighteenth century. But none of these cotton centers grew like Lancashire in northwestern England. Here, raw cotton imports tripled in the first half of the eighteenth century and, as is well known, had only begun an expansion that would change irrevocably what we mean by the word industry.

In time cotton would drive linen from its most important markets because of the cost-reducing innovations available to the late eighteenth-century cotton producers. Here we have another example of England's uncanny ability to establish a position in an industry enjoying dynamically growing demand.[12]

The dynamic of proto-industry

By the early eighteenth century large rural districts such as Maine, Picardy, and Languedoc in France, Westphalia, Silesia, and southern Saxony in Germany, Flanders and Twente in the Low Countries, Ulster, the West Riding, the Cotswolds, and East Anglia in Great Britain, and many more, overshadowed in industrial importance the old industrial cities of Italy, the Southern Netherlands, and the Rhineland. In these rural districts a large part of the peasantry had shifted from a primary dependence on agriculture, being only marginally attached to the market, to an increasing dependence on rural industry and on the merchants who supplied the materials to keep them from unemployment.

Here was an industrial organization where, superficially, the workers were independent craftsmen utilizing family labor just as their medieval guild artisan predecessor. They generally owned their means of production - the fixed capital - because even looms were not particularly expensive. What they did not possess, however, were the raw materials and the means to market their output directly. This required capital too - circulating capital tied up in the purchase of raw materials and recoverable only after the product had been made, sent to market, sold, and paid for. For example, a merchant-clothier, as the English called putting-out merchants in the woolens industry, purchased wool from a wool stapler and then sent it out, in successive stages, to spinners, weavers, fullers, and dyers before entrusting it to a cloth factor in London or some other commercial center for final sale. Because some twenty-five workers, including at least six spinners, were employed for each loom kept in operation, a large merchant-clothier might have hundreds of rural workers dependent upon him. The fixed capital owned by those workers paled in comparison to the capital tied up in raw materials, payments to workers at each stage of production, and credit extension to the factors.

Looked at from the point of view of the merchant-clothier this system was capable of being more profitable principally through reducing the turnover period of the circulating capital. Yet, this was precisely what the merchant could not control. The spinners and weavers (or nailers, smiths, etc.) worked in their own homes. Unsupervised, they worked at their own pace and might take on work for more than one merchant. The resulting delays - not to mention embezzlement of stock and uneven quality of production - had no ready remedy. In addition the merchant had to face the fact that his labor force, however devoted it was to industrial production, continued to have some form of involvement in agriculture. It was this cheap source of at least partial subsistence for the worker that the merchant relied upon to keep rural labor costs low. The other side of the coin, of course, was that the industrial labor force all but evaporated during the seasons of peak labor demand in agriculture. From the point of view of capitalists, agriculture and industry were two distinct sectors of the economy; from the point of view of the cotter population there was only the household economy.

The putting-out system, mainly because of its expansible labor force, was capable of considerably increasing the volume of output. But the extension of a merchant-clothier's enterprise beyond a certain point made it too cumbersome and time consuming to be profitable. The remedy for these twin problems of time and space was concentration. By bringing workers together in factories, where they would be susceptible to discipline, quality and the pace of work could be controlled and, most important, capital (already concentrated in the hands of the merchant) could be "saved" by shortening its turnover period. The story of this transition is not the task of this volume. However, it is important to note how the proliferation of proto-industry - retrogressive though it might appear in some contexts - acted to create conditions (concentration of capital, creation of a labor force experienced in industrial production, increase of aggregate production) that paved the way for the transition to factory production.

The restructuring of European industry also advanced through the involvement of merchants in the production process in an effort to create new production centers. This was done to break the hold of monopoly suppliers or to alter the traditional production of an area in order to take advantage of new market opportunities.

The most notable example of such merchant involvement is the Swedish iron industry. The long drawn-out war between Spain and its former possession, the Dutch Republic, disrupted the iron and munitions trade of the Prince-Bishopric of Liège, which was the principal production center in western Europe. The Dutch need for new suppliers of munitions and iron found its counterpart in the needs of the Swedish king, Gustavus Adolphus, for revenue during the Swedish-Danish war of 1611-13. This monarch granted concessions for the export of Swedish copper to the Dutch merchants Elias Trip and Louis de Geer (both emigrants from the metallurgical centers of the Southern Netherlands) in return for regular cash payments. The interests of de Geer in particular went beyond the metals trade to their production. In 1627 he moved to Sweden with Liège craftsmen to organize iron smelting and cannon production. The Dutch, who had earlier been active trying to increase armaments production in Germany, now acquired a ready supply of iron and armaments. With the Dutch as its distributors, the Swedish metallurgical industry rapidly rose to a dominant position in Europe. Her exports of bar iron rose from 6500 tons in 1620 to 17,000 tons in 1650 and 30,000 tons in 1700. England, which had been the largest producer, became heavily dependent on Swedish iron imports since she was unable to expand output much beyond the 10,000 ton level until the second quarter of the eighteenth century.[13]

Merchants frequently took the lead in expanding industrial capacity of a more modest sort. As an example we can cite the Dutch, Flemish, and English merchants resident in the Spanish port of Cadiz, who penetrated the interior to establish direct contacts with wool and olive oil producers in the late seventeenth century. By financing the acquisition of such capital equipment as oil presses they secured long-term purchasing agreements and thus cut out the local traders.[14]

Dutch merchants also affected the character of the Bordeaux region's wine industry. Because their northern markets demanded sweet wines the Dutch extended credit to French producers who would alter production. They also introduced brandy-making to make use of otherwise unsaleable wines. Such intervention is thought to bear much responsibility for the strong export orientation attained by the Bordeaux region by the last quarter of the seventeenth century.

This discussion of industrial changes runs the danger of exaggerating the growth of industrial output in Europe by passing over in silence the many old centers, particularly in the Mediterranean, that fell into ruin. Compiling an aggregate impression from a mass of highly disparate events is fraught with danger, but seems unavoidable. Iron production in Europe has been estimated to have grown from 40,000 tons around 1500 to 145-180,000 tons in 1750. While the 1750 figure appears trivial when compared to output levels of a century later, it signifies a notable increase in the usage of iron in such goods as wagons, farm equipment, and, of course, military hardware. Perhaps of greater significance than the growth of iron output, is the concentration of that output, and its consumption, in a small zone centered on the North Sea. The iron output of England and Sweden alone rose from 30,000 tons in 1650 to 80,000 tons in 1750, with England importing half the Swedish output and Holland taking much of the rest.[15]

Because of the futility of finding adequate data to estimate aggregate textile output, some historians use as a proxy the production figures of the alum mines at Tolfa, north of Rome. In the supply of alum, a mordant necessary in cloth dyeing, these papal mines for centuries had a virtual monopoly. The fall in output from 1614 to 1650 seems to confirm the view that an economic crisis struck Europe at this time. Output figures for Italian, French, and English production centers support this interpretation. On the other hand, the new draperies branch of the woolen industry grew dramatically, particularly after the crisis of 1619-22. The argument based on Tolfa's alum output is further cast in doubt by the fact that new sources of alum in England and Liège enter production at this time.

A major structural change was underway in the textile industry affecting the output mix and the location of industry. It also affected the nature of the labor force, as did contemporaneous changes in agriculture. Together, these developments probably render any statistics of commercial production inadequate to serve as an indicator of economic activity, because it seems likely that the relative importance of home versus market industrial production was undergoing an important change. Specialized agriculture and the spread of rural industry left fewer and fewer households in a position to provide for their own needs, insulated from the market.

All in all, commercial production of industrial commodities attained new levels in certain areas and created pressure for innovations to overcome the barriers to further growth. Another achievement was the expansion of merchants' involvement in industrial production. Finally, Europe's industrial restructuring stimulated the growth and spread of a new group - or class - in the rural population.

The proletariat: a new class?

Where rural industry spread, attracted by the availability of cheap labor, it created social and economic conditions that tended to foster further population growth and, hence, increased dependence on rural industry. In time the social stratification of rural industrial zones came to differ sharply from more purely agricultural districts. One can even speak of distinct ways of life, shaped by essentially different determinants, arising among rural dwellers.

The Swiss historian Rudolf Braun presents a detailed portrait of the new society taking shape in the upland areas near Zurich as a cottage textile industry spread in the region. In the 160 years after 1634 the population of this district grew nearly threefold while Zurich's population grew by less than 80 percent and that of the agricultural villages in the adjacent valleys grew by no more than 60 percent. A peasant society continued to maintain a close control over the land in the agricultural valleys; it thereby discouraged the formation of new families which threatened the economic stability of the area. In the uplands, on the other hand, the expanding employment opportunities of the putting-out industry deemphasized the importance of land. Marriage ceased to depend on acquisition of a sufficient holding, and the choice of marriage partners became less influenced by the economic assets they possessed. Not only did upland couples, with ready access to employment, marry earlier (and produce larger families) but, Braun demonstrates, among them the concept of romantic love supplanted the strategic alliance formation that continued to characterize marriage among landed peasants.

The society being created in the Zurich uplands had its counterparts wherever rural industry spread. It was a society of great insecurity because employment depended on the putting-out merchant's circulating capital, which could be withdrawn quickly whenever the conditions of distant markets, currency uncertainties, or raw material supply problems encouraged the merchant to place his capital elsewhere. Almost inevitably such a society suffered from desperate poverty. But the poverty and uncertainty, according to an analysis of the linen workers of rural Flanders, only stimulated the further growth of population and the further dependence of the population on rural industry rather than agriculture. In the Dutch province of Overijssel, the least fertile agricultural area became a center of textile production in the late seventeenth century. In the 120 years after 1675 the district's population tripled while the urban population grew by only a third and that of other agricultural districts by two-thirds.

In Electoral Saxony, where the population doubled in the two centuries after 1550, the number of full-fledged farmers remained constant, and the urban population's growth did little more than keep pace with the total population. In contrast, cottagers, people with a scrap of land who formed the backbone of Saxony's rural industry, grew fifteenfold to rise from 5 to 30 percent of the total population.[16]

In much of Europe the crystallization of this socioeconomic class of laborers and cottagers appears as a phenomenon of the seventeenth century. The responsibility for this development rests ultimately with powerful economic and political movements. However, an immediate cause of the rapid growth of this group can be located in the marriage and family formation patterns described by Braun of the Zurich uplands. In the English east Midlands villages around Nottingham the number of births per marriage (a rough indicator of fertility) was higher in villages of important rural industry than in agricultural villages, and the differential tended to increase in the course of the eighteenth century. The same differential has been observed in the southern Netherlands, around Charleroi, where mining and metallurgy spread, and in Flanders, where the linen industry spread. In three parishes in industrializing Lancashire the average age at first marriage during the eighteenth century for wives of laborers was 22.6 years while for the wives of farmers and tradesmen it was 27 to 29 years.

Much demographic research remains to be done before we can understand fully the process of population growth in preindustrial economies. When we do it is possible that we may explain it after the fashion of a group of master nailers in the Yorkshire village of Ecclesfield. In 1733 they complained of the breakdown of their apprenticeship system: the apprentices frequently broke away and set themselves up as masters, which meant that they "did frequently marry very young and inconsiderable and by that means have a great charge of children to maintain before they scarcely know how to maintain themselves."[17]

4
The dynamism of trade

European trade

By the beginning of the seventeenth century Europeans had extended their routes of trade and exploration to nearly every part of the world. It was the amazing achievement of the sixteenth century to assimilate into the western economy both the broad stretches of eastern Europe and Russia and the New World across the Atlantic. The old trade networks in which both the Baltic and Mediterranean functioned as nearly autonomous economic entities were now gone forever, replaced by a loosely articulated world economy.[1]

The centerpiece of Europe's outstretched trade routes was Spain, and, within Spain, Seville. The merchants of this city organized in the *Casa de Contratación* possessed royal monopoly privileges to exploit the trade with Spain's overseas possessions. With the discovery of silver in Bolivia and Mexico, this trade assumed international significance; according to some it became the driving force in the expansion of the European economy. As the tonnage of the fleets sent to the New World rose from 10,000 tons in the 1540s to double, triple, and in the peak year of 1608, more than quadruple that amount, the flow of silver brought back to Seville increased over sevenfold. This silver paid foreigners for the wide range of manufactured goods sent to the New World (for Spanish production was inadequate to the task), and paid for military operations and the government's foreign borrowing (for the crown automatically received a portion of the silver). Genoese bankers, and Italian, English, and Dutch traders came to depend on their Spanish commerce; the remains of the Flemish economy required the 7 million guilders per year pumped in by the Spaniards to maintain their garrisons there. How could these nations trade with the Levant, the Baltic, or Norway, when they imported more from them than those areas were willing to buy in return? They needed bullion, gold and silver coin, to lubricate these trades, and Spain was overwhelmingly the most important source. All of Europe came to depend on Spain's peculiar combination of debility and wealth. It is in this sense that the Spanish economy assumed its central position while at the same time being incapable of actually dominating the European economy.

The system broke down in the first two decades of the seventeenth century. Seville's silver imports, after a period of stagnation, began a steady decline in the 1620s, and so did the volume of exports to the New World. Demographic catastrophe among the Indian population on whom the Spaniards depended for labor - including labor in the silver mines - plus the growing cost of exploiting the mines reduced the output of silver which, in turn, reduced colonial demand for manufactured goods. At the same time, Spanish inability to prevent other maritime powers from preying on and interrupting her Atlantic trade routes compelled the colonial economies to assume a more self-sufficient posture. Perhaps such a more autarchic economic orientation would have been an inevitable feature of maturation; whatever the cause, silver was diverted into intra-American trade channels, further reducing silver exports. In a short time Seville ceased to be an attractive market for manufactured goods, and governments throughout Europe soon found the growth of their money supplies checked.[2]

The monetary chaos that resulted from experimentation with copper currencies to supplement gold and silver, and debasement and revaluations of coins - particularly in the Baltic, Germany, and Spain itself - so disrupted the marketing process that Europe was thrown into a severe economic crisis in 1619-22. The Baltic trade as measured by the tolls levied by the King of Denmark, declined almost every year from 1618 to 1630 and remained at permanently reduced levels until well into the eighteenth century, primarily because of reduced grain shipments to western Europe. Finally, in Asia, the physical expansion of European trade routes came to an end around 1650 as the last remaining economies offering possibilities for European merchants - China and Japan - inaugurated policies designed to limit strictly the trading involvement of Europeans.

International trade had grown spectacularly by exploiting the differences that existed in natural endowments, the differing relative values of gold and silver, and the differing exchange power of those metals for commodities in the distant areas connected during the sixteenth-century expansion. The ultimate expression of this speculative basis of international trade was the Manila-Acapulco trade. Because of the inordinate value of silver in Asia and the inordinate demand for silk in Europe, Spaniards found it worthwhile to send silver to Manila and exchange it for silk, which would be sent back to Acapulco, transshipped to Vera Cruz, and then sent on to Spain. Small changes in those conditions undermined this trade in the early seventeenth century.

The simple process of connecting regions of diverse economic potentials with transport links and commercial institutions can, of course, have a powerful impact by expanding markets and facilitating exchange. But the impact is likely to be once-and-for-all. At any rate, the reversals described above drew the curtain on this phase of Europe's economic expansion. European trade in the seventeenth and eighteenth centuries developed few new trade routes, nor was it buoyed by rapid population growth. Its renewed growth, overcoming the crisis of the early seventeenth century, would depend on the development of a new kind of trading system, capable of intensifying and deepening existing trade links and creating new trading opportunities where none existed before. Three achievements would impart to international trade a new dynamism: the creative intervention of merchants in production to attune output to the markets, both existing and potential; the overcoming of the limitations of bilateral exchange; and the reduction of transactions costs. (Transactions costs refer to the costs arising from the transfer - as opposed to the production - of goods. Besides the cost of transportation, the cost of acquiring information, closing and enforcing contracts, and making payments are included under this heading.)

The Iberian empires, for a variety of reasons, had not uncovered the full trading potential of their discoveries. Wedded as they were to the exploitative trading system described earlier, the economic crisis struck them and the land-based states of Europe with particular severity and created an opportunity for sea-based hegemonies to be established.

The social structure of a dynastic state enmeshed in the struggle for hegemony on the European continent certainly provides one of the reasons for this failure. The imperial commitments of the Habsburg monarchs concentrated the attention of their servants on the strategic benefits of liquid assets such as gold and silver. The massive commitments of both Spanish and colonial resources to military ambitions founded a European network of economic centers that flourished as servitors of this imperial ambition - most notably, Antwerp, the south German cities, and Genoa. They were destined to fail with the failure of their imperial patron.

The new trading system arose under the successive leadership of two states. Until about 1672 Dutch trade was in the forefront in developing commercial techniques and binding Europe through a trade network focused on Amsterdam. Beginning sometime after the Restoration, English trade played the dynamic role of constructing an Atlantic economy.

The originality of the Dutch trading system that arose in the seventeenth century derived from the long specialization of Dutch shipowners in bulk trades. As fishermen seeking employment for their vessels in the off-season, as captains in the employ of Antwerp merchants, and as Baltic traders in their own right, Dutch seafarers acquired unrivaled experience in economically transporting grain, salt, timber - even brick. When the Dutch expanded their horizons to deal in the rich trades of woolen cloth, silks, spices, and colonial goods, they competed with seafaring traditions that had been accustomed to transporting high value-low volume goods.

The Dutch specialization riveted their attention to the reduction of cost. This they achieved most spectacularly in the development of the *fluitschip*. The first such vessel, it is said, was launched in 1595, but certainly no individual was responsible for its development. The *fluit* represented an effort to maximize carrying capacity subject to the constraint of low construction cost and low operating cost. The chief innovation was in the hull. It was longer and shallower than vessels had been, while its bottom was nearly flat; fir and pine were generally used in place of the traditional oak in its construction. While the riggings of *fluits* varied, they were generally much simpler than those of other vessels of comparable size. Purists found much to complain about in these vessels: it was possible to build sturdier vessels that were more graceful and seaworthy. But it was not possible, until iron hull construction in the nineteenth century, to build vessels so admirably suited to their purpose - that is, so profitable. Conventional vessels of the same size required crews nearly twice as large, while the construction cost per ton was nearly 50 percent higher than that of the *fluits*. Because of volume production, construction costs were kept low. Large-scale purchases of raw material, the use of cranes and wind-powered saw mills, and the low cost of borrowed money gave Dutch shipyards a cost advantage that foreign imitators could not match.

Another innovative aspect of the *fluit*, one that permitted the use of light timber and maximized the amount of space available for cargo, was its specialization as a merchant vessel. In other nations, merchant vessels were expected to be readily convertible to naval use, and in any case the threat of piracy for vessels carrying valuable cargoes required armaments as a matter of prudence. The Dutch had determined from the peaceful Baltic trade that the benefits of specialization outweighed the dangers of piracy and naval attack. When *fluits* sailed in the more dangerous Mediterranean waters, they were convoyed.

The ownership and operation of the Dutch vessels was vested in hundreds of small, temporary firms called *rederijen*. Their basic form can be traced to medieval Italy, but in the Republic they attained an unusual degree of flexibility. Shares, sometimes representing an interest as small as 1/64, were purchased by investors either for a single voyage or for a longer period. The organization of seaborne trade in many small competitive firms, inexpensively formed and dissolved, permitted capital to be infused from a relatively broad public (farmers and artisans are known to have owned shares), while it permitted the investor to distribute risk among many ventures. (This same form of organization spread to industrial enterprises that required a substantial fixed investment, such as industrial windmills and refineries.)

This single-minded interest in reducing cost permitted the Dutch to offer freight charges far below prevailing levels.[3] The consequence was twofold. First, as envious rivals imbued with mercantilist notions never tired of pointing out, the Dutch engrossed much of European trade. The size of the Dutch merchant fleet in the 1670s probably exceeded the combined fleets of England, France, Spain, Portugal, and Germany. The second consequence, easily lost sight of in an era of economic crisis, was that many commodities entered trade that never could do so before - subsequently, the overall volume of European shipping increased by a substantial amount.[4]

The shipping activities of the Republic itself grew enormously in the century after the 1570s, from a core trade consisting of a trade triangle connecting Dutch ports with the Bay of Biscay in the south and the Baltic grain ports, chiefly Danzig, in the north. Merchandise sent to Iberia was exchanged for wine and salt, and in the sixteenth century, Portuguese spices, all of which found markets in the Baltic, where grain was purchased for consumption in the Low Countries. The Dutch hold on this trade triangle can be attributed, in the first place, to the fact that the Low Countries were by far the largest market for Baltic grain. Geography reinforced their dominance over Iberian or Baltic merchants in this trade triangle. At a time when information traveled no faster than people, it was impossible for merchants in either Iberian or Baltic markets to be informed about both the state of the grain markets in Danzig and the yearly Portuguese spice shipments from the East before the Dutch, midway between the two, could gain the information. The seasonal pattern of shipping further conspired to permit Low Countries' merchants to dominate trade between these distant regions.

These basic trade routes served as the foundation of the Dutch trading system, but the importance of that system rested in how the advantages in information-gathering and in low-cost shipping were exploited to increase trading efficiency. For instance, a drawback of the Baltic trade, as of most bilateral trades, was its imbalance: in this case, Baltic exports exceeded their imports by some 50 percent, requiring the Dutch to enter the Baltic with bullion. Trade with Spain, a fountain of silver, supplied this need, and, despite the bitter eighty-year long war fought between the two nations, this trade was rarely interrupted. In fact in 1640 the Republic replaced Genoa and London as Spain's financial agent for silver disbursements in northern Europe. But to minimize the need for bullion, a dependence that subjected trade to sharp contraction at every monetary disturbance, the Dutch merchants sought to increase the variety of goods offered for sale. Thus, as new trade routes were opened to the Mediterranean, Russia, and the East and West Indies, Dutch traders escaped the limitations of bilateral trade and increased the profitability of their "mother commerce." Indicative of Dutch success in this effort is the fact that the proportion of Dutch ships entering the Baltic in ballast (thus, without trade goods) was regularly 30 percent below that of English ships. Indeed, by the late seventeenth century Dutch commodity exports to the Baltic rose dramatically despite stagnation in the grain trade. In 1661-70 the Dutch carried 14.5 million pounds of colonial goods (sugar, spices, tea, tobacco, etc.) through the Danish Sound. By 1731-40 this trade had risen to 32 million pounds. The Baltic trade had long since ceased to require enormous shipments of bullion to keep its export trade from withering.

The importance of the improved Baltic trade to the Republic was, thus, threefold. Its profitability was great enough to continue to attract three-quarters of all the capital active on the Amsterdam *Beurs* (stock exchange) as late as 1666. At the same time it was the source of grain, timber, and naval stores consumed primarily in the Republic's domestic economy. Finally, and most important, the availability of these commodities - particularly grain - on the Amsterdam market laid the basis for its development as the focal point of European trade. This transformation can be said to have begun during the Mediterranean famines of the 1590s when Dutch control of Baltic grain provided a lever to penetrate the Mediterranean markets. The interlopers succeeded in parlaying their famine relief operation into a permanent commerce based on sending in textiles, furs, colonial goods, naval stores, and fish and returning to the north with oil, rice, silk, and citrus fruits. Such extensions of Dutch trade into other parts of Europe, the North Atlantic fishing and whaling ground, plus the East and West Indies culminated in the 1630s, when Dutch trade with Russia via Archangel became well established and Amsterdam stood out clearly as the entrepôt of all Europe: that is, the efficient gathering and distribution point where nearly every commodity could be bought and sold with greater ease and profit than anywhere else.

But it was not only goods that were abundantly available at Amsterdam - so was credit. With the proliferation of trade connections at Amsterdam there arose a market in bills of exchange that attracted a further increase in goods to Amsterdam. A merchant in, say, Nantes, knew that bills of exchange could easily be gotten on Amsterdam while on most other cities, bills would be subject to greater risk, cost, and delay. Thus, the Nantes merchant would be attracted to Amsterdam even though his goods might be destined for Baltic or British markets. This side of Amsterdam's commerce existed, at first, to serve commodity trade. By the last quarter of the seventeenth century bill-of-exchange specialists could be found, and by the eighteenth century Amsterdam became a money market quite independent of its commodity markets. The development of credit facilities affected transactions costs; a further lowering of such costs was achieved by the establishment by Amsterdam's merchants of institutions to reduce the costs of gathering information and making payments. These further advantages of trading at Amsterdam were achieved by the establishment of an exchange bank in 1609, a *Beurs* in 1611, and by the publication of weekly price quotations in 1613. These institutions will be discussed further in Chapter 6. Here we should note that all these improvements in the conduct of trade were eagerly received by European commerce because they helped to overcome the chronic problems faced by traders: gaining information, finding buyers, making and receiving payment, and enforcing contracts. In a Europe still plagued by the distances that separated the various commercial centers, a concentration of trade in a single place offered attractive efficiencies.[5]

This concentration process did much to turn irregular trickles of trade into large-scale, permanent flows. But the governments of Europe that saw their ports clogged with Dutch ships rather than their own did not necessarily relish the efficient services being provided them by the overly successful Hogglanders (as one English pamphleteer called them).

The commercial policies of both France and England became obsessed with reducing the Dutch hold over foreign trade. In 1601 Dutch ships outnumbered English ships in the Port of London by 360 to 207. The Navigation Acts of 1651 sought to reserve English trade to English merchants and vessels in general, but many provisions were aimed specifically at the Dutch: goods from foreign places had to come either in the vessels of that country or in English ships - not via the Dutch entrepôt; imported fish had to be carried by the English - not the Dutch who fished off the English coast. Later provisions sought to protect the English shipbuilding and sailcloth industries from the more efficient Dutch. The obvious advantage of dealing with the Dutch frequently caused these provisions to be circumvented. But a gradual erosion of the Dutch trading position was inevitable when England backed up its legislated wishes with military force in three maritime trade wars with the Dutch in 1652-54, 1665-67, and (in concert with a French invasion) in 1672. In all these wars the Dutch held their own, but the cost inevitably bore more heavily on a state of 2 million population than on England or France, states three and ten times its size, respectively. Moreover, frequent military involvement undermined the viability of Amsterdam's entrepôt function. In every war in which the Dutch were belligerents, neutral traders gained competitive advantages that would otherwise be denied them. Hamburg benefitted more than any other; this port served as an alternative entrepôt, and drew Dutch trade - particularly the sugar trade - toward itself in every period of hostility. By the eighteenth century Hamburg had become an effective rival in peacetime as well.[6]

French commercial policy became actively anti-Dutch when Jean-Baptiste Colbert served as Louis XIV's finance minister. To the mercantilist mind the long-term stagnation of the French economy seemed to be explained by the Dutch control of its foreign trade. Textile duties to keep out Dutch cloth and tonnage fees on Dutch vessels entering French ports had been enforced before Colbert took office in 1661; then there followed in rapid succession a costly attack on Dutch smuggling in the French West Indies, a high tariff wall erected in 1667, the founding of a state subsidized Company of the North to compete with the Dutch in the Baltic, and similar companies to compete in the East and West Indics. Even where these measures attained their ostensible objective their effect was, of course, to raise the costs of French commercial activity. Perhaps for this reason Louis XIV decided to invade the Republic and simply take its efficient entrepôt into his own possession. The war, just as the subsidized trading companies, failed and the French economy stayed in the doldrums for several decades more; nonetheless, the higher costs imposed on the Dutch by these actions neutralized to some extent the efficiency of their trading system. France was lost as a textile market, and while the Dutch remained the most important group of traders at Bordeaux, their share of the trade fell from 71 percent in 1651 to 34 percent in 1684.[7]

Increased costs, particularly in the last third of the seventeenth century, robbed Dutch trade of its dynamism. As the costs of defense forced up taxes, the high costs of urban living forced up wages; even drainage costs rose at the end of the seventeenth century. And as so often happens in societies when new conditions threaten their leadership, an inflexibility permeated Dutch institutions. Wealthy regents withdrew from trade rather than deal with the new competitive situation; the innovative leaders in shipbuilding, navigation, and cartography were replaced by people with an excessive reverence for past success. Only in the specialized field of international finance did the Dutch exercise real leadership in the eighteenth century.

The Dutch phase of European trade development brought

the costs of transportation and commercial transactions to a permanently lower level, and, despite the complaints of mercantilists, this lowered cost stimulated economic life throughout Europe. But while Dutch trade fluctuated around a stagnant long-run trend from the last third of the seventeenth century on, England now rose to command commercial leadership. Her new position was partly the result of having learned the Dutch techniques, but original elements also played an important role: under English leadership, a new Atlantic economy came into being.

England, unlike the Republic, shared in the severe European economic crisis of the early seventeenth century. Its trade consisted almost entirely in the export of cloth in bilateral exchanges with Netherlandish and Baltic markets. Moreover, this trade was largely in the hands of merchants organized in monopolistic regulated companies such as the Merchant Adventurers, the Levant Company, and the Eastland Company. These organizations should not be confused with the joint-stock trading companies founded in the course of the seventeenth century. They are better compared to guilds because they were essentially groups of private merchants exercising a royal monopoly privilege of trading with a certain foreign region. The English crown sanctioned such monopolies in part because they offered a convenient source of revenue. But more important was the belief that the regulated companies could exert a beneficial influence on the terms of trade facing English merchants. In a world that did not expect long-term growth of foreign markets men pinned their hopes for gain from trade on their ability to control their markets: that is, to exchange their goods on the most favorable possible terms.

But this sedentary, monopolistic trading system seemed increasingly inappropriate to English needs as traditional markets evaporated. The revival of its economy required restructuring its textile industry, as described earlier. This went hand in hand with a reorientation of English trade connections. The turning point in the international importance of the English economy can perhaps be identified as the success of English merchants in developing Iberian and Mediterranean markets for the new draperies. While they were less experienced in international trade than their rivals, the English could compensate for this with the cost advantages of their textile industry. Government commercial policies, by consistently striving to ensure the low costs of raw wool while defending its merchants with successive elaborations of the Navigation Acts, created an atmosphere in which English trade took flight after the Restoration.[8]

Then colonial activities gave a new dimension to what had been mainly a trade of selling textiles and buying merchandise. As colonial products such as sugar and tobacco came pouring into English ports (a requirement of the Navigation Acts), processing and re-exporting them to consuming markets became the fastest growing sector of English trade. The Newfoundland and Greenland fishing industries (whose catches were sold in the Catholic Mediterranean) can be added to this colonial trade. Until 1689 these trades grew explosively causing the English merchant fleet nearly to double in thirty years (although one-fourth was thought to be Dutch built), and attracting an unprecedented mass of speculative capital to foreign trade until the South Sea Bubble of 1720.

The War of the League of Augsburg (1688-97) and the War of the Spanish Succession (1702-13) slowed the growth of English trade, but by their end the English trading system had changed its fundamental characteristics. The regulated companies had fallen away; in the European trades a more competitive situation prevailed. Woolen cloth now composed only half of total exports while a diversified range of iron wares and colonial re-exports accounted for the greatest trade expansion; English merchants operated in a network extending more and more to North America, the West Indies, Africa, and India. Guided by an aggressive government and shel-

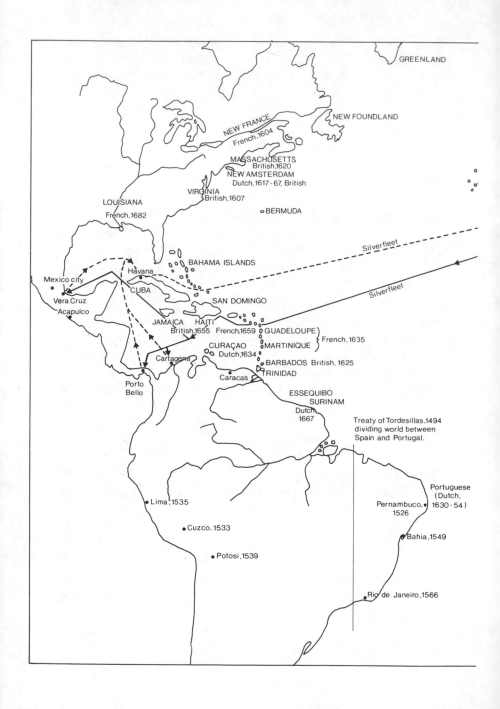

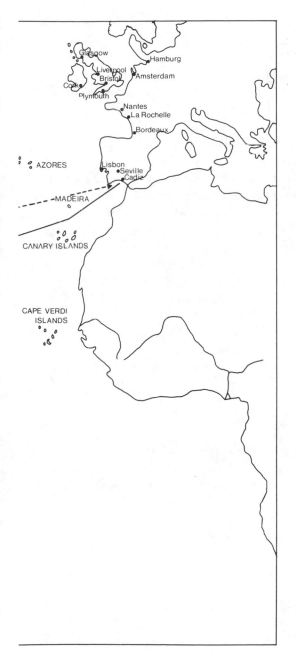

Map 2 New World,
showing colonies
and major trade
centers

tered by protective legislation, they succeeded in making London an entrepôt.[9]

The Amsterdam-centered trading system created in the early seventeenth century gave way, by the end of the century, to a multicentered trading system. London dominated this system, but, because of greater sophistication in the payments system and growth in the volume of trade, other centers - among them Amsterdam, Hamburg, Bordeaux, Lisbon - shared in exercising leadership in certain fields.

A new colonial system came into being in the seventeenth century replacing the simple extractive approach of the Iberian powers. The Dutch, French, and English all participated in this process, but the English more than the others succeeded in reorienting their economy to the non-European trades. Because the English economy took flight in the eventful decades that followed the mid-eighteenth century, historians have often assumed that a causal link connected England's colonial trades to her Industrial Revolution.[10] Although there can be no doubt that the impact of the colonial trades on the European economy was profound, does it constitute the key to understanding the industrial transformation of the century after 1750?

Non-European trade

The Dutch and English vessels that penetrated the Mediterranean in the 1590s to deliver grain to the famine stricken coastal cities began a permanent trade route. They took the place of Mediterranean merchants in many markets not only because of their success in selling their cheap, light, colorful woolens, but also because from the first decade of the seventeenth century consumers wishing pepper and spices had to turn to them. In a very short time the Portuguese empire in the East and, rather more slowly, the Spanish empire in the New World, were supplanted by the aggressive trading practices of the Dutch and the English. The public

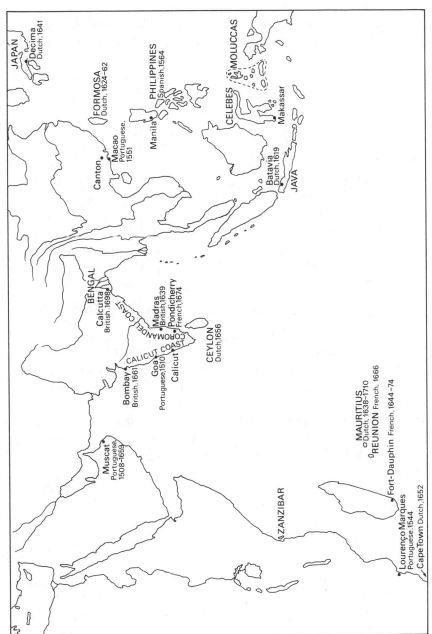

JAPAN
Decima Dutch, 1641

FORMOSA Dutch, 1624–62

PHILIPPINES Spanish, 1564

CELEBES MOLUCCAS

Makassar

Macao Portuguese, 1551

Canton

Manila

Batavia Dutch, 1619

JAVA

BENGAL

Calcutta British, 1698

COROMANDEL COAST

Madras British, 1639
Pondicherry French, 1674

CALICUT COAST

CEYLON Dutch, 1656

Bombay British, 1661

Goa Portuguese, 1510
Calicut

Muscat Portuguese, 1508–1659

MAURITIUS Dutch, 1638–1710
REUNION French, 1666

Fort-Dauphin French, 1644–74

ZANZIBAR

Lourenço Marques Portuguese, 1544
Cape Town Dutch, 1652

Map 3 Asia, showing colonies and major trade centers

institutions erected by the two Iberian powers to supervise their trade monopolies were exceedingly bureaucratic and dominated by aristocratic officeholders devoid of expertise in navigation and trade. When in the 1590s the northern merchants' initial expeditions to the Indian Ocean found Portuguese resistance small and trading profits high, the response was immediate: merchants in London and many Dutch trading cities pooled capital and sent out more vessels. By 1600 the scale of activity had so escalated that many merchants feared that chaotic competition among the enterprises would glut European markets.

In England, where the larger merchants were concentrated in London, a remedy was quickly achieved: following the example of the regulated companies that presided over so much of English trade within Europe, they acquired royal sanction for a single company to exploit the Asian trade. They subscribed 30,000 pounds to finance the initial sailings. In the Dutch Republic jealousy among the merchant groups in the six cities that were active in the trade held up cooperation. It might never have come had the government not seen the political advantage to having a strong, unified institution to strike at the economic strength of Portugal - then a possession of the Spanish crown. The leadership of Johan van Oldenbarnevelt achieved a single company, the United East India Company (henceforth, the VOC, for *Verenigde Oostindische Compagnie*). It was divided into six chambers and presided over by seventeen directors selected from merchant members of the chambers. This gave it a rather ramshackle organizational structure, held together through its two-century existence chiefly by the common outlook of the directors. Its initial capitalization of 6.5 million guilders was ten times that of its new English rival. These two companies both differed from their Iberian counterparts in that they were vaguely semiprivate rather than aristocratic.[11]

They transformed the East Indies trade very quickly. Throughout the sixteenth century some fifty to seventy vessels per decade left Lisbon for the East. By the 1610s and 20s departures from Europe rose to 250, half of them Dutch. Thereafter there is little further growth until the 1650s and 60s when the 400 vessels per decade level was attained, the Dutch continuing to account for at least half. The maximum yearly tonnage (assuming all ships returned to Europe - which is by no means true) rose from some 11,000 to about 19,000 in the course of the century, and escalated gradually in the eighteenth century. Although the European value of each ton from the East Indies was extraordinarily high, these are not enormous capacities. If such a flow of goods from Asia could hardly have exerted a profound impact on more than a handful of Asian locations, the same was not necessarily true of its impact on Europe. An indication of the effort required to secure these Asian goods is the fact that the VOC, in its two-century existence, sent ships to Asia manned by a total of 1 million men, only a third of whom ever survived the five-year round trip to set foot once again on European soil.[12]

The example of the English and Dutch companies encouraged other nations to follow suit later in the century. The French East India Company formed in 1664 was the greatest of these, but there were others. Dutch merchants excluded from the VOC monopoly established the East India Companies of Sweden and Brandenburg as a means of penetrating the lucrative trade routes. Their success sparked a spate of companies designed to trade in the New World, where the ossifying Spanish administration daily showed itself unable to provide basic trading functions in the area it claimed as a private economic preserve.

Within a few decades European merchants whose trading traditions, derived from the Middle Ages, had been characterized by the coexistence of numerous private, short-term ventures and competitive markets found themselves forming enormous monopolies, state sanctioned and supported, intended to endure for an indefinite period of time. What was the significance of these new institutions?

The novelty of the great chartered trading companies could

have escaped no one living in seventeenth-century Europe. In an economy composed almost entirely of family enterprises or, at most, temporary combinations of a handful of merchants, there now arose enterprises with an existence - a personality - independent of the persons who ran it, a permanence that transcended the biological limitations of family firms, and a size far in excess of any private economic units hitherto known. Toward the end of the seventeenth century the Dutch East India Company employed directly 12,000 persons. Standing behind these new characteristics was the principal novelty: the existence of a large permanent stock of capital.

Hundreds of merchants subscribed 6.5 million guilders to establish the VOC in 1602 and in 1621 the Dutch West India Company (henceforth WIC) began with over 7 million guilders. And while the English East India Company and other trading companies founded later were more modestly capitalized, reinvested profits gave most companies control over a large capital stock. Much of it was fixed capital, invested in ships, shipwharves, warehouses, trading posts, and military installations - even plantations. Most, as befits trading companies, was circulating capital, invested in commodities intended for sale. However, the great length of the voyages created long delays in the realization of capital sunk in commodities, and as new vessels were sent to the East before earlier departures had returned, it rapidly became apparent that the traditional means by which merchants engaged in joint ventures had settled their accounts were unworkable.

Translating this realization into a new concept of the trading firm took time. For the first fifty years of its existence the English East India Company vacillated between treating each voyage as a separate enterprise and reinvesting trading profits to finance future voyages. Only in 1657 did the Company establish a permanent stock of trading capital. The Dutch company was more precocious in this respect. In its original charter it was intended that accounts would be settled after ten years. But when that time came, in 1612, the directors, faced with having to realize nonliquid assets scattered all over the world, refused to permit a withdrawal of capital. They advised subscribers wishing to liquidate their holdings to sell their shares in the Company on the Amsterdam *Beurs*. In this *ad hoc* way the VOC and the other companies following its example took on the form of joint stock companies.

Because modern capitalism is dominated by joint stock companies - or corporations - there is a natural tendency to see the great trading companies as a major step in the development of capitalism. There are reasons to believe this viewpoint is superficial. From the East India companies to the later companies founded to exploit the slave trade and the New World plantations, none - right to their end - ever established accounting procedures that reflected an understanding of what "capital" is. Even the VOC did not keep consolidated accounts, which only reflected the fact that underneath their unified exterior, the companies tended to operate as decentralized enterprises in which their various activities frequently seemed not to relate to each other except perhaps in a constant striving to gain a "monopoly." Some authors hold that the confused organization of the companies only reflected the mentality of an *ancien régime* that did not feel a need to distinguish and clarify aims or act consistently to fulfill them. But this is certainly an unfair characterization of the mentality that created the *fluitschip* and organized the Baltic trade. It is more likely that the combination of not always compatible missions embodied in the trading companies accounts for the form they took.

The formation of joint stock companies enjoying a trade monopoly in some part of the world may have been necessary to mobilize the resources required for highly speculative trade in distant places. But it is unlikely that they would have arisen from the competitive, small-scale trading structure that characterized most European trades had it not been for the intervention of the state. We have already seen how government leadership was required to bring the rival municipal trade organizations of the Dutch Republic together to form the VOC. The WIC was even more a political venture. Its formation to prey on Spain's New World trade was timed with the lapse of the twelve-year truce between Spain and the Republic. So many merchants were wary of the enterprise that the Government's treasury contributed a million guilders to insure its formation - and played on religious motives to encourage investment from others. The French companies, founded under Colbert's guidance, were utter creatures of the state. In England merchants had long been accustomed to trading under the protection of government sanctioned monopolies. Still, among English investors one can distinguish between merchants with an eye to profit and aristocratic investors whose motives mixed profit, patriotism, status, and expansionist fervor.[13]

Although the activities of the joint stock companies may have been very important in the development of Europe's economy, their form and their methods of operation were probably less an expression of developing capitalism than the result of pragmatic efforts to bind trading energies to the political strategies of the state.

The economic role of the companies formed to trade in Asia was to buy pepper and spices for sale in Europe. These commodities enjoyed a strong demand because they were required to render palatable dried meat and fish. This demand had its limits, however, and as the English and Dutch competed with each other and with the Portuguese, the volume of pepper and spices sent to Europe began to glut the markets and depress prices. This became painfully apparent after 1648. Shipments remained high despite sinking prices because the rival companies each hoped a trade war would drive out their competitors and give them a monopoly position. By 1652 this was clearly not to be; the Dutch company's warehouses were gorged with a three-year supply of pepper. The Dutch were able to control the markets for certain spices by taking control of strategic spice islands in the Moluccas, but pepper was produced in many areas, and many Asian commodities could, in any case, be obtained from long-established native traders.

In an effort to bring order back to the pepper trade, the VOC embarked on military operations to exclude rivals from the foremost pepper sources. This resulted in a partial success in 1680 with the conquest of Bantam, whose sultan had operated a pepper emporium open to all traders. These problems of glutted markets, rising protection costs, and other political schemes imposed on the companies by their governments put an end to the initial burst of trade expansion at the beginning of the seventeenth century. Many lean years followed, but the companies overcame these limitations in the second half of the century and greatly increased the volume and profitability of their trade. Two innovations in their activities warrant our attention. One reduced their dependence on pepper as an import; the other reduced their dependence on bullion as an export.

The problem of glutted markets for pepper and spices was overcome when the English and Dutch companies began to diversify their trade by returning to Europe with tea, coffee, silk, cotton, and copper. For example, the value of pepper and spices in the Europe-bound ships of the VOC was 50 and 18 percent respectively as late as 1650. By the end of the century pepper and spices each made up only 11 percent of the value of Asian goods. Silks and cottons now accounted for half while dyestuffs, copper, tea, and coffee each accounted for between 4 and 8 percent.[14]

The Asian trades were extremely one sided in that the Europeans could offer virtually nothing that Asians would accept in exchange for their commodities - except bullion. Both the English Company and the VOC regularly paid for 80 to 90 percent of their purchases with gold and silver coins. This threatened to limit the growth of the trade in Asian commodities because of mercantilist objections that the Asian trades drained Europe of bullion. There also arose periodic difficulties in supplying the Asian trades with sufficient bullion to elicit an increased volume of commodities. To reduce the dependence on bullion, the English and Dutch began participating in inter-Asiatic trades. The Dutch, for example, purchased calicoes in India, elephants in Ceylon, and copper in Japan, to sell again in the Moluccas and Java in order to increase the volume of spices sent to Europe. By the 1640s the VOC maintained eighty-five vessels in Asian waters exclusive of those heading to or from Europe, and this intra-Asian fleet continued to expand until the early eighteenth century. The trade with Japan, where the Dutch exercised a monopoly as the only European traders from 1634 until the nineteenth century, was principally directed toward this activity.

As the highly elastic demand for these new commodities made itself felt, the VOC went so far as to organize production by bringing coffee plants from the Persian Gulf to Java. The total importation of coffee to Europe rose from nothing in the early seventeenth century to 66 million pounds by 1750, most of the growth occurring after 1690. Tea, first imported by the Dutch in 1609, still cost a prohibitive 6 to 10 pounds sterling per pound on the London market in 1650. The shipments of the English East India Company rose fivefold between 1690 to 1703 when the price had fallen to 16 shillings per pound. But large-scale tea shipments could not begin until the 1720s when China opened the port of Canton to all European traders. Here, where the two giant companies could exercise no monopoly power, the minor East India companies of the Swedes, Danes, French, and Austrian Netherlanders were particularly active. By 1766, 15 million pounds of tea left Canton, most of it destined for consumption in northern Europe.

Calicoes, the cotton cloth of south India, provided the companies with their largest revenue producers. Shipments to Europe rose from negligible levels in the mid-seventeenth century to 240,000 pieces for the English and 30,000 pieces for the Dutch company in the 1660s. By the beginning of the eighteenth century the English imported 861,000 pieces and the less well placed Dutch about 100,000 pieces. Thereafter the English market was closed by legislation that aimed at protecting the domestic textile industry from the popular Indian fabric.

When the joint stock companies with monopoly rights in the New World were founded, their economic mission was less apparent than those of the East where the Europeans simply participated in the ongoing trade of Arabs and Asians. The Western Hemisphere lacked a large population and a sophisticated economy. It did have Spain and its mines, however, so the political mission of the companies was crystal clear - to interlope on the silver-lined Seville-Atlantic trade. This was originally the main activity of the Dutch WIC; indeed, its only enormous profits came in 1628 when its Privateer-Commander Piet Heyn captured the Spanish Silver Fleet lock, stock, and barrel, for a one-day profit of over 11 million guilders. However, the cost of outfitting privateers was hardly compensated by such occasional windfalls, and it became apparent that the extractive colonial economy of Spain had to be supplanted by a new colonial economy if the English, Dutch, and later the French companies active in the Atlantic were to prosper.

Mercantilist theory suggested the form that the new economy should take: it should produce raw materials for processing in the motherland. The Portuguese in Brazil and the English in the Caribbean and North America had explored the possibilities of sugar and tobacco production, but increasing production required a growing labor force and securing this expansion met with problems. Colonists, on whom the English depended, were not sufficiently numerous while Indians, on whom the Spaniards relied, suffered a demographic catastrophe. Africans were imported by Portugal, whose papal-sanctioned claim to the trade of Africa made them monopolists. The slave supply made available in the

New World was not great; however, the Portuguese commercial lethargy at this time did not promise a rapid change. It was left to the nonmercantilist Dutch to show what could be accomplished. In 1637 the WIC, flush with Spanish booty, captured sugar-producing northeastern Brazil, and at the same time took over Portuguese slaving ports on the Gold Coast of Africa. It set about moving slaves to Brazil to expand sugar production. The sugar was shipped to Amsterdam where it was refined for markets in which each increase in supply seemed to develop further the sweet tooth of the European consumer.

Political events (and a Dutch decision that keeping the Portuguese salt trade was more important than trying to recapture the Brazilian sugar trade) forced the Dutch from most of Brazil in 1645. Left with slave posts in Africa, sugar refineries in Amsterdam, and a fleet of ships, they set about to save their investment by encouraging sugar production on English and French islands. With their privateering base of Curaçao set up as a depot for the slave ships, they supplied the region with slaves. Since Portugal had broken away from Spain in 1640, Spain ceased granting its *asiento* - a monopoly slave-supplying contract - to the Portuguese. The Spanish market was wide open for the Dutch, and to increase the demand for slaves, they encouraged sugar production on Barbados, where a white population dependent on tobacco production was suffering the effects of glutted European markets. Another wave of Dutch planters left Brazil in 1654. Because the first Anglo-Dutch war made them unwelcome on the English islands, they moved to the French islands of Martinique and Guadeloupe. As sugar output rose on English and French islands throughout the 1650s and 60s, the Dutch dominated the slave and carrying trades. Thereafter, England's Navigation Acts and France's bans on Dutch trade with French islands, loosened the Dutch grip on the Atlantic commerce, but the basic direction of the New World economy was by then well established.[15]

To illustrate the nature of the Atlantic trade we can use the records of an eighteenth-century company: vessels sailed to Africa where they bought slaves, providing in exchange textiles (57 percent), guns and gunpowder (24 percent), spirits (10 percent), and household goods (9 percent). The slaves were sold in the Caribbean, together with European manufactures - including cheap linens for the slaves - in exchange for sugar, tobacco, and various lesser staples which were then returned to Europe.[16] A recent effort to ascertain the magnitude of the slave trade clearly shows how the growing volume of slave shipments in the seventeenth century was linked to the development of the Caribbean islands (see Table 3). As sugar plantations spread on Barbados, Antigua, Jamaica, and in the eighteenth century, on St. Dominique, the volume of sugar exported to Europe skyrocketed. Shipments to London rose from very low levels in 1640 to an average of 17,000 tons in 1663-69, 19,000 tons in 1699-1701 - when the price had fallen to half the 1640 level - and 46,000 tons in 1750-54. French output growth began later but reached even higher levels in the eighteenth century. From 1600 to the American Revolution, New World sugar production grew tenfold, from 20 to 200 thousand tons. Tobacco production also grew enormously; after the initial glut in the 1640s, demand grew to permit English shipments to increase from 9 million pounds in the 1660s to 38 million pounds in 1699, and 55 million pounds in 1750.

The spectacular growth of the new colonial economy had, to say the least, far-reaching consequences. Our purpose here is to focus on but one of them: the impact on the European economy.

Karl Marx felt very certain about the impact of the non-European trades. In one of the most memorable passages in *Das Kapital* he wrote:

> The discovery of gold and silver in America, the extirpation, enslavement, and entombment in the mines of the aboriginal population, the beginning of the conquest and looting of the

Table 3. *Atlantic slave trade, 1601-1760 (in thousands)*

Destinations	1601-25	1626-50	1651-75	1676-1700	1701-20	1721-40	1741-60
Old World	12.8	6.6	3.0	2.7	-	-	-
Spanish America	75.0	52.5	62.5	102.5	90.4	90.4	90.4
Brazil	100.0	100.0	185.0	175.0	292.7	312.4	354.5
British Caribbean	-	20.7	69.2	173.8	160.1	198.7	267.4
French Caribbean	-	2.5	28.8	124.5	166.1	191.1	297.8
Dutch Caribbean	-	-	20.0	20.0	120.0	80.0	80.0
Danish Caribbean	-	-	-	4.0	6.0	3.3	6.7
British North America	-	-	-	-	19.8	50.4	100.4
TOTAL	187.8	182.3	368.5	602.5	855.1	926.3	1197.2
Average per year	7.5	7.3	14.7	24.1	42.8	46.3	59.9
Percentage of total to Caribbean	0	12.7	32.0	53.5	52.9	51.1	54.5

Source: Philip D. Curtin, *The Atlantic Slave Trade, A Census* (Madison, 1969), pp. 119, 216.

> East Indies, the turning of Africa into a warren for the commercial hunting of blackskins, signalised the rosy dawn of the era of capitalist production. These idyllic proceedings are the chief momenta of primitive accumulation.

The colonial trades produced windfall profits, a primitive accumulation of bounty which, when transferred to Europe, acted as the starting point of real capitalist production. The parade of West Indian planters and East Indian nabobs who returned to Europe with handsome fortunes would seem to confirm this view, but when we turn to consider the profitability of the trading companies that conducted the great bulk of these activities, a different picture emerges. The WIC paid a few big dividends when its captains captured Spanish booty, but it usually paid none at all and in 1674 fell into bankruptcy. A new company took its place, but its infrequent dividends rarely exceeded 4 or 5 percent. When it was dissolved in 1730 the shares sold on the Amsterdam Stock Exchange at an enormous discount. The general opinion of the Dutch merchants, about where their best opportunities for profit existed was clearly expressed in 1645, when they objected to efforts to regain Brazil on the grounds that it could provoke Portugal to close its salt pans to Dutch traders. Not only was Caribbean sugar more important than New Amsterdam; the European salt trade was more important than the sugar trade.

The Royal African Company was founded in 1672 to increase the English share in the slave trade and in this mission it succeeded. Between 1672 and 1712 it dispatched 500 ships to Africa, delivered 100,000 slaves to the Caribbean plantations, and imported 30,000 tons of sugar to England. In the same period it was a resounding financial catastrophe. Although it paid dividends in its early years, it also borrowed heavily and ended its life heavily in debt. The South Sea Company, whose purpose after 1713 was ostensibly to execute a thirty-year monopoly license (the *asiento*) to supply Spanish colonies with slaves, found the trade as unprofitable as had the others. A small Dutch slaving company, operating in the eighteenth century, made a net profit on only 59 of its 101 voyages; its long-run annual rate of return did not attain 3 percent.[17]

These examples do not prove that no one made money in the slave trade. The Dutch found it very rewarding indeed when they controlled Brazil. But when they supplied slaves to dozens of markets in competition with other slave traders, they could no longer balance supply and demand. The costs of maintaining slave posts and Caribbean depots, financing lengthy voyages, and extending credit to finance slave purchases involved large fixed expenditures. The slightest change in international commodity markets could depress revenues and turn profit into loss.

It was, in short, both a very speculative trade *and* a very competitive trade. Whatever profits there were in the slave trade apparently disappeared through the entry of more participants. The same can be said for the planters who bought the slaves. The expansion of plantation agriculture intensified competition and drove down the price of all the staple exports to where only a few planters, favored by possession of the best soils, made any profit - or, technically, captured a quasi-rent. In Africa, too, the large number of slave suppliers apparently prevented them from benefitting from the strong demand for slaves. Here its chief impact may well have been to attract such large numbers into the slave capturing business as to divert labor from productive economic activities. There is a tragic irony in the slave trade: the "commodities," the buyers, and the sellers all lost, although some lost more than others. If there were gainers from the trade it appears to have been European consumers who were able to buy sugar, tobacco, and cotton at prices far lower than they would have been in the absence of a too-elastic labor supply for plantation agriculture.[18]

The companies trading in the East Indies enjoyed a greater financial success than their western counterparts. The greatest of them, the VOC, paid dividends after 1634 which averaged 18 percent of the face value of its shares. In six consecutive years beginning in 1715 the company paid dividends of 40 percent. But because the *Beurs* value of shares rose far above face value, few investors actually received such returns. Moreover, the company contracted large debts; it closed its doors with over 130 million guilders of debt. In general, modern accounting methods would considerably diminish these profit rates; after about 1730 they would expose persistent losses. Even more important, as the historian of the VOC's trade concludes, the company's pre-1730 profits were moderate by comparison with the results of Dutch shipping and commerce within Europe.[19]

If the homely Baltic trade generated more profit than did the richly-laden Indiamen, one reason for this was contributed by the non-European trades. Traders to the Baltic and Mediterranean brought with them less bullion and a greater quantity and variety of consumer goods that originated in the East and West Indies. The demand for tea, sugar, calicoes, tobacco, coffee, and spices did much to enliven the traditional trade routes of Europe.

Another approach to linking the non-European trades to the growth of the European economy focuses on growth of markets for European manufactures. If, as Adam Smith asserted, the division of labor is limited by the extent of the market, and if the domestic market is fragmented and poor, then it follows that an economy must capture more and more foreign markets to act as a forcing agent for industrial development. The historian Eric Hobsbawm follows this line of reasoning when he argues that the economic crisis of the seventeenth century was overcome as England, because of successful mercantilist rivalry with Holland and France, concentrated into her hands a large portion of world trade - particularly, the rapidly growing Atlantic trade.

Of course, the growth of a nation's foreign trade does not necessarily create a forced draft to fan the flames of industry.

The East Indies trade was almost entirely an import trade; European industry never produced goods attractive in Asian markets. In the decades after 1713 France was remarkably successful in developing its Caribbean islands. The ports of Bordeaux and Nantes grew rapidly as the slave and sugar trades grew, if anything, more rapidly than those of England. Sugar imports from French St. Dominique grew twice as rapidly as from English Jamaica while secondary staples such as coffee, indigo, cotton, and cacao were far more important in French commerce than in English. Overall, French foreign trade between 1716 and 1748 grew at the rapid annual rate of 4.1 percent. But New World markets for French manufactures did not grow at nearly this rate. In fact the Atlantic trades of France never developed beyond a series of intense but temporary booms in commodity imports.

Few nations enjoyed a more buoyant growth in colonial trade in the first half of the eighteenth century than Portugal. The beginning of gold shipments from Brazil in 1693 generated an intense demand there for manufactured goods. Portugal could not satisfy this demand. In a manner reminiscent of the sixteenth-century Spanish economy, the gold passed through Portugal into the hands of foreign economies more capable of providing manufactures, shipping capacity, and financial and insurance services. Brazilian trade made Lisbon once again a focal point of the European economy. It also enriched the Portuguese monarch sufficiently to finance the construction of the monastery-palace of Mafra and enriched Lisbon's bourgeoisie sufficiently to finance a large increase of imports. But none of these economic impulses penetrated far beyond Lisbon itself. The capital functioned as a relay, passing its Brazilian trade on to - primarily - the English, whose trade with Lisbon grew nearly fourfold in the first half of the eighteenth century.[20]

Indeed, the only nation for whom the Atlantic trades seemed to play a dynamic role in its national economy was England. In the first half of the eighteenth century some 85 percent of English exports were manufactured products. The traditional woolen exports, whose markets remained in Europe, fell to under half of total exports as miscellaneous manufactures - principally cotton cloth, housewares, and iron products - rose to account for a quarter of English exports. These commodities found vent in the New World - primarily in the protected markets of the North American colonies. But before we conclude that the colonial trades "caused" English industrial growth, two questions should be answered. First, how did the colonies pay for the manufactured goods? Their economies were dependent on the sale of staples in the mother country; hence, their purchasing power depended directly on the condition of European markets for their sugar, tobacco, and the like, as well as military remittances for fortifications and the maintenance of troops. Because mercantilist policies strove to make a closed circuit of the colonial trades, it seems inevitable that we must search for the sources of dynamism in Europe rather than in the New World plantations.

Secondly, did foreign markets in fact grow faster than domestic markets? Precious few records stand ready to assist us in answering this question. We know that food prices fell to very low levels in the early eighteenth century under the impact of the agricultural revolution. This increased purchasing power in many social groups, the spread of retail shops, plus records of increased consumption of many "luxuries" support the view that the exported share of textiles and ironwares output may not actually have grown in the first half of the eighteenth century.[21]

The reader having followed our argument thus far will surely not be surprised to read that, in the author's opinion, we must qualify any argument that a growing colonial trade stimulated the European economy with the proviso that this stimulus was not automatic. It could act only where the domestic economy was responsive to the new opportunities thus created. Whatever the facts may show once adequate evidence is compiled about the exported percentage of total output, the European economy probably gained more from its non-Western imports than from the colonial export markets it acquired.

Consider the "demonstration effect" that non-western imports exerted on the European economy. The importation of Chinese and Japanese porcelain gave rise to imitations in Holland, where delftware was created, in Germany, where the first European porcelain was made, and in England, where by the early eighteenth century potteries enjoyed a growing mass market. Tea and coffee found an acceptance in Europe that changed social customs (and increased the demand for porcelain). Tobacco not only changed social customs, it also occasioned the establishment of institutions that succeeded in extracting from eager smokers vast tax revenues, and provided European agriculture with a labor-intensive cash crop that brought prosperity to many otherwise poor rural districts. The importation of Indian calicoes uncovered a widespread demand that threatened the established woolens and linens industries of Europe. When England prohibited the importation of calicoes to protect its woolen industry, a domestic cotton industry arose to supply the new market; in time, of course, it became the country's largest industry and the pioneer in mechanized production.

As we consider the eagerness that characterized the European desire to consume these new products and its ability to finance their imporation, our attention is directed from the intercontinental and European trades to the regional economies. In some of them the volume of trade was growing enormously - the product of productivity advances and institutional changes that stimulated mass demand.

5
Urbanization and regional trade

Units of economic life

The historian must take care to avoid having the availability of documents dictate what is and is not important in the economic life of the past. Governments that did little else invariably tried to control and tax the import and export of goods. As a consequence customs records are available from quite early dates to illuminate the major trends of international trade. Likewise, European trade links with other continents are well-documented thanks to the privileged monopolies that were erected everywhere to defend national interests and enrich royal coffers. In contrast, the hundreds of thousands of Europeans who labored to provision local markets dealing in the mundane necessities of everyday life were not often the object of systematic record keeping. Consequently, their role in the European economy is easy to ignore, or more seriously, to dismiss as inconsequential - as an inert process of repetitive transactions incapable of injecting dynamic change in the economy.

The altered character of agriculture, industry, and government described in this volume supports the hypothesis that regional trade evolved in scope and organization during the seventeenth century. If it continued to lack the drama of international trade, it no longer lacked its dynamism. Indeed, it is not impossible that the explosive growth of the East and West Indies trades will ultimately be explained as a consequence of a revitalization of the hundreds of regional trading economies into which Europe was organized in early modern times.

Despite the tentative efforts of royal administration to deflate the egos of urban magistracies and impose some common economic regulation on their states, the European economy in the seventeenth century can, for many purposes, continue to be understood best as a collection of regions, with cities as their focal points. This structure, inherited from the Middle Ages, was not to be transformed utterly until the growth of the new factory cities of the nineteenth century.

Urbanization

In 1600, just as in 1300, Europe was full of cities girded by walls and moats, bristling with the towers of churches and charitable institutions. The inhabitants maintained guilds which organized and regulated industrial production, selected magistrates to run courts and administrative organs, and held regular markets which served as the principal link between cities and their rural hinterlands. The sale of both urban industrial and rural agricultural goods was regulated to protect the consumer's interest. Regulations strove to suppress middlemen between producer and consumer and to maximize the hinterland that supplied the urban markets. And, just as in earlier centuries, the cities, as repositories of industrial skills and commercial expertise, continued to have an economic impact on their hinterlands far greater than their size alone would suggest.

Within this ancient structure there arose significant changes in the role of cities. In the course of the seventeenth century they were becoming at once more and less than they had been earlier. We can see this varied process of change best by beginning with their demographic characteristics.

In order to determine the market impact of urban populations, some global assessment of urbanization, the percentage of the total population residing in cities, would be useful. No overall figures are yet available, but such reasonably reliable regional data as we now possess show that the percentage of the population living in cities was no higher in 1750 than it had been in 1600; it was apparently lower than the urban percentage attained at the crest of the demographic expansion that arrived in the 1620-50 period. In Electoral Saxony 31 percent of the 1550 population lived in 143 cities. By 1750 the population had doubled, mainly in the first half of the period, but the urban population had grown to only 36 percent. In Lippe, in western Germany, town dwellers made up 28 percent of the population in 1590. The Thirty Years' War hit the region's small cities hard, reducing the urban population to 21 percent in 1700. However, the decline of the towns had other causes as well, for the contraction persisted to the census of 1776, when only 15 percent of Lippe's population lived in the province's four towns. The German historian Julius Beloch provides us with a comprehensive survey of Italian population trend. Italy north of the Papal States possessed 14 cities of over 20,000 inhabitants in 1600. Together they numbered 665,000, or 12 percent of the total population. By 1650 the same cities possessed only 526,000, and a century later, in 1750, their combined populations had recovered the 1600 level, but now made up only 10 percent of the total population. Urban decline in Spain was, if anything, even more pronounced than in Italy. In both countries the recurring famines and plague epidemics of the early seventeenth century caused urban losses that, in the unfavorable economic context of the Mediterranean basin, could not be made good for many decades.[1]

Once we begin to examine individual cities, it becomes apparent that the aggregative figures obscure as much as they tell. In the course of the seventeenth century the demographic fortunes of cities varied enormously with their social and economic functions. And while overall urbanization made no gains, the size distribution of European cities was radically transformed.

Princely residences and centers of absolutist administration

Map 4 Europe, showing major cities and approximate population in 1700

grew in a spectacular manner. Madrid is the classic example of the new capital city. When the Habsburg crown settled on Madrid as the permanent capital for its vast empire in 1561, it had but several thousand inhabitants. Supported by nothing more than government employment, this centrally located city grew to 65,000 by 1600 and 170,000 by 1630. Paris and London possessed more varied functions, it is true, but their administrative and attendant social roles were central to their explosive growth. In the mid-sixteenth century, Paris had some 130,000 and London 60,000 inhabitants. They were already by far the largest cities north of the Alps. By 1650 both were approaching the half million mark - unprecedented in western Europe. London continued to grow after the mid-seventeenth century, but in the next century attention is focused on the capitals of northern and central Europe. When the Danish King Frederick III assumed absolute powers in 1660, Copenhagen was a city of 23,000 inhabitants. A century later it numbered 93,000. The contraction of Swedish power notwithstanding, Stockholm doubled its population in the century after 1650. When the Great Elector made his agreement with the Junkers in 1653, Berlin numbered 12,000 inhabitants. The growth of Prussian absolutism is mirrored in the growth of the capital. In 1740 Berlin numbered 90,000 inhabitants, 21,000 of which were military personnel. In the same period Vienna grew to an even larger size, and even among the minor capitals, such as Hannover and Munich, rapid growth was in evidence.

Absolutist governments had no monopoly on the need for large administrative centers. The decentralized Dutch Republic managed to transform The Hague from an overgrown village of a few thousand at the time of the Revolt to the nation's third largest city by the mid-eighteenth century. British rule in Ireland raised Dublin from a town of 18,000 in 1650 to a European social center of 130,000 a century later. And we have yet to mention the purest expression of absolutism, Versailles. Raised from a small village by Louis XIV's decision to build his combination palace-office building in 1667, Versailles numbered 60,000 by the end of the *ancien régime.*[2] (It is not completely certain what this number means, however, because reckoning such a settlement's population poses problems similar to reckoning the population of a college town.)

A second group of cities that stands out because of its extraordinary growth comprises the Atlantic ports. The port cities of the Mediterranean and Baltic seas do not share in this growth, nor do Seville, Lisbon, and Antwerp, the sixteenth-century centers of Iberian trade. But from Hamburg to Cadiz, the major ports - including Liverpool, Bristol, and Cork in the British Isles - grew by 250 percent between 1600 and 1750. Prospering as entrepôt centers, re-exporters of colonial goods, centers of the slave trade, processors of sugar and tobacco, and provisioners of the Indies fleets, these commercial centers were the most demographically dynamic bourgeois cities of Europe.

The cities of a third group are conspicuous not so much by their size or growth as by their novelty. They are the creation of social and political currents without earlier parallels. New standards of naval architecture together with strategic policies commonly labeled as mercantilist gave rise to naval stations that supported entire cities. Portsmouth and Plymouth in England, and Brest and Toulon in France each become very considerable places by the end of the seventeenth century for this reason. Colbert, as part of a Herculean effort to advance French naval and commercial power, founded the new port cities of Brest, Cette, Lorient, and Rochefort. The grand absolutist strategies that inspired their creation had earlier inspired Sweden to found the port of Göteburg in 1611. Spas and resorts, the foremost being the English city of Bath, are the other novel forms of urbanism that attained importance in the century after 1650.

The impact of colonial, commercial, and naval policies on urbanization becomes even more impressive if we turn our attention to the New World and East Indies colonies. The rise of such settlements as Philadelphia, Kingston, and Batavia and the rapid growth of older colonial cities such as Rio de Janeiro was obviously related to the growth of European commerce. While the trading interests of Europeans in the non-western regions were primarily import-oriented, they did export the European city itself. Many of these foundations remained for centuries more closely associated with the mother country than with their surrounding territories. Consequently, their contribution to the growth of Europe's urban markets should not be passed over.[3]

So far we have emphasized the growth sectors of European urban life. Most cities did not grow significantly after the demographic upswing of the sixteenth century. The cathedral towns, centers of provincial administration, inland commercial centers, and industrial cities all experienced checks to their development. In the north the Reformation undermined the inflow of revenue to some old religious centers; everywhere urban industry faced the powerful trend toward rural relocation; interior cities found themselves at a growing disadvantage in competition with coastal commercial centers. All was not lost, of course. Many cities compensated for the decline of the urban textile industry by fostering new industries requiring special skills or trading connections (Delft, Lyons); others evolved important roles as the commercial and financial centers of industrial hinterlands (Ghent, Amiens). Finally, and of particular significance for the development of regional trade, provincial capitals tended to become social centers, attracting landowners to buy townhouses and patronize a growing variety of luxury trades. Still, the net demographic effect was often stagnation and, in the Mediterranean basin, decline. Such commercial and industrial cities of ancient reputation as Nuremburg, Cologne, Ghent, Mechlin, Strasbourg, Angers, Dijon, failed to keep up with their regions' populations, while Valladolid, Toledo, Segovia, Padua, and Vincenza declined absolutely.

By the end of the demographic expansion of the sixteenth century, western and central Europe were dotted with some 200 cities of over 10,000 inhabitants. In the following century it is unlikely that the new additions to this category greatly outnumbered the deletions. But two significant changes did occur: first, by the late seventeenth century urban population was shifting to selected centers in northwestern Europe and along the Atlantic coast; second, the larger cities were gaining at the expense of the smaller. Trade, finance, and government were increasingly attracted to a relative handful of the hundreds of cities with which medieval society endowed Europe.

In sum, while urban Europeans did not become relatively more numerous, they did become concentrated in fewer cities. Between 1600 and 1750 the number of cities over 100,000 grew from eight to thirteen; those in northern Europe grew from two to six. Cities of 40 to 100,000 inhabitants increased from twenty-five in number to thirty-four; those in northern Europe doubled from thirteen cities to twenty-six; cities of 20 to 40,000 declined in the Mediterranean, but doubled from twenty-five to fifty in the North. While 4 percent of the northern European population lived in cities of over 20,000 at the beginning of the seventeenth century, nearly 8 percent did so by 1750.[4]

The cultural and economic differences between urban and rural dwellers are well known; what still needs to be emphasized, however, is that the cultural, economic, and demographic impact of cities grew more than proportionally with their size. The daily life of the inhabitants, the logistical problems of provisionment, the institutions of distribution, the role of urban migration - all of these were qualitatively different for large cities.

The impact of the new metropolises was greatest in northwestern Europe. This region had always been known for its relative urbanization. But after the 1570s the Flemish and northern French industrial cities were dwarfed by the explosive growth of Paris, London, and the cluster of cities in the province of Holland which in this century have come to be identified as the *Randstad*. The *Randstad*, a circle of nearby cities including Amsterdam, Haarlem, Leiden, The Hague, Delft, and Rotterdam, can be best understood as an integrated urban region. Paris, London and the *Randstad* in the 1570s collectively embraced some 370,000 inhabitants. In the next century each grew to surpass the 400,000 mark. By 1700 one and a half million people lived in them.[5] (See Figure 4.)

The existence of these unprecedented human agglomerations could not help but set people in motion. Cities, from the time of their earliest development, have always attracted migrants who seek their fortune away from their childhood homes. Cities of a few thousand inhabitants could easily acquire sufficient guild apprentices and domestic servants from their hinterlands. Ties of kinship and god parentage often served as the link that brought villagers into a city. Such short-distance migrants were likely to maintain some contact with their home villages.

Altogether different was the volume, distance, and motive of migration to the new metropolises. In the first place, the need of these cities for recruits so far exceeded that of smaller cities that their immediate environs were incapable of satisfying the demand. This state of affairs was only partly the result of their rapid growth. Even when they ceased expanding, the great cities, because of their frightful mortality, needed a constant flow of new arrivals to replenish populations that, in isolation, would inevitably die out. Before the nineteenth century cities virtually devoured people, and the larger the city the more voracious its appetite. Contemporaries were well aware of this problem. One of the most exhaustive accounts of urban mortality we possess is a three-volume work by Johann Peter Süssmilch, the mid-eighteenth century Chaplain of the Prussian Army. He believed high urban mortality was part of God's plan; a nation that wished to have a

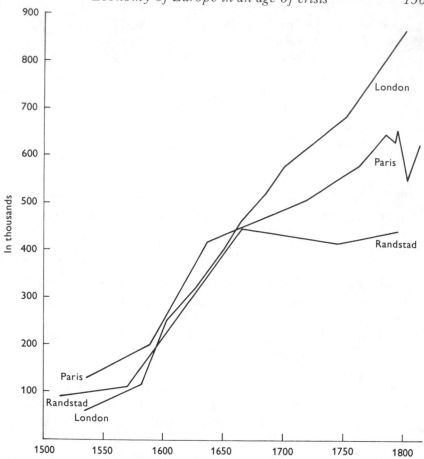

Figure 4   Population of London, Paris, and the Dutch "Randstad"

growing population sufficiently healthy to perform military service, he implied, should avoid having large cities. Prussia was not an urban nation, but the explosive growth of eighteenth century Berlin must have influenced Süssmilch. He enlisted the aid of Prussia's parish ministers to calculate crude death rates for a ten-year period around 1740. In 1056 villages the average death rate was 26.0 per 1000 inhabitants; in twenty small cities it rose to 30, while in large cities, the death rate shot up above 40 per thousand. In 1688 the English statistician Gregory King had uncovered the same pattern. The death rate of villages was 29 per thousand, that of small cities 33, that of London 42. London's mid-eighteenth-century death rate hovered around 50. Mortality varied directly with density, and in large cities it almost inevitably stood far above the level of fertility. The result was a net deficit that had to be made good through immigration.[6]

The trek to the city was a constant feature of European life, even when the cities were not growing. The 1740 population of Paris, had it not been replenished by migrants, would have been reduced by 9 percent in ten years. Rome, a city of 138,000 in 1702, would have very nearly died out within ninety years. In fact it grew by 25,000 in that interval, the product of an average yearly influx of 1500 persons. This, of course, is a net figure. Many more entered such a city each year; the net immigration figure is the result of deducting those who depart to live elsewhere. Some sense of the role that newcomers played in the large metropolises can be gained from examining the marriage registers of Amsterdam. Throughout the century after 1660, when the city's population was roughly constant, persons born elsewhere made up over half the participants of marriages contracted in the city. In 1757 a contemporary expressed the view that two-thirds of London's adults were born in the provinces or had come from "distant parts." Already in the 1630s the spectacle of thousands of provincials entering Paris every year inspired Théophraste Renaudot to propose the establishment of an employment office, the *Bureau d'Adresses*. His scheme appealed to the city's magistrates, who were preoccupied with the problems of vagabondage and lawlessness, as a means of enabling countryfolk to obtain employment as soon as they arrived in the capital.[7]

The great cities of the seventeenth century were full of outsiders; they could not have existed without them. One does not have to wait until the nineteenth century to find great masses of uprooted people forced to adjust to a new way of life. Not only did the great preindustrial cities attract thousands away from the countryside, but the changing character of peasant agriculture in many areas robbed many rural dwellers of the option of staying. The seventeenth century, thus, sees a large part of the population on the road, moving to new, thinly populated, rural locations as well as to the large, densely populated cities. The impact of the former rural industrial migration has already been considered. What was the impact of the urban migration?

The English demographic historian E. A. Wrigley attempted to assess the impact of London in the century after 1650. Its growing population and excessive mortality were such that, if one assumed migrants were typically about 20 years of age, the survivors of almost one-sixth of all English births would be living in London 20 years after their birth. This refers only to net immigration. Once temporary migrants are added - for which no hard figures exist - the portion of adult Englishmen who had had a direct experience with London life becomes even larger. Similar statistical exercises can be applied to Paris, the Dutch cities, and the other growing capitals of the Continent. They point to the conclusion that a significant proportion of northern Europeans for the first time were coming into contact with cities quite different from the closed, corporative, medieval city or the towns dominated by the local landed society. These places continued to exist, but they were now overshadowed by the metropolis where family life was less dependent on kin relations, where dealings between individuals could no longer be based entirely on custom and status, where strangers had to rely on contracts in their dealings.[8] The consumption patterns in such a competitive urban setting, full of people from different regions and even different countries, was bound to be more susceptible to novelty. People exposed to such an environment who returned to the countryside must have had a leavening influence there as well.

The demographic and sociological impact of rural industrial regions chiefly affected production. The demographic and sociological impact of the new metropolises chiefly affected consumption and the organization of the local and regional trade which supplied these unprecedented concentrations.

The grain trade

The most important trade was invariably that which secured urban food supplies. In economies with meager and often precarious agricultural surpluses, concentrations of nonagricultural population stood in an exposed position. Municipal regulations dating from the Middle Ages sought to secure foodstuffs on favorable terms in two ways: first, by forbidding the food surpluses of a city's hinterland from being sold elsewhere and, second, by requiring producers to sell directly to the urban public at regulated open markets. Middlemen and speculators were anathema in a marketing system designed to maximize competition in the retail market. Occasional royal edicts attempted to control the flow of grain or its price, but generally the grain trade was a municipal concern. In this way the supply areas of each town came to be carefully delimited.[9]

The task of supplying nonagricultural populations of enormous size - whether in cities, rural industrial areas, or in armies - created a demand that could not be met by this time-honored approach. A city of 100,000 or 400,000 required a qualitatively different sort of supply network from a city of 10,000 or even 40,000. By the mid-seventeenth century Paris required 3 million bushels of grain per year, the brewers and bakers of Amsterdam made use of 1.3 million, Madrid and Rome each consumed nearly a million bushels. In each case continued reliance on the deliveries of local farmers was out of the question. The solution to the problem was not so easily discovered. In the mid-sixteenth century Venice found its supply areas, spread throughout the Adriatic, reserved by local authorities to meet the demand of a growing population in south and central Italy. The response of the Venetian government was to encourage Venetian landownership on the *terraferma,* the city's mainland possessions. Many other factors combined with the need for a secure food supply to increase enormously the land owned by the Venetian aristocracy in the first half of the seventeenth century. The food supply problem became acute in the Mediterranean long before the seventeenth century. The enormous cities of Italy had long drawn their supplies from distant production centers. They were joined in the course of the sixteenth century by the growing Iberian cities and the demand of settlers in and sailors to the New World. The approach to urban provisionment was to use royal power to batten on grain producers.

In Spain maximum grain prices were fixed in 1539; Spain also controlled Sicily, long the chief granary of the western Mediterranean. Here the export of grain was channeled to the politically and economically appropriate destinations through a system of export licenses (*tratte*). The disincentives of these controls combined with the grave technical and social weaknesses of Mediterranean agriculture to limit the supply response to the growing demand for grain. By the second half of the seventeenth century, Sicily had ceased being a dependable granary for anyone; the island's overriding problem had become the supply of food to its own overgrown aristocratic cities.[10]

Long before then, in the decade beginning in 1590, the Mediterranean faced a famine crisis which marks a turning point in its economic history. The efforts to secure grain for the enormous and growing cities of the Mediterranean had been unable to overcome the inelasticity of supply. Indeed the net effect of the restrictions on trade and growing exactions on the peasantry, which amounted to a kind of "refeudalization," was to exacerbate the problems. Short-term relief of grain supply problems arrived in the early 1590s in the form of Dutch and English ships laden with Baltic grain. Periodically during the next half century, northern - particularly Dutch - grain ships alleviated the region's chronic famines. The northern fleets sailing through the Straits of Gibraltar symbolized the passing of commercial supremacy from the Mediterranean, where it had been vested since early medieval times, to the North Sea. One feature of this new supremacy was a more successful handling of the food supply problem.

In the north the Dutch evolved the most dramatic solution. The Baltic trade over which Dutch merchants gained mastery in the late sixteenth century was both the foundation of their international commercial empire (described earlier) and the supplier of their intensely urbanized and economically specialized nation. The grain moving westward through the Danish Sound found by far its largest markets in the Dutch Republic. Amsterdam, the arrival point for Baltic grain, became a grain entrepôt as well. Her merchants were well-situated to supply other countries suffering from famine conditions - such as Italy in the 1590s. But while Baltic grain served this temporary and marginal role elsewhere, it fed the largest portion of the Republic's urban population. In many years the 70 to 80 percent of Baltic grain transported in Dutch bottoms - some 300 ships from Danzig alone - supplied no other markets. When before had such a large urban population been dependent for the bulk of its food supply on such distant suppliers? While Venice's distant supply areas dried up, forcing the city to pursue a policy of commercial involution, Amsterdam and the other Dutch cities operated an efficient fleet of *fluits* which annually carried enough grain to feed well over half a million people.

A celebrated historian, wishing to emphasize the importance of the great intercontinental trades, once asked rhetorically what could be "the importance of . . . this potluck trade of the Sound and its barges, dragging prudently their fat stomachs under foggy skies?"[11] Prosaic it certainly was, but the establishment of a permanent bulk trade over such a distance must nevertheless be regarded as one of the major accomplishments of the early modern economy. It enlarged enormously the potential for specialized production and efficient commerce that were the main sources of productivity growth before the Industrial Revolution.

A more straightforward approach was used in securing the grain supplies of London and Paris. Paris, situated in the center of a rich grain producing region, had long been supplied by river barges from Picardie and Champagne and wagons from the surrounding Ile de France. By 1637 Paris was said to require over 90,000 tons of grain, far more than these regions could spare. The growth of the army and of Versailles caused the requirements to grow throughout the next century. As Paris reached further outside its environs for its food supply the careful delimitation of supply areas worked out in the sixteenth century was completely broken down. "The Rouenese market area is invaded, the Loire valley is tapped, the Breton granaries pour their supplies into the boats of Parisian merchants."[12] This state of affairs forced the abandonment of two cherished ideas: that local communities should have first claim to locally produced foodstuffs, and that middlemen and wholesalers should be forbidden. These beliefs did not die without a struggle. Right up until the Revolution - indeed, until the railway age - local authorities and bands of aggrieved peasants and workers tried to uphold the ancient restrictions on the movement of grain. However, we find the royal government and its agents, the intendants, upholding the rights of wholesale merchants to engage in a free grain trade. The mid-seventeenth century, when Paris ended a century of phenomenal growth, witnessed a rash of peasant uprising provoked by the fiscal exactions of the crown and the removal of foodstuffs that the tradition of localism dictated should first be offered for local use. But peasants were not the only group who were forced into a national market. The small cities that had long relied on the surpluses of their traditional hinterlands also suffered. The bourgeoisie of such places also sought to defend a localism which the alliance of metropolis and central government felt obliged to dissolve.

In England the localist resistance to the expansion of London was overcome with greater dispatch and thoroughness. The sixteenth-century city's supply area consisted of the adjacent home counties plus East Anglia, which sent its grain along the coast. In the seventeenth century the growing city's supply lines spread up the Thames valley to the Midlands and up the eastern coast to Yorkshire. By the mid-eighteenth century all of England south of the Humber was devoted to supplying the largest city of Europe. In 1725 it was calculated that Londoners yearly consumed 2.5 million bushels of flour, 20,000 sheep, 60,000 calves, and 187,000 swine. The 23,000 horses housed in the city's stables required vast quantities of hay and oats. The 2 million barrels of beer consumed in the metropolis required further imports of malt and barley.

The supply of such a market could not be left to chance. An army of wholesale merchants, factors, and cattle drovers deployed itself throughout the English countryside. The medieval structure of the nearly 700 market towns was altered to suit the new requirements. Inland trade abandoned the smallest markets and migrated to the larger towns. The scale of commercial dealings increased causing many local markets to specialize as trading centers for some particular commodity. Finally, many transactions were negotiated by professional middlemen in commercial inns rather than on the open market. In short, food marketing throughout most of England became reorganized to supply efficiently the London market.

The role of the state was one of acquiescence. The local justices of the peace were empowered to secure local food supplies through enforcement of the ancient laws against forestalling, the private purchase of commodities before they were offered for sale at the public market, and regrating, the purchase of commodities with the intention of selling them again at the same or a nearby market. These statutes, sometimes employed to harass unpopular traders, were rarely used to prevent the feeding of the metropolis. They were finally abolished and the practices of middlemen were finally legitimized by the Grain Act of 1663.[13] One reason for the lower level of localist resistance was the success described earlier of landowners and commercial farmers in increasing supply. By 1700 the government's concern was not how to keep a volatile urban population fed but how to clear the national market of a growing oversupply of grain.

Energy supplies

The preindustrial city's fuel supplies came from nearby woodlands. Today it seems odd that woodlands were placed near the city gates along with horticultural gardens. The enormous transport costs of this bulkiest and most cumbersome of basic commodities dictated its nearby location. The problems that arose when the capital cities reached unprecedented size are dramatically illustrated by the case of Madrid. As the Castilian capital grew to 170,000 inhabitants in 1630, charcoal, the city's heating and cooking fuel, had to come from more and more distant places. Ultimately, much of the city's yearly charcoal consumption of 12,500 tons travelled over 50 miles. It was transported, moreover, by thousands of pack animals and mule-drawn wagons. The further growth of Madrid was limited by the steeply rising cost of fuel and transportation which resulted from their highly inelastic supply.[14]

The more severe climate of northern Europe caused the demand for fuel to be considerably greater than in the Mediterranean area. It is no coincidence, therefore, that two of the greatest concentrations of urban population in the north should have developed novel solutions to their fuel supply problems. Their solutions not only permitted them to continue expanding but laid the foundation for the rise of fuel-intensive industries and stimulated economic activity over extensive hinterlands.

The virtually forestless Dutch Republic had long relied on peat, the oxygen-starved, decayed plant life found in abundance throughout this region of marsh and moor. Through much of the sixteenth century peat had been dug mainly by peasants on a casual basis. Brewers were the only users with a sufficient demand for peat to warrant hiring peat diggers and organizing production on a permanent basis. The rapid growth of Holland's cities after the revolt against Spain forced changes in the peat industry. Casual production in the peat bogs of central Holland no longer satisfied the demand. Rapidly rising peat prices created an army of professional peat diggers. They also triggered a response among the noblemen of outlying provinces who began forming companies to dig canals into the more distant virgin peat bogs to supply the urban markets of the maritime region. The large investments required proved to be beyond the means of these enterprising provincial nobles; one by one their companies in Groningen, Drenthe, and Overijssel fell into the hands of urban capitalists from the western cities. By the mid-seventeenth century several hundred thousand tons of peat annually departed the Zuider Zee ports serving the Overijssel and Drenthe fields, and this represented but a minor portion of the total output.

The massive investments that permitted the low-cost and large-scale exploitation of these bogs had far-reaching effects. The low peat prices at the consumption centers stimulated the development of a wide variety of fuel-intensive industries. Amsterdam became the sugar refiner of Europe by 1650; Haarlem became the bleacher of German linen. The brick and ceramics works, soap boiling, brewing, distilling, and the salt-refining works all owed their locations in the Republic in large part to the elastic fuel supply. In the producing regions of the interior provinces, peat industry investments stimulated many related activities. The new canal network created to move the peat provided low-cost transport for agriculture which, by itself, could not have borne the cost of such investments. At the same time the fields stripped of their peat could be turned into productive farm land through the application of manure, including urban night soil, which the peat barges carried cheaply as return loads. Despite the possibilities of reclamation, the spread of exhausted peat bogs necessarily set Dutchmen to ponder what would become of them when the peat should run out. The author of a mid-eighteenth-century account of the province of Friesland, a major center of peat digging, wrote:

> That there exists in all of Friesland a great deal of peat is apparent from the large transportation of the same in many peat-barges both internally and abroad. Still, the same is diminishing constantly; someone had made a guesstimate that there are still available only 300 to 400 years worth of peat in the Friesian moor . . . Should it come to pass that the peat in Friesland were exhausted then the inhabitants would definitely be unfortunate for they have no wood. But, if it is true, as has been reported to me and which is believable, that [the peat will grow back in the exhausted bogs] this would become of use to our distant descendents and who knows what changes can occur in the meantime![15]

Despite the many advantages of peat, we now know it was not to be the wonder-fuel of industrialization. London had the good fortune of being supplied with a substance capable of releasing a more intense heat than peat: coal. Complaints of timber shortages in England date from Elizabethan times. In fact, timber prices rose far more rapidly than those of other commodities in the early seventeenth century. Had London continued to rely on wood we can be certain that her growth would have been severely limited by the intensified competition with the construction, metallurgical, and shipbuilding industries for the nation's dwindling timber supplies. Still, the transfer to coal for heating, cooking, and industrial purposes was not a simple matter. In the first place the population had to become reconciled to the stench and smoke of the new combustible. The lower price of coal helped this education process along rather nicely. A more difficult problem was overcoming the quality deterioration that often came when coal was substituted for wood or charcoal. Experimentation resolved this problem in one industry after another until the ultimate obstacle to the industrial use of coal was overcome when a coke-fueled iron-smelting process was discovered by Abraham Darby in 1709.

The explosive growth of output of each industry as it began substituting coal for timber was both cause and effect of London's growing market. Through the continuing process of empirical investigation and willingness to accept a new - not altogether pleasant - environment, coal came to dominate London's fuel supply. Between 1605 and 1705, a century in which the city's population doubled, coal consumption multiplied sixfold. In the next twenty years it grew by half again, reaching the annual level of 475,000 chaldrons (of about 2800 pounds each).[16]

This concentrated demand for coal did more than anything else to stimulate the development of the Newcastle and Sunderland mine fields and to build up an efficient fleet of coastal vessels - colliers - to transport economically hundreds of thousands of tons of coal annually to the Thames. Under the pressure of this traffic the colliers grew in average capacity from 73 tons in 1606, to 248 tons in 1700, and to 312 tons by 1730. The trade came to employ thousands of seamen and became prized in official circles as the "nursery of seamen" - a convenient reserve transferable to naval duty in time of need. The ability of mundane domestic trades to act in as dynamic a fashion as the glamorous intercontinental trades was recognized by a mid-seventeenth-century poet who exclaimed:

> England's a perfect world! has Indies too!
> Correct your maps: Newcastle is Peru.[17]

Transportation facilities

The volume of regional trade grew to a distinctly higher level of magnitude in the seventeenth century. This occurred despite the absence of any significant growth of population. It reflected, instead, a profound redistribution - both social and spatial - of the European population: the largest cities gained at the expense of the smaller, the proportion of the rural population specialized in either agriculture or industry grew, and the number of soldiers enrolled at any given time in the new standing armies of the absolutist monarchs increased as the custom of providing for their provisions gained acceptance. All these developments meant that the passive portion of the population which rarely entered the market as either buyers or sellers diminished. Indications of these changes can be observed throughout Europe, but not everywhere did they have free rein to expand the volume of regional trade. Where transportation facilities remained inadequate, a ceiling existed to contain this commercial expansiveness.

Sicily offers the most notorious example of an export economy hobbled by inadequate transport and commercial facilities. In the seventeenth century the grain surpluses of this monocultural economy moved to the coast on muleback. At the coast hardly any harbor facilities existed to send the grain to its destinations. Instead, porters waded into the water bearing sacks of grain to transfer them to lighters which, in turn, brought the grain to ships riding at anchor away from the unimproved "harbors." The century after 1650 saw an impressive building boom in Sicily, but it consisted entirely in the construction of country villas for the nobility: over 200 were begun in the vicinity of Palermo alone. Clearly, none of the available investment funds found their way into transportation improvements. When Goethe traveled through Sicily in 1787 he found that even on the main roads, rivers could be crossed only by fording. At one point he could not proceed except by being hoisted across a river by a band of burly peasants. The Spanish rulers of the unhappy island regarded its grain surpluses as a national asset to feed armadas and cities. But they did nothing to prevent Sicily's exports from declining in the seventeenth century except attempt to deny needed foodstuffs to the island's own cities.

In Spain itself transport facilities were little better. When Philip II raised Madrid to the dignity of capital city for a vast empire, the fact that an enormous new city would grow in the center of Castile escaped no one. The best way to improve communications in this region was to make the river Tagus navigable from Toledo to the sea at Lisbon. This ambitious and expensive project was begun with royal backing in 1580. Despite considerable technical difficulties, the project was completed in 1587, but shortly thereafter inadequacies in the engineering work were exposed. Then, with the guiding hand of the constructing engineer removed through death and the king's attention diverted to more pressing matters, the opponents of the project took the offensive. The owners of mills along the river protested the loss of their rights while local landowners hurried to levy tolls on passing traffic. Finally, the city of Seville, with a stake in an alternative route to central Castile, sought to prevent the necessary repairs on the Tagus navigation from being carried out. By 1600 navigation on the Tagus once again had to be abandoned.

The energy exerted on this negative policy was not available for constructive activities. Seville's own trade required the dredging of its river, the Guadalquivir, which was silting up, and the construction of a bridge to span the river. Neither was done during the city's prosperous decades and by 1650, "Seville," as its recent historian puts it, "is no longer Seville." In the 1630s the proposal to link the Monzanares and Tagus rivers with a canal was submitted for consideration to a committee of theologians. Those not astounded by the selection of such a group to pass on the merits of the project will not be surprised at their recommendation: if God had intended the rivers to be connected, He would have made them so.

Castile and its growing capital were left to rely on overland transport which, given the region's terrain, meant pack animals and mule-drawn carts. In an effort to increase the supply of carters, the crown strengthened the legal privileges of the carters' guild in the 1590s. They could thereafter graze their mules along the routes without hindrance from local farmers. As Madrid continued to grow, more and more mules were needed. In 1757, for instance, the supplies entering the city would have loaded 600,000 pack animals or 150,000 carts. These mules had to be fed, yet, at the same time, the growing capital required increased food supplies, which required an expansion of arable land. In years of insufficient harvests in central Castile, Madrid had to be supplied from abroad, which, in turn, required mule convoys traveling the great distances from the sea.

The burden of an inefficient transportation system that claimed resources needed to feed the population obviously pressed down on the Castilian economy. It is no coincidence that the growth of Madrid was paired with the collapse of Toledo, the largest city of central Castile in the sixteenth century. The royal capital simply drew to itself the inelastic supply of muleteers, carters, and grain. A road building program was not begun until 1767, and then the chief purpose of the new royal roads was strategic rather than economic. [18]

The French response to the growing demand for improved transportation facilities was more positive. The Parisian penetration of regions that had previously supplied more local consumption centers received important royal support. In the first decade of the seventeenth century Henry IV's finance minister, the Duke of Sully, had encouraged a scheme to build canals connecting the Seine to the Loire, the Loire to the Saône, and the Saône to the Meuse. His interest in these measures had little to do with the needs of local commerce; he saw them as part of a grand strategy to divert international trade from routes controlled by the Habsburg crown. While nothing became of the grand strategy, Sully did actively promote the Braire canal connecting the Loire to the Seine. During his years in office nearly one million livres were spent on this project, so important to the growth of Paris. Its completion was delayed until 1642 and further improvements in navigation had to wait until Louis XIV and Colbert. With their backing, the navigability of the Loire was enhanced and work was begun on the canal Crozet, linking the Somme to the Oise, a tributary of the Seine. In 1734, when this work was completed, Paris stood at the center of a serviceable canal network penetrating much of northern France.

The strength of absolutist government, its ability to push policies through the often immobilizing localist obstructionism that was endemic in early modern European society, was also capable of making massive misinvestments. Colbert's pet project, the cutting of the *Canal de Deux Mers*, serves as an example of this weakness. This 150-mile canal that connected the Mediterranean Sea with the Garonne River and, thus, the Atlantic Ocean stood more as an engineering and administrative achievement than as an economic asset. To assure its construction Louis XIV showered on its financier and designer, Pierre-Paul Rignet two lucrative seigneurial jurisdictions plus a seigneurial monopoly on canal revenues. But, after completion in 1691 the canal's use never matched Colbert's (or Rignet's) expectations for it. The bulk of its traffic was always local grain while its high maintenance costs enforced a neglect that made the higher reaches of the 100-lock route frequently unserviceable.

A network of royal roads was slowly developed to augment the French canal and river network. The budget of the Royal Road Administration suffered from neglect after Sully's energetic road and bridge building of the first decade of the seventeenth century. His expenditure levels apparently were surpassed only at the beginning of the eighteenth century when the Royal Road Administration budgets rose from

870,000 livres per year to 4 million livres by 1770. Much of the 40,000 kilometer road network planned in 1738 continued for decades to exist only on paper, but the major routes connecting Paris with the frontiers were in place by mid-century. As a consequence of this investment, coaches between Paris and Lyons that required ten days in 1660 required only five days in 1770.

It was characteristic of absolutist governments that at the same time that they improved transport facilities, they were busy elaborating and codifying a complex and burdensome system of internal tariffs. This, of course, negated much of the beneficial impact of new roads and canals. Colbert's Tariff Ordinance of 1664, carved France into a large central zone, "Five Large Farms," and numerous smaller zones, the "Provinces Reputedly Foreign." The latter, although provinces of France, were treated as separate countries in matters concerning trade. To see how trade was burdened by such a system we can follow Franklin Ford's description of a shipment entering the city of Strasbourg, an old imperial city on the Rhine acquired by Louis XIV only in 1681.

> When a freight wagon rumbled over the Rhine bridge, westbound, or when a barge docked at the Boatmen's Quay . . . what the shipper had to pay the farmers of royal customs depended entirely on where his goods were ultimately delivered. If they were disposed of inside Strasbourg, the central collectors would receive nothing. If they were going only to Colmar or some other Alsatian town, representatives of the farmers-general, stationed at the city gates, would assess up to 50 percent of the normal French tariff on some items, but others, especially foodstuffs, passed duty-free. If the consignment was for Paris or Besançon, it would pay the full rate, later, at the customs frontier. The same regulations theoretically applied to shipments eastbound, out of the interior, from Alsace, or originating in Strasbourg. A complex system of deposits and clearance slips was designed to protect the royal farmers against fraudulent declarations of destinations.[19]

A French internal customs system effectively carved this largest of European states into a number of separate economies, but its impact on obstructing trade was as nothing compared with the tolls and privileges that plagued the Holy Roman Empire. Until well into the nineteenth century on the Rhine River goods were subjected to the staple rights and guild privileges of the cities of Cologne and Mainz. No goods could pass either city without first being unloaded and offered for sale (regardless of the intended destination of the goods) and then being loaded into the river vessels of the municipal boatmen's guild which exercised monopoly rights on river transport from their cities. On the Oder River disputes between the cities of Stettin and Frankfurt a/d Oder provoked Stettin, at the mouth of the river, to close it to trade for over a century after 1562. The Peace of Westphalia of 1648 only worsened matters; by removing all semblance of central authority from the Holy Roman Emperor nothing could restrain the mushrooming of tolls by Germany's numerous independent princes and cities.

In contrast to this sad strangulation of trade in central Europe stood the Dutch Republic, a byword for mobility in the seventeenth century. It was, of course, almost naturally endowed with a good network of internal waterways, but the seventeenth century witnessed a massive investment in new and improved canals. The expansion of peat digging, as described earlier, occasioned a large addition to the Republic's navigable waterways, but of even greater importance were the new intercity tow-path canals built between 1632 and 1665 to provide direct links between every important city in the maritime region of the nation. This decentralized state was not devoid of the obstructionist efforts of cities anxious to protect ancient toll privileges, and it had no monarch capable of overriding such narrow views. But, in contrast to Spain, the appeal of the benefits of the new routes proved superior to the appeal of obstruction. Several million guilders were invested to build 500 kilometers of new canals. By the 1660s they produced some 38 million passenger-kilometers of transportation each year and had sufficiently lowered costs to permit Amsterdamers to send their dirty wash to Haarlem and Gouda to be cleaned in the pure waters available there.

The canal age of England began in the 1760s. By then the Kingdom possessed 1400 miles of navigable water, half of which had been created by engineering works between 1600 and 1760. (In contrast, the combined German states had only 300 miles of canal or canalized rivers.) These improvements took the form of extending navigation to the upper reaches of the Severn, Thames, Ouse, and Trent river systems. To connect these basins together to serve a national market, reliance continued to be placed on coastal shipping and on a spreading network of turnpike roads.

The ineffectualness of laws that placed the burden of road maintenance on local parishes led Parliament, in 1662, to experiment with a new approach in the passage of a turnpike act. This act entrusted a stretch of notoriously difficult road to a group of trustees who were given the right to levy tolls in exchange for committing themselves to upgrade the road. Here, too, there arose opposition from all types of vested interests. But the noteworthy fact is the persistent spread of this legal device after 1700 until a network of turnpike roads was fashioned consisting of thirteen main routes radiating from London extending nearly 1600 miles by 1750. As a consequence, road transport costs tended to decline during the first half of the eighteenth century while the rudimentary stagecoach services begun after the Restoration were able to expand to provide service to every corner of the Kingdom. The eight to twelve days needed to travel by coach from London to Exeter in 1673 were reduced to four to six days by 1760.[20]

The capacity of trade expansion to be translated into economic growth varies enormously among economies. In early modern Europe that capacity was enlarged where transaction costs were reduced and where the social structure and the pattern of urbanization enlarged the percentage of the population that depended significantly on the market. By no means did these conditions prevail everywhere.

There arose a considerable disparity among regions in their ability to respond to trade opportunities. By the eighteenth century a clear distinction could be made between the Dutch Republic, and the Atlantic ports of France and Germany, on the one hand, and the interior regions of Europe on the other. In the former, the concentration of international trade was matched by the invigoration of regional trade. This accomplishment was the result of an almost imperceptible process of institutional and organizational innovation plus a reshuffling of the population. Thus, although no spectacular transport innovations appeared, mundane investment in roads, canals, and coastal vessels achieved significant increases in the speed of passenger travel and reductions in the cost of freight carriage. In these regions, the everyday commerce in necessities altered its structure to accommodate to the concentrated demand emanating from the great metropolises, the military and naval installations, and the spreading rural industrial districts. Among these favored regions, England stood out because of its ability, already apparent by the mid-eighteenth century, to integrate its industrial sector most fully into the Atlantic trading system.

6
Capitalism creating its own demand

The character of demand

When examining an economy dependent upon human and animal power modestly supplemented by wind and water for the energy to produce its goods, we quite naturally assign special significance to those measures that raise output beyond the meager limits that seemed to be imposed by technology. But the feebleness of productive power was not the only obstacle to the attainment of higher living standards. Keynesian analysis makes us aware of the role played in the modern economy by the demand for goods in securing an economic state in which resources are fully utilized and investment plans are carried out.

In the preindustrial economy underutilized resources and chronic underemployment testify to the frequent inadequacy of demand. It might be judged uncharitable to accuse our ancestors - people whose labor was physically taxing in a way we hardly know - of idleness. But it existed, and for good reason, as Adam Smith explained: "It is better to play for nothing than to work for nothing." Technical and natural constraints explain a part of this idleness: the rigors of winter bottled northern shipping fleets in their ports (typically only 2.5 percent of the ships passing the Danish Sound did so in the three winter months); the rhythm of agricultural production enforced seasonal unemployment on farm laborers. These constraints on economic efficiency are well-known.

Less well-known is the fact that failure of demand contributed heavily to this problem of underutilized resources. Indeed, a great deal of seasonal unemployment in agriculture is not natural at all; it is the result of markets too weak to warrant the use of the available labor force in more labor-intensive production. Here, long before the technological breakthroughs of the Industrial Revolution, was a means by which higher output levels might be achieved.[1]

But how could demand be increased? Contemporaries had little faith that this could be done. In fact, the economic "theory" of early modern Europe, mercantilism, was quite clear about the nature of demand; one of its basic premises was that markets were static. Charles Davenant, the English observer of economic affairs, expressed this view in an all-encompassing way:

> For there is a limited stock of our own product to carry out, beyond which there is no passing: as for example, there is such a quantity of woollen manufactures, lead, tin, etc. which, over and above our own consumption, we can export abroad, and our soil as it is now peopled, will not yield much more; and there is likewise a limited quantity of these goods which foreign consumption will not exceed.[2]

In such an economy lowered prices could only result in lowered revenue; there could be no expectation of a compensating increase in volume. It was firmly believed that to increase one's trade, new markets would have to be added to old ones. As Francis Bacon put it early in the seventeenth century, "the increase of any estate must be upon the foreigner (for whatsoever is somewhere gotten is somewhere lost)." Inevitably, foreign trade seemed to be a species of warfare.

The belief in static markets was so strongly held that evidence to the contrary, notably the adoption by common people of dress and consumption habits previously confined to the rich, was received as a symptom of moral and economic disorder. Such consumer behavior would drain the state of its treasure at the same time that it undermined God-ordained status distinctions. Sumptuary laws - invariably futile - continued to be enacted to obstruct the downward diffusion of upper-class fashions.

Merchants who viewed their markets in this way can perhaps be excused for shifting their attention to money lending and crown financing if they had the chance. Those who remained active in trade tended to see their best chance for gain in catering to a relatively narrow range of urban and elite customers. In these markets the vagaries of fashion promised to reward the lucky with sudden increases in demand, and even the merchant not so blessed could compensate for the small volume of his trade with large profit margins on each sale. But these traditional markets could not support the long-term development of the entire economy. By the beginning of the seventeenth century merchants were gradually putting together substantial accumulations of capital, yet investment opportunities created by simple extension into new areas were being depleted. Capitalists could not indefinitely continue to confine their activities to the limitations of the highly stratified market structure of European societies.

Still, the problem remained. How could demand be expanded on a sustained basis? Only then could capital accumulation proceed unimpeded, and only then could the chronic underemployment of preindustrial economies - the seasonal idleness of the farmer, the casual employment of the day laborer - be suppressed. Two demand-limiting characteristics of the preindustrial economy had to be dealt with.

In the dominant agrarian sector a large portion of peasant households were marginal consumers. Their passivity derived not simply from poverty: peasants' use of their productive resources to meet household needs first and to market only the surplus meant that only a small portion of their total output passed through the market. Consequently, they depended on the market for very little of their consumption. Moreover, small changes in the economic climate could cause large numbers in rural society to retreat from the market. The thinness and volatility of the peasant market discouraged investors from committing capital to it.

In the wage earners' sector, households had no alternative to purchasing goods through the market, but the expansion of demand from this sector was limited by a "backward bending labor supply curve." That is, if wages rose, workers preferred to work less rather than to buy more. For instance, in the fifteenth century when labor scarcity drove wages to unprecedentedly high levels, the number of working days diminished as laborers observed more and more saints' days. Few economic concepts were more firmly entrenched as conventional wisdom than this belief that workers strove for a "target income" and that higher wages did not increase the demand for goods but only deprived the economy of labor. Sir William Petty expressed this view in the 1670s in his *Political Arithmetic.*

> It is observed by Clothiers and others, who employ great numbers of poor people, that when corn is extremely plentiful, that the labour of the poor is proportionately dear: and scarce to be had at all (so licentious are they who labour only to eat, or rather to drink).

In the eighteenth century observers remained loyal to this dogma:

> Scarcity, to a certain degree, promotes industry . . . the manufacturer [i.e., worker] who can subsist on three day's work will be idle and drunken the remainder of the week . . . The poor in the manufacturing counties will never work any more time than is necessary just to live and support their weekly debauches.[3]

The creation of a vigorous home market could not proceed without removing these obstacles. To remove them required confronting deep-seated structural characteristics of the society. We would credit seventeenth-century merchants and manufacturers with more imagination and radicalism than they possessed by saying that they acted to create a social order compatible with expanding demand. The evidence, such as the quotes above, shows the opposite to be true. But in pursuing more immediate and practical goals governments, peasants, landowners, and merchants often took important steps to enlarge the market economy and thereby recast the social order.

The growth of the proportion of the population dependent on the market during the period 1600-1750 can be confirmed by noting the doubling of the population of the larger cities of northern Europe, the farmers' shift of emphasis toward livestock raising and the production of fodder, industrial, and horticultural crops, and perhaps most significant the explosive growth of the cotter and landless populations among whom rural industry spread. The consequent reduction of the number of passive households should not be confused with an increase in per capita income: the two did not necessarily go hand in hand. Indeed, the angry and fearful complaints about the poor in the seventeenth century stem from the new visibility of an enlarged, permanent class of casual wage laborers. But this new class, just as surely as the rich, was part of a social stratification gradually taking shape that tended to reduce the number of households that produced primarily for home consumption.

A more active force compelling market involvement in the seventeenth century can be found emanating from the state. Absolutist and constitutional governments alike developed permanent bureaucratic and military structures that greatly increased their day-to-day impact on the population. The growth of government expenditure was supported by a bewildering variety of taxes and fiscal expedients most of which fell disproportionately on the lower classes. In a modern economy regressive taxes would reduce consumer demand. But to the extent that they fell on peasants only marginally involved in the market economy and workers with target incomes, they forced an increase in market-oriented production to pay the taxes that supported the growth of government demand. Examples can be cited into the nineteenth century of peasants whose only market involvement occurred just before tax payments fell due.

In the modern economy the growth of demand is not left to chance. Producers and merchants strive to anticipate and even mould public tastes. By offering and advertising irresistible goods the economy can induce consumers to work longer, and even take second jobs in order to acquire a new, coveted commodity. In the early modern society strongly held beliefs about the permanence and sanctity of the social hierarchy tended to limit the ability of merchants to foster new consumption patterns, but during the seventeenth century the necessary social tolerance could be found, particularly in the new metropolises, to permit merchants a dynamic market role.

New commodities from Asia and America, new household luxuries, and status objects for ordinary people were being popularized and made available in retail shops (another innovation of the period). The impact of desirable goods newly available on local markets could be just as far reaching as farm enclosure or rural industry in increasing market dependence. The peasant who bought a pair of shoes or cotton calicoes in the market ceased making their equivalents himself. He not only entered the market to buy, he also entered the market to sell because a portion of his household's labor was diverted from self-provision of crafts to market production of food. When thousands of households shift their production and consumption habits in this way, the economy benefits from trade creation and specialization. The economy becomes more productive even though no technological advances have been introduced.

By no means did these developments in social structure, taxation, and the creation of wants overcome all the limitations of demand. But they made a discernible difference that permitted the aggregate demand for goods and services to exhibit enough sustained growth in certain regions to encourage new initiatives in increasing production. In the following discussion we will describe the growth of demand and the upgrading of expectations and standards by considering in turn the component parts of an economy's aggregate demand: consumer demand, investment, government demand, and foreign (in this context, non-European) demand.

Consumer demand

What trends did personal income exhibit in our period? Two variables exerted the greatest influence: the state of the harvests and the rate of population growth. The former affected personal income in the short run; the latter was more of a long-term factor. Periodic harvest failures exerted a direct and pervasive influence on the distribution of personal income. Poor harvest yields first affected the farmer. Although prices were likely to rise sharply, only the larger farmer, who regularly sold big surpluses on the market, was in a position to benefit. The smaller farmer, who produced a marketable surplus only in good years, was likely to have nothing to sell. Indeed, he might find himself compelled to buy grain in such a year. Next to be affected were the cottagers and day laborers who depended on harvest labor for their cash income. Small harvests reduced the demand for their labor, with obvious consequences. Finally, we must consider the industrial worker: his cost of living shot upward at just the time that employment was reduced for lack of demand. Demand for manufactures was hurt by unemployment in agriculture and the diversion of purchasing power into basic foodstuffs. In years of good harvests, the analysis can be reversed.

These harvest-led cycles were temporary, but could nonetheless have far-reaching effects. As described in Chapter 2, a severe harvest failure could so strengthen the position of large farmers and landlords and so plunge the lesser folk into debt that a long string of good years might be insufficient to reverse its impact on the social structure.[4]

Turning to the long-run trend, we must consider factors that affected labor productivity. The preindustrial economy, with the exception of cottage industry, was one in which labor was subject to sharply diminishing returns. Consequently, changes in the level of population directly affected labor productivity and, ultimately, wages. Rapid population growth almost always was accompanied by land scarcity in agriculture and glutted labor markets in the other sectors of the economy. Even when wage rates remained fixed, their purchasing power fell as the demand for basic foodstuffs outstripped the ability of agriculture to increase the supply. Should the population of such an economy decline, the survivors' income would benefit from the larger per capita quantity of productive resources - particularly land - and also from the relatively strong demand for labor. At the same time, the prices of staple foodstuffs would tend to fall (because demand for necessities is inelastic and a smaller population would buy less, despite the more attractive price).[5] Such market conditions produced a golden age for the wage laborer (whose income rose while his costs fell), but these same conditions produced something less than that for the landowning farmer, particularly the grain farmer.

Assessing the overall impact of such an era on consumer demand is not easy. The falling price of basic foodstuffs depresses grain production, but the resulting increase in the discretionary income of wage earners increases the demand for dairy products, beverages, and manufactures for which demand is more elastic. The shifting pattern of demand combined with the redistribution of income from landowners to wage earners creates, at the very least, economic dislocation. The century following the Black Death was such an era and the century that began between 1600 (in the Mediterranean) and 1660 (in the north) was another. The evidence is compelling that the economic dislocation of the fourteenth century created a genuine depression - that the benefits accruing to certain groups and sectors were more than compensated for by the decline of others.[6] But the seventeenth-century stagnation differed in important respects from its predecessor.

In Ireland, Germany, Poland, Denmark, and the Mediterranean countries varying combinations of plagues and chronic warfare and insecurity caused a substantial decline in population. Price trends and income redistribution stimulated certain industries but, as after the Black Death, total consumer demand probably fell considerably. Elsewhere, and particularly in northwestern Europe, the price trends described above arose *without* a fall of population. Stagnation or a slow upward trend characterized the seventeenth-century populations of the Dutch Republic, the Southern Netherlands, England, and, apparently, France. As in the rest of Europe, grain prices fell, but, in most of northwestern Europe, reduced demand was not the cause. Rather, the weak grain prices reflected glutted markets that were the result of increased output.[7]

Consequently, in this region of Europe we find real wages rising without a sharp fall in population. Of course, the long-term downward drift of grain prices threatened the incomes of the agricultural population, but, as noted in Chapter 2, this regional deterioration was tempered by the introduction in this region of technical advances which tended to lower costs at the same time that they facilitated a shift in emphasis toward relatively profitable livestock products. To these factors should be added the changes in social stratification and urbanization described in earlier chapters, which increased market participation. Consumer demand, under these varied influences, was not simply channeled into x at the expense of y: rather, it grew absolutely to usher in new standards for both urban and rural populations.

Figures 5 and 6 illustrate what was happening to the incomes of wage earners. Several time-series of nominal wages, wages expressed in current money units, are presented in Figure 6. A striking characteristic of most series is their "stickiness." After the inflationary pressure of the early

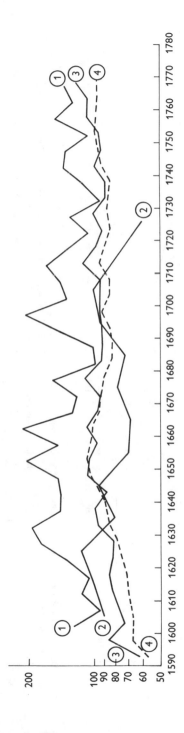

Figure 5 Cost-of-living indicators

1 Price of Prussian rye at Amsterdam. Five-year averages in guilders per last.

2 Average price of cereals (wheat, rye, millet, rice) at Milan. Ten-year averages indexed 1701-10=100.

3 Price of a composite unit of consumables in southern England. Five-year averages indexed 1650-74=100.

4 Cost-of-living index for Leiden. Five-year averages indexed 1650-74=100.

Sources:
1 N. W. Posthumus, *Nederlandsche Prijsgeschiedenis*, vol. I (Leiden, 1943), pp. 573-76.
2 Aldo de Maddalena, "Preise, Löhne und Geldwesen im Verlauf der wirtschaftlichen Entwicklung Mailands," in Ingomar Bog, et al. eds., *Wirtschaftliche und Soziale Strukturen im saekularen Wandel*, vol. II (Hannover, 1974), p. 486.
3 E. H. Phelps Brown and Sheila V. Hopkins "Seven Centuries of the Prices of Consumables, Compared with Builders' Wage-Rates," *Economica* 24 (1956), appendix B.
4 N. W. Posthumus, *De geschiedenis van de Leidsche lakenindustrie* vol. III (The Hague, 1939), pp. 1014, 1082.

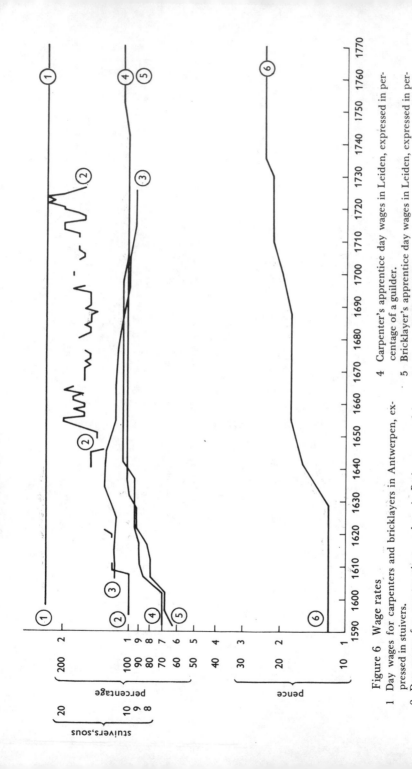

Figure 6 Wage rates

1 Day wages for carpenters and bricklayers in Antwerpen, expressed in stuivers.
2 Day wages for construction workers in Paris, expressed in sous.
3 Average wage in Milan. Ten-year averages indexed 1701-10=100.
4 Carpenter's apprentice day wages in Leiden, expressed in percentage of a guilder.
5 Bricklayer's apprentice day wages in Leiden, expressed in percentage of a guilder.
6 Day wages of building craftsmen in southern England expressed in pence.

Sources for these data will be found at the foot of the next page.

seventeenth century subsides, wages are fossilized, sometimes for over a century at a time. Only major events bring any changes, and they are, with few exceptions, upward adjustments. Figure 5 presents price data for grain as well as two attempts at calculating "cost-of-living" indexes. Dividing Figure 6 by Figure 5 would give us a real wage index, but because of the grave problems standing in the way of calculating a statistically acceptable cost-of-living index (we know next to nothing about rents, retail prices of nonfood items, and the actual composition of expenditures among the various consumption categories) that step has not been taken here. Nonetheless, the figures show clearly enough that purchasing power of wage earners rose in the century after 1650.

It is in this context of favorable demand conditions that the enormous expansion of tobacco, sugar, coffee, cacoa, and tea imports to Europe should be explained. By itself, the cost-reducing impact of commodities made possible by large-scale plantation production hardly seems sufficient to explain the European economy's absorption of these commodities in volumes that altered the daily life of broad strata of the population.

Nowhere are the new standards of comfort and style more apparent than in the large cities. Indeed, much of what we have come to understand as European urban life - hotels, opera houses, theaters - came into being in this period. Retail shops gained widespread acceptance by about 1700; they supplemented the traditional retailing carried on at periodic markets and by hawkers and peddlers - which, of course, continued to exist. The new shops sold many goods, notably

Sources of data in Figure 6 (p. 186)

1 E. Scholliers, *De levenstandaard in de XVe en XVIe eeuw te Antwerpen* (Antwerp, 1960), p. 140.
2 M. Baulant, "Les salaires du Bâtiment, 1490-1726," *Annales.*
3 Maddalena, "Preise, Lohne und Geldwesen," p. 486.
4 and 5 Posthumus, *Lakenindustrie,* pp. 1014, 1082.
6 E. H. Phelps Brown and Sheila V. Hopkins, "Seven Centuries of Building Wages," *Economica* 23 (1955), table I.

colonial wares and textiles, but they were particularly important as purveyors of fashion to the larger portion of the population now able to aspire to a more refined material culture.

The demand for French fashions became sufficiently important to suggest to Louis XIV that his court should be used deliberately to publicize new fashions abroad. It was even theorized in Holland that the Sun King deliberately sought to popularize French luxuries among the austere Dutch middle class. Aside from the moral decay induced by addiction to French fopperies, such a weakness would presumably reduce the savings rate and, hence, the commercial and financial strength of the Republic. This strategy was clearly the product of a diabolical mind.

At the same time, oriental fashions brought to Europe in small quantities along with the spices and pepper uncovered a burgeoning demand that rapidly attracted European imitators. Lacquer work, caned furniture, porcelain, and calicoes were the most important of these. The Dutch shipped over 3 million pieces of Chinese porcelain to Europe in the first half of the seventeenth century. Civil strife in China then cut off the supply but the demand for porcelain had grown so that only domestic imitations could hope to satisfy the new markets. After 1650 the city of Delft found a new importance as a ceramics center, and in England small local potters came to face the competition of the semi-industrial firms of north Staffordshire which captured large markets by adapting oriental designs to their products. North Staffordshire production increased tenfold in the first half of the eighteenth century.

Besides retail shops, cities came to possess coffee houses and cafes to serve the demand for coffee and the new alcoholic beverages - brandy, gin, and rum. If it was true that the poor only worked to earn enough to drink it was apparently not true that they had a "target drinking quota," for "official" gin production in England rose from 500,000 gallons in

1680 to 4 million gallons in 1727 to over 7 million gallons in 1751. To this must be added a growth in legal rum imports from none in 1700 to 800,000 gallons by 1750. By the end of the seventeenth century alcohol had become a major growth industry in northern Europe. The only Dutch industrial city to grow in the eighteenth century, Schiedam, did so on the strength of its gin industry.

As gin drinking increased, so did newspaper readership. London's first daily, the *Daily Courant*, was established in 1702; by 1709 eighteen dailies appeared in the city. For Europe as a whole newspaper sales have been estimated at 7 million copies per year by 1753. The expanding population with the money and literacy to buy newspapers also demanded other services that spread among the major cities after 1650. Postal services came to replace the municipal and commercial messenger services that had sufficed to serve the limited needs of merchants since the Middle Ages. The more settled conditions brought on by the Peace of Westphalia permitted rapid expansion of the German imperial postal service operated by the princely family of Thurn and Taxis. In 1660 the postal officials of Amsterdam cooperated with it to organize a regular 56-hour horseback service to Hamburg and points north and east. In the same year Amsterdam inaugurated a service of twice-weekly mail boats to London. By 1670 the Republic was crisscrossed by a network of nightly mail routes connecting every city. In France the value of the postal monopoly rose from 1.2 million livres in 1673 to 8.8 million in 1777.

Street lighting spread in the major cities during the same period. Paris began to hang lanterns in 1667; by 1700, 65 miles of city street were illuminated, using 200,000 pounds of candles annually. In London a joint stock company, the Convex Lights Company, endeavored to illuminate city streets beginning in 1684. It is, perhaps, a reflection of the growing relative backwardness of the Mediterranean, that Venice acquired street lighting only in 1732.

Fire protection also had to be upgraded. The bucket brigades on which cities had relied since the Middle Ages no longer seemed to suffice in the great metropolises. The hand-powered water pump first used in Holland in 1668 spread to Paris in 1704. By 1723, twenty-two of the contraptions, capable of sending a jet of water to the upper floors of houses, functioned in the French capital while Amsterdam stationed seventy of them around the city.

These municipal services developed in societies where the standards of private comfort were also being upgraded. Among the well-to-do, leaded windows, French furniture, and tapestries were acquired while the use of carriages for movement about the cities became *de rigueur*. The need to use carriages was reinforced by the elaborate new fashions, for which the streets were far too muddy and filthy. Thus, by 1636 some 6000 private and public-hire coaches transported the rich in London, while the official estimates of coaches in use in Paris rose from 4000 in the 1630s to 20,000 by 1700.

The growing crowds of beggars, vagabonds, and casual laborers in the larger cities certainly did not share in the new comforts. Contemporary accounts of their wretchedness give the impression that urban life had descended to a new low point, at least in the scope of the poverty problem. But between these rootless masses and the very rich there existed a considerable group that enjoyed some elementary improvements. The growing volume of peat and coal used in home fires for heating and cooking plus the increasing importance of whale and vegetable oils for lighting and soap production are clues that simple comforts were now in the reach of large numbers.

If these new consumption habits are unimpressive to us, they were sufficient to convince contemporaries that they were living in a new age. Jan ten Hoorn, in the introduction to his 1679 guide to the public barge and coach routes and inns of the Netherlands, wrote enthusiastically of the new, effortless mobility then available to a large public. He described earlier decades as though they had been virtually barbarous, and related, in passing, that his grandmother had told him that in her day soap had not been in common use.[8]

Not everyone greeted the new comforts with enthusiasm. In England an anonymous "Lover of his Country and Well-Wisher to the Prosperity of the King and the Kingdoms" attacked the stage coaches that were established on many routes after the Restoration as destructive to horsemanship, encouraging effeminacy, and undermining both the social and the economic order. By making travel easier, he objected, stage coaches tended to reduce the grandeur of the traveling gentleman at the same time that they drained the provinces of money that could now easily be spent on London luxuries.

Because the price trends of the century after 1650 did not favor agriculture we might not expect the new taste for comfort and luxury to spread to the country districts. The impact of market trends varied greatly among types of farming, and our knowledge of peasant consumption standards is far from complete. But the examination of the inventories of the possessions left by deceased peasants in parts of England and the Dutch Republic show impressive improvements. They are, in fact, hard to reconcile with the apparent squeeze on agricultural profits in those areas. Friesian dairy farmers acquired curtains, fancy tables and chests, mirrors, and wall decorations (even paintings) after 1650. Bibles and books became more common and the formal costumes festooned with silver buttons and, for the women, gold head ornaments began to appear. The average number of linen shirts owned by large farmers rose from four around 1600 to over ten by the end of the century. After the 1690s ceramic dinnerware supplemented the wood and tin utensils they had long used, and clocks were being hung on their walls.[9]

We cannot assume that the new material comforts of the Friesian farmers were characteristic of rural dwellers everywhere. Agriculture in Friesland was highly commercialized and the farmers formed a prosperous minority in a countryside filled with more humble craftsmen and laborers. Moreover, in the neighboring province the more isolated peasants enjoyed very few of the comforts of the Friesians. The spread of commercial agriculture was still very uneven, but where it existed there arose a significant new demand for consumer goods.

Investment

It is hard to put one's finger on the demand for capital goods in preindustrial economies. The capital sunk into mills, forges, furnaces, navigation improvements, and the like rarely attained impressive levels. Most capital was circulating - invested in raw materials, inventories, and credit extensions. Moreover, the modest sums sunk in productive equipment were scattered over wide areas. The demand for capital goods under such conditions rarely had a major impact on the economy.

A significant exception to this was provided by the growing volume of seventeenth- and eighteenth-century trade, which created a derived demand for shipbuilding and its many related industries. This investment demand was highly concentrated around the growing Atlantic port cities where the handling and processing of bulky cargoes also generated an investment demand for such industrial installations as sugar refineries, mills, breweries, distilleries, and warehouses.

As the volume of coal shipped from Newcastle grew, as the number of ships sent yearly to the Indies rose, and as the fishing and whaling industries expanded, more and more capital was attracted to shipbuilding. Available estimates of the total tonnage of the European merchant fleets cannot be accepted without reservation, but the trend they show is unmistakable: the total tonnage is thought to have grown from 600 to 700,000 tons around 1600 to over 3 million tons in 1786. The bulk of this tonnage was in the hands of the Dutch, English, and French, with the Dutch in the lead throughout the seventeenth century and the English in the forefront by the mid-eighteenth century.[10]

As the production of oceangoing vessels grew - after the 1650s the Dutch alone may have built 500 per year, at an average cost per vessel of 8000 to 10,000 guilders - the demand for timber, tar, pitch, turpentine, sailcloth, rope, and metal fittings rose. Supplying these materials required the development of new facilities and the tapping of new production areas. For example, the strong demand for resin and turpentine so enriched the monopolistic Baltic suppliers that Dutch merchants - the chief purchasers - entered southwestern France to organize a rival production center.

Timber, in demand as both a fuel and a construction material, posed the greatest problem. The merchants of maritime nations scoured Germany, Scandinavia, and the Baltic states and even imported from North America. The Dutch built specially proportioned ships to haul timber from Norway. When these supplies became inadequate they turned to the Baltic from which the annual westward flow of timber rose from 100,000 in the 1660s to 1.5 million pieces in the 1730s.

The most far-reaching impact of the growing demand for timber came not from efforts to increase its supply but from efforts to find substitutes for its use. As the competing users for timber drove up its price in many areas, the expansion of fuel-intensive industries came to hinge on finding substitutes for wood and charcoal.

The pioneering of English and Southern Netherlands' industrialists in the use of coal in brewing, dyemaking, and salt boiling permitted investment in larger, permanent fixed capital facilities. However, substituting coal for wood and charcoal was not a straightforward matter in all industries. Only through experimentation with grades of coal and types of furnaces did industrialists find ways to gain acceptable results using coal in baking, brick and pottery making, and malting. By the end of the seventeenth century London industrialists, challenged by the enormous market at their doorsteps, had overcome many of these difficulties. One application, of enormous potential importance, remained to be achieved: using coal fires in iron smelting. The release of sulphur fumes in the combustion of coal undermined. the quality of the iron. This problem posed a formidable obstacle to the use of coal in the iron industry, but as the demand for iron goods grew in both English domestic and colonial markets, the advantages of being liberated from dependence on local timber resources provided the necessary stimulus: in 1709 the iron-master Abraham Darby achieved the crucial breakthrough at his forge in Colebrookdale.

Agriculture, the largest sector of the economy, generally was the weakest source of investment demand. The poverty of most peasants, the discouragement provided by most tenure arrangements, and the desire of landlords for immediate income combined to keep investment at a level barely sufficient to maintain the existing capital stock in working order. Exceptions to this norm arose in those regions identified earlier where the consolidation of large, commercialized farms was underway. The massive investments of English landlords during the parliamentary enclosure movement (the enclosure of open-field villages under the authority of Acts of Parliament) that began in the mid-eighteenth century did not mark the beginning of a new era of agricultural improvements. In the preceding century enclosure by private agreement plus such measures as the construction of water meadows and the purchase of imported clover to improve pastures all required major commitments of capital.

Similarly, the first two-thirds of the seventeenth century saw impressive sums invested in reclamation in the coastal areas of many nations. Besides this capital-broadening investment, capital deepening also occurred: most of the polders, windmills, and sluices built in the Dutch Republic during this period were not to win new land but to improve the quality of existing land. In those favored regions where such investments were increasing agricultural output, a derived demand was generated for services and farm equipment that directly affected the occupational structure of rural areas.

The various craftsmen in most rural communities seem to have been small farmers who sought to supplement their agricultural earnings by following a trade. The weak demand for their services in a peasant community, where most households sought to avoid expenditures on goods or services they might supply for themselves, prevented more specialization than this. In those regions where agricultural investments established a commitment to the market, the farm demand for the services of smiths, carpenters, wheelwrights, boatmen, and the like increased substantially. In the Dutch province of Friesland farmers doubled their ownership of wagons and boats in the course of the seventeenth century and increased their ownership of kettles, vats, and pails made of metal. In the same period the overall value of farm equipment rose from no more than 10 to 17 percent of the total value of farmers' movable property. The same trend has been observed in the English county of Sussex where equipment rose from 4 percent of total farm inventory value in 1611-59, to 7 percent in 1660-99, and 9 percent in 1700-44. Standing behind this trend were the replacement of two-wheeled carts by four-wheeled wagons and the more widespread use of metal parts in farm equipment, most notably the introduction of the iron plow.

This upward trend in the amount, and particularly the metal content, of farm implements is easy to overlook. But, given the size of the agrarian sector in the preindustrial economy, even small increases in demand could have a large aggregate importance. For instance, in a region where farmers switch from a three-course to an alternate husbandry rotation, the increased area requiring plowing each year by itself would generate a demand for plows and for horses (and, hence, horseshoes) that is likely to have exceeded the increase in iron-demand from any other single source.[11]

In those regions where agricultural specialization produced this growing demand for equipment (as well as for consumer goods) the role of village craftsmen changed. In rural Friesland, for example, a 1749 census shows smiths, wagon- and boatmakers, and carpenters, as well as shoemakers, bakers, and millers, to be far more numerous than in adjoining provinces where commercial agriculture had made much less headway. Moreover, the value of the craftsmen's tools and materials plus the scarcity of livestock among their possessions show that their trades had ceased being by-employments: they were now as specialized as the farmers they served.

The growth in investment demand from the peasant sector was apparently confined to several regions of northwestern Europe; the demand for construction was more widespread. (For the sake of simplicity both residential and commercial construction will be considered together.) Where large-scale commercial agriculture gained ground, the demand for larger farm buildings expressed itself in the development of new rural architectural styles and in the use of new building materials, such as brick and tile. The new farmhouses found in England and the Dutch Republic exhibited a growing appreciation for privacy and a desire to separate servants from their employer's household as parlors and separate sleeping chambers were added to the one or two multipurpose rooms that had previously sufficed the peasant household. The rural villages also adopted more substantial building styles; the period from 1570 to 1640 has been identified as one in which rural England was rebuilt and in which the vernacular styles one now associates with the English countryside were devised.[12]

The growth of the large cities, and the gradual replacement of fire-prone timber with brick construction in nearly all of them, generated a great demand for brick. The physical expansion of Amsterdam required such vast amounts of building material that a single brick buyer in 1660 was in a position to contract for 100,000 bricks from each of twenty-four separate brickworks for two consecutive years. The Dutch Republic also exported brick and tile, particularly to England and the German states along the North Sea coast, where they supplemented traditional supplies of stone and timber. The rebuilding of London after its devastating fire of 1666 presented an opportunity to raise the standards of urban constructions. The resulting demand for brick could only be met by domestic brickyards. As means were found to replace wood with coal in the kilns, the industry grew rapidly in the decades after the Restoration.

No visitor to Europe could fail to recognize a final form of construction demand, that for palaces and country houses. One need not dwell on the 66 million livres spent by Louis XIV on Versailles or the 250,000 pound cost of Blenheim (eight times the initial capital invested in the East India Company) built for the Duke of Marlborough. Besides these great piles there arose, particularly in the late seventeenth and early eighteenth centuries, hundreds of smaller houses.

In Holland the old nobility could afford little more than repairs on their uncomfortable medieval structures, but the urban regents now built scores of handsome country houses within a short distance of their cities. The new fashion spread as far as Sicily, where the aristocracy, long resident in Palermo, felt a need for country places; in short order over 200 were built in the vicinity of the capital. We are not describing the rebuilding of the seats of ancient landed families - rather, what we have here is a sort of urban colonization of the countryside pursued by urbanized nobles, plus mercantile and governmental families. In the course of the seventeenth century the establishment of country villas and estates at not too great a distance from the cities occurred around many major cities - as anyone can still see who travels in the hinterlands of Venice, Naples, Bordeaux, or Hamburg.

England experienced the greatest building boom. A modest country house might have cost as little as 3000 or 4000 pounds, but something more substantial, like Petworth House, rebuilt in the decade following 1688, cost over 20,000 pounds. Because 90 percent of the disbursements were paid out within the market town of Petworth itself - mainly for labor and materials - the impact of such a project on the local economy could be substantial.

Whether it was a harmful or a beneficial impact depended on whether these expenditures occurred when the local economy was fully employed (in which case the construction could force the contraction of more productive undertakings) or underemployed (in which case it would mobilize idle resources, pump purchasing power into the economy, and stimulate productive output in general). It is not known if there was any counter-cyclical timing to great house construction, although it seems unlikely that someone bent on having a new mansion, and willing to relocate physically whole villages in order to open up a pleasing vista, would have exercised the restraint needed for such a policy.

Another form of investment to which ambiguity adheres is expenditures on "human capital formation," or education. Did the responsible authorities (mainly Church, municipal government, private associations) divert significant amounts of money into education, and did these amounts increase in the course of the seventeenth and eighteenth centuries? We cannot yet answer these questions; the few scraps of available evidence point to a varied pattern of educational investment.

In higher education a great expansion boom swept over Europe in the late sixteenth century. By the 1630s some 2.5 percent of English males of university age entered these institutions. In the Dutch Republic the figure may have exceeded 3 percent. These were extraordinary levels given the occupational structures of that time, and they did not last. All over Europe enrollment levels fell in the course of the seventeenth century. (In England the enrollment level of the 1630s was not regained until World War I.) This was, perhaps, just as well. During the boom the universities in most countries came under the control of aristocratic interests for whom these institutions functioned as centers of legal training and bureaucratic advancement. Such dominance both unleashed on society an oversupply of lawyers and undermined the ability of universities to pursue true scholarship.

The largest commitment of resources, and a gradually expanding one, was made at the mundane level of elementary schooling. Education was only one of the motives behind the spread of church schools, private tutors, and municipal schools for the poor. Still, they had their effect. Male literacy rates (as measured by the ability to sign one's name) stood at 30 percent in England around 1650; a similar percentage was true in France in 1688-90. In the following century they rose by 60 percent in France and doubled in England. These averages obscure marked regional differences: French improvement was concentrated in the north, east and far south, the center of the country remaining very illiterate; in England, the great grain-growing belt stretching from East Anglia southwestward toward Wiltshire remained notably illiterate. Literacy also rose in this period in Prussia and Scandinavia, while - judging from later evidence - the Mediterranean and eastern Europe did not advance at all.

By the mid-eighteenth century the ability to sign one's name had spread to half of male Frenchmen, but to only 27 percent of French women, 60 percent of Englishmen (over 40 percent of women), and 85 percent of male Amsterdamers (64 percent of the women). This achievement required a significant commitment of resources; what is still unclear is what this gradual rise in literacy meant for the economy.[13]

Significant increases in consumer and investment demand were recorded in the seventeenth and eighteenth centuries. But the great regional variation and the persistence of retrogressive habits, particularly in the investment sector, make the demonstration of this development difficult. In contrast, the growth of government expenditures in the seventeenth century is obvious, massive, and ubiquitous.

Government demand

Few European states - whether absolutist or constitutional - could boast of a rational tax system. Simply keeping tax rolls up to date was beyond most of them. To understand the nature of the growing tax burdens being imposed on the European economies we can consider the French tax system, which is often regarded as the classic example of petrified inequalities and exorbitant collection costs.

The principal French tax, the *taille,* fell on real property. The clergy and nobility enjoyed exemption, although with the complication that the exemption was "personal" in France north of the Loire (that is, any property owned by these classes was exempt), while in the south the exemption attached to the land (that is, only such land as had in some sense originally been exempt). The *taille* fell principally on the remaining commoners, among whom the burden varied enormously among residents of the *pays d'élection,* where the crown levied the tax directly, the *pays d'état,* where provincial assemblies voted and collected the tax, and most important cities, where local privileges exempted some or all of the property from the *taille.* This does not exhaust the possibilities of discrimination among taxpayers; within each region the tax level would vary among villages, because the assessment, likely to be a relic of bygone days, was levied on the villages as a whole without much regard to changes in population or prosperity affecting the villages since the assessment had been made. Because the nobility was exempt from the *taille* this tax endowed noble status with a considerable economic premium. Supposedly it was in the French government's interest to prevent entry into the nobility (a process that eroded the tax base and increased the burden of the peasantry), but the royal treasuries were generally not above capitalizing on the value of noble status by selling titles and, particularly, official posts that led to the acquisition of noble status.

The indirect taxes included the *gabelle,* an excise on salt, and the *aides,* excise taxes on wines, liquors, tobacco, candles, soap, and other articles of consumption. Because they fell on all classes, the government, particularly under Colbert, was eager to increase them. Excise taxes were, of course, a very crude device for tapping noble wealth; the main result of their increase was to inhibit the growth of domestic markets.

The whole tax system was basically a legacy of the fifteenth century. Efforts to reform it, such as Vauban's 1707 proposal for a 10 percent income tax on all classes, invariably met massive noble resistance. One new direct tax designed to compensate for the exemptions of the *taille* was the *capitation.* It called for the division of the population into twenty-two categories, each with its own yearly head tax. This levy, which taxed the privileged orders heavily, was introduced in 1695 and lasted three years. In 1701 it was revived, but then it included several modifications designed to moderate its impact. Nonetheless, it remained as the only direct tax to which the nobility was annually subject. The only way the tax system could be improved was to increase the net yield to the royal treasury after the deduction of collection costs. Colbert was able, briefly, to increase the treasury's share of tax revenue collected by the tax farmers but ultimately this reform measure also failed. The state depended too much on the tax farmers. In the absence of a banking system the tax farmers provided the treasury with short-term credit to close the gap between the steady outflow of expenditures and the lumpy, often delayed inflow of tax receipts from the countryside. This indispensable service, plus the enormous sums collected from the tax farmers through the sale of their offices, made the state unwilling to anger them by reducing their profits.[14]

Once the net tax revenues reached Paris, they were recorded and administered with the greatest difficulty. Only the crudest budgets existed to guide expenditure and the clerks continued to keep accounts in Roman numerals into the eighteenth century.

The backwardness of French fiscal administration (and much the same description applies to many governments of this period) is highlighted when compared to its Dutch counterpart. In the Dutch Republic, Stadholder Maurice of Nassau had commissioned experts to apply double-entry bookkeeping to state finances in the early years of the seventeenth century, and Arabic numerals were in general use. The public bodies responsible for establishing budgets gained a reputation for integrity, not least because the books were inspected yearly by a committee of provincial delegates. Throughout the seventeenth century the Republic's government was able to float an enormous public debt on the basis of international confidence in its fiscal institutions. Unlike the French crown, or the English until 1693, it did not have to depend on a small, privileged circle of creditors. The advanced state of Dutch public finance can be at least partly explained by the fact that municipal governments were the first European public authorities to gain experience in public finance and public debt management, and the Republic was, in a sense, a union of municipal authorities.

When we turn to the actual taxes levied and the manner in which they were collected, we see a state of affairs much closer to French practice than to Dutch reputation. Tax anomalies and inequalities abounded. Despite the overwhelming importance of commercial wealth, real estate bore the brunt of the direct tax burden. Moreover, Holland's real property tax assessments were not altered for a full century after 1632 (indeed the allocation of central government taxes among the seven provinces remained unchanged for even longer), despite widespread changes in population and regional prosperity. Here, too, tax farmers controlled the excise tax collections; each year the collection privileges on forty-three separate excises were sold to the highest bidders. This system produced social discord that generated the most significant riots in the Republic's history.

With crude fiscal devices such as these, in societies of more or less constant population, and with money of more or less constant value, the European states managed to increase their revenues and expenditures many times over in the course of the seventeenth century. (The generation after the War of the Spanish Succession apparently felt the need for a respite. Peacetime tax levels tended to stabilize in the eighteenth century.) French public revenues rose from an annual average of 20 million livres in 1600-04 to 100 million livres in the first two decades of Louis XIV's personal reign. In the war years at the end of the century, revenues had pushed up yet farther to well over 200 million livres but expenditures had far outdistanced them. The royal debt, about 300 million livres at the beginning of the seventeenth century, and much reduced under Mazarin, stood at some 2 billion livres by 1715.

English government expenditures rose tenfold in the century following the end of Queen Elizabeth's reign. After the onset of Danish absolutism in 1660, government revenues rose nearly threefold by the 1730s. In Holland, large increases in tax revenue notwithstanding, the public debt rose from 1 million guilders in 1579 to 140 million in 1655, and to over 400 million a century later.

The rising tide of government revenue exposed by these examples had two general effects: that which affected the taxpayer in his efforts to pay has already been considered; the impact of government expenditures on the economy remains to be discussed. Two categories account for the great bulk of government expenditure in this period: military expenses and the costs of court and bureaucracy. Of these, the first was by far the most important; in years of peace it claimed over half the French budgets, while the public debts of most states were entirely the result of military operations.

These enormous military expenditures were not simply a consequence of the frequent wars of the period: they also reflect the new standards of preparedness required for land and naval forces by the late seventeenth century. Until about 1600 armies of over 30,000 men were rarely put in the field.

Moreover, these armies consisted chiefly of mercenary soldiers and recruits brought together by a military contractor; they would be released at the end of the campaign. Innovations in the Spanish and French armies forced a gradual abandonment of these practices in favor of the maintenance of much larger standing armies. France, which maintained the largest standing forces, attained peacetime levels of 150,000 men by the late seventeenth century; her wartime military strength (and war years were nearly half of all years) could reach 400,000 troops. Such armies exceeded 5 percent of the male population between the ages of 16 and 40, but several smaller states outdid populous France in this regard. The peak strength of the Swedish army attained 110,000 men, while the normal strength of the Prussian army rose from 29,000 under Frederick William, the Great Elector, to over 83,000 under King Frederick William I in 1739.

The costs of maintaining these forces created unprecedented problems for governments and exerted novel pressures on the economy. The Spanish government found that in order to maintain its standing force of 60 to 70,000 men in Flanders, it had to send a yearly average of 7 million guilders to Antwerp throughout the first half of the seventeenth century. These infusions became essential to the international economy of the Southern Netherlands, but effecting the transfers so strained the commercial facilities of Antwerp and even London, that Spain eventually was forced to rely on its enemy, the Dutch, to act as its agents in making disbursements in northern Europe.[15]

The new standing armies required distinctive uniforms for the first time between 1670 and 1700, and commissaries were established to supply them with food and other goods. The resulting orders for equipment, simply by their size and concentration, did much to increase the scale of industrial production. In England the shoemaking industry of Northamptonshire grew after 1650 as a result of large military orders. Metallurgy and leather tanning were similarly stimulated, while in France the textile industry of Romortain in the Orléanais rose on the basis of orders for army uniforms.

Naval development was equally revolutionary. The counterpart of the *fluitschip*, the specialized merchant vessel, was the specialized fighting ship. Maintaining a naval fleet obviously entailed greater expense than conscripting merchant vessels for naval duty in time of war. The English fleet was built up in the 1630s by Charles I (using the infamous ship-money tax), but its major growth occurred under Cromwell. Between 1649 and 1660, 207 naval vessels were built, and naval manpower increased from 4000 sailors under Charles I to 16,000 in 1660. However, even this figure was exceeded between 1714 and 1763 when the tonnage of the English fleet doubled. By 1758 the royal shipyards, which had employed a total of only 1000 men a century earlier, employed 3800 men as shipwrights and caulkers alone.

In France naval construction took flight under the leadership of Colbert. When he became finance minister in 1661, the fleet consisted of 30 vessels; at his death in 1683 there existed 176 vessels in operation and 68 more planned or under construction. The firepower of the French navy rose from 1045 cannons in 1661 to 12,000 in 1677.

Whole new towns arose to build, maintain, and supply these vessels. Plymouth became the largest city in the southwest of England largely on the strength of its naval station. Louis XIV and Colbert built the cities of Brest and Rochefort to serve as arsenals and naval stations. Late in the eighteenth century the French naval stations employed some 10,000 workers during peacetime.

A notion of what the maintenance of naval fleets cost can be gained from the records of the Admiralty of Amsterdam. This was but one (albeit the largest) of the five Dutch admiralties. In the thirty-seven years following 1714, during which the fleet was reduced from fifty-seven to thirty vessels, sank to a decidedly second-rate position, and engaged in little action, the Admiralty nevertheless found it necessary to spend a yearly average of 2 million guilders; nearly half of this sum could be attributed to the wharves, arsenals, and rope-making works.[16]

A final source of extraordinary military expenditure arose in the last quarter of the seventeenth century as the massive fortresses designed by Vauban for France's frontier defenses gained general European acceptance. The new defensive strategies required the construction at strategic points of engineering wonders of enormous cost.

All these military developments taken together constituted a challenge to the European economy equally as important as their political and administrative consequences. By the 1680s Mars demanded the use of as much as 5 percent of the male population aged 16 to 40. Because most of the labor thus mobilized was apparently otherwise underemployed (armies were recruited from the poorest classes and the poorest regions), the net effect of military growth was to increase aggregate demand without greatly reducing output. The demand fell primarily on the textile, heavy metals, and shipbuilding sectors. Demand for cannons and muskets provoked the most notable response; a whole new industrial economy arose in Sweden to meet that demand (see Chapter 3, pp. 107-8), while in England efforts to increase output resulted in the application of the reverberatory furnace to nonferrous metals (in the 1690s) and, ultimately, the use of coal in iron smelting.[17]

After military expenditures, the largest category of government spending was in support of royalty, court, and bureaucracy. In a peacetime year of Louis XIV's reign, 1689, 16 percent of government expenditures went to the royal and princely households, the court, and others favored with sinecures and royal subsidies. Paris, as Madrid, Berlin, and many smaller court cities, is generally regarded as having been reliant on such expenditures. Even London, after it had captured European commercial leadership from Amsterdam, depended heavily on the government's transfer payments to the rich. Werner Sombart regarded London's trading profits in 1700 as inferior to the 700,000 pound civil list allocation granted by Parliament to William III. When all those subsisting from interest on government bonds - whose number swelled in the eighteenth century - are added to those living from royal offices and subsidies, the role of government in pumping funds into the great cities, and hence fostering the concentration of demand that was a chief feature of the economy, becomes indisputable.

Along with the stimulus that a concentration of demand in large cities can provide to industry and commerce, there existed a compensatory danger. The social structure of cities dependent on government offices, subsidies, and bondholding tended, naturally enough, to be dominated by courtiers, functionaries, judicial office holders, divines, aristocrats, and lawyers. Personal service and the luxury trades employed the working population, and industry found itself at a disadvantage in competing for workers. More seriously, the recipients of such privileged incomes could forget that consumption also requires production. Thus, a resident of Madrid in 1675, Alfonso Núñez de Castro, could fail to see the connection between the decadence of the Spanish economy and the tax revenues that propped up his over-opulent city when he declared:

> Let London manufacture those fine fabrics of hers to her heart's content; Holland her chambrays; Florence her cloth; the Indies their beaver and vicuña; Milan her brocades; Italy and Flanders their linens . . . so long as our capital can enjoy them; the only thing it proves is that all nations train journeymen for Madrid and that Madrid is the queen of parliaments, for all the world serves her and she serves nobody.[18]

Foreign demand

The foreign (non-European) demand for goods has already been considered in Chapter 4. To the extent that it depended on military transfers to the colonies and on colonists' income derived from sales in Europe, it was clearly not an autonomous phenomenon. Moreover, autonomous or not, the question still remains open whether the export volumes were sufficiently large to affect significantly the overall economy. However, what concerns us here is the concentration of this demand at the handful of Atlantic ports that dominated the colonial trades. Such demand could, of course, percolate back into the hinterlands of the ports. Orders for cheap linens to clothe slaves gave the rural industries of Flanders and Brittany seemingly inexhaustible markets, while the demand for guns and hardware for the African and North American trades played a large role in the growth of the Birmingham area iron trades. But the disproportionate benefit accrued to the port cities, where industries and commercial services enjoyed new levels of demand as Navigation Acts or their equivalents funneled colonial demand to them.

Many retrogressive economic characteristics persisted into the eighteenth century to choke the potential growth of aggregate demand. Too many landlords and peasants tended to invest their capital in extending their landholdings, thereby redistributing income and driving up land prices but doing nothing for agricultural productivity. Governments, despite their avowed mercantilist interests in industrial development, spent revenues in such a way that industrial growth was no more than an accidental fringe benefit. And we should not lose sight of the fact that such demand growth as occurred exhibited an extremely uneven distribution through Europe.

Yet, when trying to gather our various observations into a composite picture, the positive developments seem most noteworthy. Among the wage earners, real income rose even though there was no catastrophic fall of overall European population. The backward bending labor supply curve seems to have been gradually breaking down as a widening range of simple consumer goods became available; all classes of society except the poorest exhibited a strong interest in upgrading standards of comfort. Finally, a variety of factors, among them government policy, military expenditure, and colonial trade, combined to concentrate the growth of demand in the great capitals, the Atlantic ports, and their hinterlands, where it could most effectively generate improvements in production and distribution.

7
Capital accumulation and the bourgeoisie

The sources of capital

The economic institutions of earlier centuries were concerned chiefly with control over land and labor. Although these factors of production did not lose their importance in the seventeenth century, they were joined by capital as the third factor that now played a sufficiently large role in much of Europe to warrant the development of new institutions and customs. The terms "capital" and "capitalism" did not yet exist with the meanings we attach to them today, and, as we have seen, accounting practices, even in the greatest enterprises, did not often make a clear distinction between capital investment and operating expenses. But, still, large accumulations of capital existed, and a distinct class - or, perhaps, congeries of groups - exercised discretion over the bulk of nonagricultural capital. Capital and those who controlled it were gradually becoming a pivotal factor in economic life. Great interest has long been expressed in the rise of this new situation, but it has not been matched with great understanding. Two notions exert a strong influence on this topic: primitive capital accumulation and the (ever) rising middle class. Neither is enormously helpful in analyzing seventeenth- and eighteenth-century economic life.

Theories of economic development that gained widespread acceptance in the two decades after World War II placed a great emphasis on inadequate capital accumulation as a bottleneck in the growth of poor economies. An economy with little capital, so the argument went, suffered from low productivity. The population lived close to subsistence and, as a consequence, had little ability to save from their incomes to increase the capital stock. A vicious circle trapped the economy in poverty.[1] The policy implication was that infusions from outside the poor economy, through foreign investment and aid, were necessary to break the vicious circle. If the preindustrial European economies were of this type they obviously could not have been financed by a pre-existing developed economy. This line of reasoning identifies as the fundamental question about the growth of the European economy: how were the initial accumulations created?

Statistical investigations of the eighteenth-century European economies have undermined the basic premises of this approach. In the first place, at least some economies were no longer hovering around a subsistence level. The estimates of British national income made in 1688 by the statistician Gregory King set per capita income at a level far above that of modern Asian and African economies (two or three times as high, as nearly as can be determined). He believed that Dutch income was even higher. In the second place, the capital requirements of most industrial and commercial ventures were not large. Institutions existed for the pooling of capital from several investors, and commercial credit supplemented the working capital of many enterprises. Finally, there are enough examples of rapid accumulation of capital through ploughing back the profits of enterprises to dismiss the notion that an overall shortage of capital could have been the principal obstacle to economic growth.[2]

The persistent decline of interest rates in the seventeenth century lends what is perhaps the clearest support to the view that capital was not peculiarly scarce - indeed, that a borrowers' market existed. The Dutch enjoyed Europe's lowest interest rates; the return on government bonds, which paid 8.33 percent in 1600, fell to 6.25 percent in 1611, and 5 percent in 1640; after 1672 they hovered in the 3 to 3.75 percent range and continued to be oversubscribed. By the mid-eighteenth century, bonds often yielded less than 3 percent, and contemporaries estimated that 14 million guilders yearly sought investment objects in the Amsterdam money market. Much of this capital was placed abroad, where interest rates were higher. The official English maximum interest rates, which stood at 10 percent until 1624, fell to 6 percent in 1651, and 5 percent in 1714. In the Italian principality of Piedmont, government bonds followed a downward course very similar to English trends, while in Genoa the remarkably low rate of 1.5 percent prevailed for a time. These rates do not cover all types of borrowing, and there were governments, notably the French, that continued to find high interest rates of around 8 percent necessary to attract capital. But such high rates embodied a substantial risk premium; the general trend throughout most of Europe was for interest rates to diminish in the course of the seventeenth century.[3]

If large capital supplies characterized the European economy before the growth of full-fledged industrial capitalism, could this have been the result of windfalls? Could colonial exploitation, state-sanctioned expropriations of land, and the price inflation have created a primitive capital accumulation which laid the foundation for the later growth of the European economy. Where Marx argues that "divorcing the producers from the means of production" was crucial to the development of both a free labor market and a home market - requisites of a capitalist economy - we can only agree. The social stratification process described in Chapter 2 had the clear result of furthering capitalist relations in the countryside. The fact that peasants and aristocrats alike, in legal settings of varying descriptions, behaved in ways that prompted such stratifications of rural populations creates some ambiguities; it would appear that we can only partially

understand "peasant expropriation" as an institutional creation - that is, a response to the exercise of power by a ruling
group. But there was a second type of primitive capital
accumulation. Did, as Marx put it, "the treasures captured
outside Europe by undisguised looting, enslavement, and
murder [float] back to the mother-country and there [be]
turned into capital"?[4] It would be difficult to deny that the
capital stock at the disposal of eighteenth-century Europeans
must have originated somewhere. But the notion that special
windfall gains were a prerequisite to "real" capitalist growth
(that is, dependent on the exploitation of free labor) certainly focuses attention on the wrong aspect of capital accumulation in early modern Europe.

One can easily find many examples of rapid capital
accumulation, both dramatic and prosaic, in our period. To
use examples from the Dutch Republic, we can match the
Dutch East India Company's average yearly divided distribution of 18 percent on the original subscribed capital with the
17 percent yearly return on the capital invested in the drainage of a large lake in north Holland. Or we can compare the
increase in the number of Amsterdam capitalists with taxable
wealth in excess of 100,000 guilders from 5 in 1585 to 200
in 1674 (a sixfold increase on a per capita basis) with the
nearly fivefold growth in the taxable wealth of Gouda capitalists with over 10,000 guilders between 1599 and 1680
(while the city's population grew very little). Amsterdam's
wealth derived in part from spectacular long-distance trading
ventures; Gouda's, on the other hand, stemmed from exceedingly commonplace regional transport and manufacturing activities.

No, the key to understanding the growing power of capital
in the European economy is not to be found by searching for
esoteric sources of capital; rather, it rests with the solution to
the problem of preserving and keeping productive the capital
stock already in existence. In other words, a major weakness

of the European economy that had to be overcome was not
the inadequacy of capital, but the misinvestment and dissipa-
tion of capital.

Bourgeois aspirations

This brings us to the second misleading concept: the
rising bourgeoisie. Bourgeois families in most European
economies, if they rose, rose out of the bourgeoisie and into
the aristocracy. As long as the reference group of the
bourgeoisie was the aristocracy, the economy suffered an ongoing hemorrhaging of capital from trade and industry. To
many bourgeois families - though not to society as a whole -
the return to invested capital seemed greater when it was
invested in military, administrative, and judicial offices,
dowries, and agricultural land. When commercial activity en-
countered problems - as in the early seventeenth century -
this alternative seemed particularly inviting. Thus, we see the
combination of contracting trade and rapidly growing
dowries in Piedmont, England, Venice, and France in the first
half of the seventeenth century. Likewise, judgeships in the
Parlement of Paris - perhaps the highest dignity available to a
bourgeois Frenchman - could be had for 18,000 livres in
1605, but cost 140,000 livres in 1660. The sale of offices was
common to many states, but nowhere did it figure so
prominently as in France. Tax assessors, refuse collectors,
registrars of births, marriages and deaths, mayoral and other
municipal offices (after 1692) - in short, every imaginable
office - was sold. It is said that in six years after 1692 some
170 million livres was raised by playing on bourgeois vanity
in this way.

The return to bourgeois capital invested in offices was not
paid purely in the form of "status," of course. Many offices
were lucrative because of the rights to collect fees that they
conferred. Tax farmers, who purchased the right to collect
taxes in a given area, could keep all money collected above a

fixed amount due to the treasury. But whether the return was primarily monetary or social, the fact remained that commercial capital was converted into government revenue used to cover day-to-day expenditures or was transferred in marriage contracts and land transactions from commercial families to aristocratic families.

The most visible representatives of the seventeenth-century bourgeoisie are the innovative merchants whose work wc have considered in earlier chapters: men such as Louis de Geer, who developed the Swedish metallurgy industry; or Jean de Neufville, who, beginning penniless, conducted his silk business in Frankfurt and Amsterdam with such success that at his death he left an estate of 800,000 guilders; or the numerous and anonymous developers of the West Indian sugar trade, the Dutch shipbuilding industry, and the new draperies of England. To contemporaries, an even more conspicuous bourgeois group was the well-connected financiers, particularly those who served the state. Men such as Samuel Bernard and Antoine Crozat, leaseholders of lucrative French government monopolies, ranked among the very richest people of their age. Hiding behind this top layer of innovators and financiers was a much larger portion of the bourgeoisie whose economic life was passive, if not utterly ossified. Particularly in the provincial cities, the bourgeoisie was anything but rising as its capital was channeled into an inert noncapitalist sector composed of agricultural land, administrative offices, and government securities.

In the southern French city of Montpellier, commerce and industry faded away in the century after 1550; the decline of the commercial bourgeoisie found compensation in the growing wealth of the nobility and clergy, but particularly in the explosive growth of fiscal officials and judicial officeholders, many of them recently ennobled. By the mid-seventeenth century administrative and fiscal functions supported the city, and the bourgeoisie readily adapted itself to the new opportunities offered by the absolutist state. An almost identical social transformation affected seventeenth-century Dijon, the provincial capital of Burgundy, which increasingly came to live from agricultural and seigneurial revenues.[5]

Toulouse, one of the largest cities of southern France, possessed in the fifteenth and sixteenth centuries a vigorous bourgeoisie active in the textile industry and the woad trade. By the eighteenth century the city's bourgeoisie was puny, consisting of a few textile merchants and grain traders of local importance and purveyors of luxury goods for the aristocracy. It was now the aristocracy that dominated the city's life. Of the total wealth of Toulouse residents, half was invested in land, 20 percent in urban property, and another 20 percent in annuities and bonds. All the chief institutions of the city - from the convents to the university - were aristocratic. What had happened? The competition faced by the woad industry from the colonial production of indigo - a cheaper substitute for blue dye - had its effects, no doubt, but more important, surely, was the constant, ongoing efforts of bourgeois families to elevate themselves into the ranks of the aristocracy. By purchasing land and paying feudal recognition fees to the king, one could gain the right to purchase an ennobling office. Once a title and rank were acquired, a family was expected to live *noblement* - that is, from the passive revenues of land and bonds, rather than from business income - and this they proved only too eager to do. This, after all, was what the rising bourgeoisie was all about to them.[6]

The same problem of a hemorrhaging of bourgeois capital plagued the northern industrial cities of France. In Amiens an effort to trace the names of the principal textile merchants through successive tax lists found that only about a fifth of the surnames present in 1589-90 could be found in 1625; between then and 1711 the surviving surnames were, similarly, about a fifth. The sons of rich merchants abandoned their fathers' professions, preferring careers as officials, military officers, clerics, or, more typically, preferring to live from their investments and property. Thus, in the seventeenth century the upper bourgeoisie of Amiens drew some 60 percent of their income from land and bonds. In nearby Beauvais the same forces were at work. A study of the Danse family, the greatest linen merchants of the town, shows them constantly placing their business profits in rural property, acquiring nobility and, in 1757, liquidating their business interests altogether.[7]

With every crisis in agriculture, urban families bought up farmland from peasants and the old nobility alike. Step by step, a new nobility - the *noblesse de robe* - was forming based on judicial and administrative offices, urban property, government bonds, and agricultural land. And below the level of titled nobility a great mass of bourgeois families lived *noblement*. An eighteenth-century observer declared that people retired from active commerce of their own free will when they had accumulated an estate insuring them of a yearly income of between 3000 and 4000 livres. By no means was this phenomenon unique to France. In Piedmont the policies of Carlo Emanuele II and Vittorio Amedeo II succeeded in getting the middle class to buy offices and support absolutism just as effectively as did Louis XIII and Louis XIV. Between 1713 and 1742, 84 percent of higher and 98 percent of lesser offices were held by the bourgeoisie. And here, too, these offices were the bridge that carried the wealthiest of the middle class into the nobility. Neighboring Lombardy, under Spanish rule, showed the same characteristic.[8]

Nowhere was the depletion of the bourgeoisie more disastrously complete than in Spain. In a society where the prestige of nobility hardly needed to be bolstered, the state, through its taxing policies, made noble status a virtual necessity. The *hidalgo* (nobleman) was exempt from taxation, and the status could be purchased (the sale of *hidalgo* status became an important source of revenue). As the economy declined and taxes rose, there was a flight into the nobility and the Church (some 5 percent of the population was noble in 1787; one estimate has 8 percent of the adult male population in the priesthood during the reign of Philip IV). Because everyone with capital bought *hidalgo* status, government bonds, and government offices, the consequent withdrawal of capital from trade and industry insured that the nation's economic weakness would not be directly confronted for some time to come. The cities, which had earlier conducted trade in wool and textiles, became populated with courtiers, clerics, high functionaries, and judicial figures. As a government minister said of Valladolid in 1688, "It seems that this city is made up principally of consumers only."[9]

Those nations that had no glittering tax-exempt aristocracy to draw away bourgeois talent and capital were in a better position for economic growth. Indeed, English observers of the Dutch Republic attributed much of its success to the custom of sons succeeding their fathers in their businesses. This gave young merchants both more experience and more capital than their foreign rivals. But the merchants of a bourgeois republic were not immune to the blandishment of the aristocratic life. We have already noted how the commercial nobility of Venice transformed itself into a landed class during the seventeenth century. In Holland agricultural income never replaced commercial income, but in the eighteenth century the passive incomes from offices and bonds assumed an enormous importance. In Amsterdam's 1742 tax assessment, the largest single group of taxpayers, 1709 of 12,655, were *rentiers.* The fact that the *burgemeesters* of Amsterdam filled directly some 3200 offices suggests that here, just as in France and Spain, *empleomania,* an economy of office-filling dominated by nepotism and patronage and financed by more or less corrupt methods, attracted a large portion of the bourgeoisie.

In previous chapters we noted that a backward bending labor supply curve, to the extent it was characteristic of the wage labor force, had to be eroded if a capitalist economy was to flourish. It might be added that a backward bending supply curve of bourgeois talent and capital also had to be eroded. How could an economy develop if its leaders moved out of active commercial life at the first opportunity?

Max Weber thought this attitude toward money-making was altered by Reformation - particularly Calvinist - theology. The believer was enjoined to regard his worldly activity as part of the unfolding plan of God, and in his role as a steward, to "pursue," as Weber put it, "profit and forever renewed profit, by means of continuous, rational, capitalistic enterprise."[10] Such a protestant ethic could be of obvious use in reducing the hemorrhaging of capital. But whether or not such an ethic existed, it did not alone determine economic behavior.

Investment opportunities

The bourgeois behavior described above was not wholly a consequence of the aspiration to enter the nobility or an insufficient appreciation of Calvinist theology. It was also a consequence of an economy with investment opportunities that were too limited. A merchant successful in his line of trade was likely to find that his trade could not expand fast enough to absorb his constantly growing stock of capital. What was he to do with his surplus funds? Similarly, a successful merchant, looking to the future, could fear that should he suddenly die, his wife and children would be unable to carry on the complex dealings in which he habitually was involved. How could he invest his capital to give his family a secure, uncomplicated income? Until the seventeenth and eighteenth centuries, the European economy offered but one general solution to these problems. Wherever feudal tenures had been dissolved sufficiently to create a land market, the merchant could hope to diversify his investment portfolio by purchasing land.

In this context, the century after 1650 stands out as a

period in which a large expansion of investment opportunities was achieved. Negotiable titles to wealth and a market in which they could readily be bought and sold came into existence in Holland and England, thereby offering a potential escape from the chronic problems of misinvestment and diversion of capital.

Government debt was the most widespread and earliest investment option. Of course, wealthy banking families - such as the Medicis and the Fuggers - had lent money to monarchs for centuries. What spread in the seventeenth century was a funded government debt in which the payment of interest was budgeted and the debt, in the form of bonds, was negotiable. This less risky form of lending funds to the government attracted capital from a much broader group than had earlier provided royal loans. The Dutch Republic led the way in this form of government finance. Its ability to instill confidence in investors enabled it to borrow vast sums at unprecedentedly low interest rates. This inspired other governments to do the same. As long as the English debt was the personal responsibility of the monarch, the only regular lenders were a specialized group of London financiers who, because of their scarcity and because of the high risks they took, extorted high interest rates for their services.

In 1672 a vast improvement was made in English finances when a beginning was made to assign specific revenues to cover new borrowings; subsequently, in 1693 a true national debt was established by declaring Parliament rather than the crown as the guarantor of the debt. The government now acquired a vast borrowing capacity at decidedly lower rates. But the other side of the coin is equally important: a relatively broad class could now invest their capital with confidence in government bonds and annuities.

This important aid to stable government finance did not spread everywhere. The failure of France to carry out a similar reform kept her finances in a precarious position throughout the eighteenth century. The French government continued to rely on loans from large financiers who demanded in return offices (particularly tax farms), status, and high interest rates. As we shall see, the hostility of this powerful group to the *Banque Royale,* established in 1716 to finance a funded debt, was instrumental in its failure in 1720. Funded debts were also rare in the German states. During and immediately after the Thirty Years' War, when the absolutist princely states took shape, the princes came to rely for their financial backing on banking families called *Hoffaktoren,* or *Hofjuden* (court Jews). The legal and social disabilities of the financiers and the relatively primitive financial structure of central Europe created a strong and long-lasting partnership between the necessitous princes and the ambitious court financiers, the most important of whom became Christians and received noble titles.

Where government bonds and annuities existed they added an element of flexibility to the portfolios of bourgeois families, but they were not an unalloyed improvement. When they succeeded in attracting large masses of capital from commerce and burdening the generally regressive tax systems with interest payments to be transferred to the well-to-do bond holders, these debt instruments reduced employment and redistributed income from the poor to the rich at the same time. Spain is, again, the classic case. The growing, tax-exempt *hidalgo* population proved to be eager purchasers of government bonds, *juros.* Such was the demand for *juros* (or such was the unattractiveness of alternative direct investments) that they were purchased despite repeated state bankruptcies in which short-term debts were consolidated (at unfavorable terms) into new *juro* issues bearing lower interest rates. By the 1660s the state found itself paying 9 million ducates per year in interest on this funded debt. This was double the interest payments in 1600 and represented about two-thirds of Castile's total annual revenues. Not surprisingly, payments became extremely irregular in the last decades of the Habsburg regime.

Besides government debt, there arose in the seventeenth century a growing market for mortgage debt. Wherever secure titles to land had evolved, it was possible for landowners to borrow money by pledging their land. But this was only a first step in creating a supply of capital available for long terms. As long as lenders could call back their loans on demand, a borrower risked too much if he used his loan for long-term purposes. In England the courts came to the opinion, in the 1630s and 40s, that borrowers could not be made to repay the principal of mortgages so long as they paid the interest. The lender's ability to recover his capital was protected in this matter by making it easier to assign the mortgage to another. On these terms a flourishing mortgage market arose as both the demand for mortgages (particularly to finance country-house construction) and the supply of long-term mortgage capital grew enormously. In France it is thought that a considerable amount of bourgeois landowner-ship derived from the foreclosure of mortgages, but, just as with the growth of government debt, this form of investment did not inevitably benefit the middle class. For example, in Spain and Sicily the mortgage indebtedness of the aristocracy reached such phenomenal proportions that the state intervened to sanction the repudiation of these debts rather than witness a wholesale transfer of property rights. Such measures struck at the root of the concept of private property, but even lenders could be found supporting aristocratic debt repudiation. In a society where everyone was parasitically dependent on feudal rent, any measures that kept the aristocracy afloat and consuming were accepted with relief.[11]

Neither government bonds nor private debt instruments were a guarantee against misinvestment - far from it! - but their expanded availability gave the bourgeoisie important flexibility in the disposition of their surplus capital. The explosive growth of the demand for negotiable titles to wealth can be gauged from the rise of joint-stock securities.

From our earlier discussion of the English and Dutch East

India Companies it is apparent that the permanence and negotiability of shares evolved gradually. By the mid-seventeenth century their character was well defined, and share prices were quoted along with commodity prices in London and Amsterdam. Thereafter, and particularly after the 1670s, joint-stock shares became extremely popular. Eager buyers drove up the value of East India shares (both English and Dutch) to four and five times their face values, while in England investors rushed to place capital with the scores of new joint-stock companies being formed. Fifty-six were formed between 1681 and 1718, and many, particularly trading companies such as the Royal African and Hudson's Bay Companies, found investors so eager that they were oversubscribed despite the fact they offered the unattractive combination of modest return and great risk. The market value of all English joint-stock shares (including the Bank of England) grew nearly fivefold between 1695 and 1717, when the total value reached 21 million pounds.

An embryonic stock exchange was taking shape; share prices were widely disseminated and the negotiability of shares enhanced. Thus, shares became convenient to buy at the same time that a new land tax (introduced in 1677) and the drying up of the land market made landownership less attractive to bourgeois families (the land market declined as aristocratic wills increasingly included legal devices that prohibited heirs from selling off their land).

The bond market also funneled a great deal of bourgeois capital toward the joint-stock companies. The companies raised increasing amounts of their trading capital by floating bonds as falling interest rates made bonds a cheaper source of capital than new stock issues. Such bonds - nonspeculative, bearing fixed yields, and redeemable - found eager buyers who looked upon them as the ideal investment for the support of wives and children. By 1685 women owned directly 20 percent of the bonds of both the East India and Royal African Companies.[12]

The popularity of joint-stock company shares culminated in a speculative frenzy in 1719-20, when 190 new companies were founded in England alone and share prices rose to extremely high multiples of face values. From the perspective of the modern economy, saturated as it is with financial speculation, there is something appealingly naive about the gusto with which transparent schemes were proposed and the eagerness with which investors accepted promises of easy riches. But the bubble of 1720 is also a telling expression of the abundance of capital then searching for a suitable outlet.

Actually, there were two distinct crises - one in France, the other in England. The French crisis focused on two institutions founded by John Law, a Scot who had gained the confidence of the Regent in the years of transition that followed the death of Louis XIV. Law's two creations were the *Banque Royale* and the *Compagnie des Indes,* a joint-stock company formed in 1719 by amalgamating all the rival French trading companies previously in existence. Law's initiatives (and his ambitious plans to reform French fiscal and monetary policies) stirred a hornet's nest of opposition. Court financiers with a stake in Law's failure floated a rival company in the hope of depriving Law's schemes of investors. In the ensuing competition there arose a speculative mania in the shares of the companies. When it finally became clear that Law's company could never be sufficiently profitable to justify the inflated share prices, the bubble burst, Law's schemes - both good and bad - fell into disrepute, and he was forced to flee the country.

In England the speculative bubble focused on the South Sea Company. This joint-stock enterprise promised enormous profits on the basis of its acquisition in 1713 of the Spanish *asiento* (an exclusive slave-trading concession wrung from Spain in the Treaty of Utrecht) and its plans - broached in 1719 - to fund the government's public debt. As speculators bid up the company's shares, a raging bull market began to affect all companies. In this climate stockjobbers tried their luck by floating stock issues for scores of new companies, many with no apparent purpose.

In September of 1720, with the rise of Robert Walpole to the position of Prime Minister, the climate in which the speculative bubble flourished suddenly vanished. A strict new "Bubble Act" - supported by the South Sea Company - prevented banking, trading, and industrial promoters from forming joint-stock companies without specific acts of Parliament.[13]

Neither the French nor the English collapse led directly to economic crisis; the bubbles were too emphemeral for that. However, the reaction to them did delay - particularly in France - the growth of stable, trusted financial institutions that might have aided in channeling capital from savers to investors.

The financial machinations of 1720 do not represent the first of the great speculative bubbles that have marked capitalist society. Nearly a century earlier a speculative mania swept Holland. Because a large variety of negotiable titles such as joint-stock shares and government bonds were not yet available, investors satisfied their craving for speculation with tulip bulbs.

The tulip was introduced to western Europe from Turkey in the decades after 1554. By 1600 it was found to do well in the sandy soils of westernmost Holland, and men of wealth eagerly purchased the novel and beautiful flowers. The flamed or double-colored tulips were particularly sought after. Each year, between June, when the tulips were dug from their beds, and September, when they were replanted, there arose an active trade in bulbs. Buyers hoped that their bulbs would grow excrescences which could then be sold in future years. As Dutchmen began accumulating ever larger stocks of capital, their interest in investment diversification spread to, among other things, the bulb market. The key development was the creation of a futures market. Speculators sold bulbs still in the ground in anticipation of the successful growth of excrescences. Because immediate delivery of goods was impossible, bulbs came to be bought and sold repeatedly, the sellers without bulbs and, as long as prices kept rising, the buyers without cash. The plague outbreak of 1635-36, perhaps by spreading a certain fatalism among the population, kicked off the most frenzied episode of the Tulip Mania. Now the small investor entered the tulip market. Small quantities of common bulbs were offered to suit the pocketbooks of weavers and bargemen, while the explosive growth in the number of transactions inspired the streamlining and simplifying of contractual agreements.

By February of 1637 individual bulbs were changing owners hourly and fetching prices in the thousands of guilders. Then the realization came that most buyers would never be able to pay up and that many sellers would never be able to deliver. The inevitable crash followed, but it would be wrong to say that economic life gained nothing from this preposterous speculative mania; the techniques of futures markets and of handling a large volume of transactions that had evolved could be used another day. In 1734 a hyacinth mania swept Holland, and in 1751, 1763, and later years, Amsterdam's financial operations - the most sophisticated in the world - suffered from speculative crises in large part because of futures trading.[14]

Short-term credit and banks

The growing range of investment opportunities opening up in the course of the seventeenth and eighteenth centuries was not confined to long-term investments. In an economy where circulating capital greatly overshadowed fixed capital in importance, it was inevitable that short-term credit extensions should constitute a major form of investment. Such credit, generated by virtually every significant mercantile transaction, was embodied in the bill of exchange, a credit instrument dating from the Middle Ages. When a merchant sold a commodity to a buyer, he drew a bill on the buyer which stipulated the payment due (embodying an interest rate) and the due date. The buyer signed the bill, indicating his acceptance; the creditor then held the bill until it matured, when he expected payment, most likely from the buyer's correspondent in the creditor's city. In the early seventeenth century the repayment period for bills of exchange commonly ranged from one to three months. But, in the course of the century, a combination of lengthier trade routes and stronger bargaining positions for buyers tended to stretch out the repayment period; by 1700, six to twelve months was common. This trend, by tying up circulating capital for longer periods, could have hamstrung commerce unless more capital could be attracted to the bill market and the available capital could be used more efficiently.

Consider the problem of, say, a putting-out merchant who drew a bill on (extended credit to) a buyer of his wares. What if our creditor had bills of his own to pay before the due date, or simply wanted his cash immediately? The medieval bill of exchange would have been unable to accommodate his wishes, for it generally specified that payment be made to the person - usually the creditor - designated on the bill. That is, it was not generally negotiable.

In the sixteenth century Italian bankers in the most advanced commercial centers began to lift this limitation by making bills negotiable. A century later this practice spread to northern Europe. Laws confirming the negotiability of bills were promulgated first in the Dutch Republic (1651), followed by France (1673), England (1704), and Spain (1737). Thus, by the eighteenth century bills of exchange could be either discounted or endorsed. The creditor wanting his money before a bill matured could now call on merchant-bankers who were willing to buy bills. To compensate themselves for the risk they took (and for what was in effect a loan to the bill holders), the bankers paid something less than the face value of the bill - that is, they discounted the bill.

Alternatively, the creditor may have used the bill to pay a debt of his own by endorsing it - signing it and committing himself to pay the sum should the original debtor default - and offering it to his creditor as payment. This next creditor could have used it in the same manner, so that when the bill finally matured, it might have a long string of endorsements to ensure the holder that he would be paid, if not by the original debtor, then by each endorser in turn.[15]

The use of bills in this way was a major step in supplementing the money supply through credit creation. It gave a distinct financial advantage to the great commercial centers, such as Amsterdam and London, where these new practices became commonplace. But it also created the setting in which merchants with capital accumulated in their own trade could put it to the service of others by discounting bills, and, eventually, performing other financial services. By the mid-eighteenth century many Dutch merchant houses had ceased being traders altogether; their capital was now used to finance the commerce of others through acceptance banking, bill discounting, and insurance. Almost everywhere in Europe there were merchants who acted as local bankers by discounting bills and facilitating the making of payments to distant places. As a consequence, it was now possible to deposit one's funds with a banker or goldsmith who would pay interest in exchange for the right to use the deposit in his business or in making short-term loans.

The culmination of the financial innovations outlined here - which are thought by some to constitute a true financial revolution - came with the establishment of public banks. In Italy, where banking traditions reach back to the Middle Ages, many cities possessed banks which served the needs of merchants by accepting deposits for safekeeping and effecting transfers between the accounts of members who traded with each other. They were not intended as lending institutions, although some granted loans to their city governments. North of the Alps Italian financial wizardry had been slow to take root. The superiority of Italian techniques had given its merchants considerable trade advantages for centuries, but in the seventeenth century the gap was closed - indeed, reversed.

Long-distance finance had depended on periodic fairs to bring bill-of-exchange dealers together so they could settle accounts. Among the major financial centers of the sixteenth century were Lyon and Antwerp, which functioned as more or less permanent fairs, plus Piacenza, Burgos, and Frankfurt. The development of public banks made these fairs seem increasingly old-fashioned. It is interesting to note how they decline in importance first in western Europe; in Germany the Frankfurt fairs function until after 1648 and the Leipzig fairs even longer. In Russia, the fairs of Novgorod persist far into the eighteenth century.

The first public banks in northern Europe were imitations of the Italian institutions. The Bank of Amsterdam, established in 1609, was the most notable of these. Its purpose was to serve the commercial needs of the city by bringing order to the currency and by making transfers among the accounts of member merchants. Not without difficulty, the Bank accomplished the first of these goals by accepting the enormous variety of circulating coins and converting them to a standard currency of account for all record keeping purposes. The accepted coins plus bullion bought from the West India Company were then sent to the mints for conversion into standard, full-valued coins useful in international trade. The Bank performed its money-transfer (giro) service with efficiency because of the legal provision requiring that every bill of exchange exceeding 600 guilders be made payable through the Bank. This compelled virtually every merchant to open an account.

The Bank of Amsterdam and similar institutions established in Hamburg, Nuremberg, and Rotterdam introduced Italian practices to northern Europe, but they did not truly function as modern banks because they did not discount bills of exchange or issue bank notes. The revenues of the Bank of Amsterdam, for example, came almost exclusively from its minting function and a service charge on giro transactions; its charter made no provision for lending the deposits. In fact, the banks gradually did make credit available. The Bank of Rotterdam faced embarrassment during the war crisis of 1672 because of its extensive financing of merchants engaged in the Westphalian linen trade, and the Bank of Amsterdam gradually and discreetly enlarged its practice of extending short-term loans to the city treasury and the Dutch East India Company. But such credit-creation remained an unofficial practice accessible to only a small, privileged sector of the economy.

The most important advance in the Bank of Amsterdam's activities came after 1682, when its long-established services to commodity merchants were extended to include traders in precious metals. As a center of the international trade in gold and silver coin, Amsterdam attracted large stocks of precious metals. Beginning in 1682 merchants could deposit such stocks waiting for sale with the Bank and receive a modest rate of interest. The equivalent in bank money was then credited to the merchant's account and in acknowledgment the Bank issued a receipt of deposit which was fully negotiable. Moreover, these receipts were traded on the *Beurs* to protect their face value from changes in specie values. Traders in precious metals were now able to conduct an extensive trade with limited capital. In the eighteenth century the Bank of Amsterdam functioned as a great reservoir of precious metals, mediating the irregular inflow of gold and silver from the New World with the demand for various types of currency from all over Europe. The existence of this stock helped stabilize exchange rates in Amsterdam, which encouraged the circulation of bills of exchange as negotiable instruments of credit. It also dampened price fluctuations caused by sudden changes in the volume of circulating currency.[16]

The first public bank to issue an actual circulating paper currency was the Bank of Stockholm, established in 1656. This innovation was inspired by the inconvenient size and weight of Swedish coins. To take advantage of Sweden's copper output the government established a copper currency whose larger denominations weighed many pounds. Consequently, the public eagerly accepted the paper currency offered by the Bank. Of greater moment than this curiosity was the establishment of the Bank of England. With its creation a new chapter of banking history began.

The Bank of England came into being in 1694 in order to accommodate the government's need to borrow from a wider circle than the band of London goldsmiths who for decades had been - not without great controversy - the chief royal creditors. Involvement in the seemingly interminable wars against France made the need for long-term borrowing particularly intense in the 1690s. The bank scheme, put forward by a Scot active in the colonial trade, called for subscribers to lend 1.2 million pounds to the government in return for an annual interest payment of 8 percent, secured by the revenue of specific taxes plus the right to found a bank. The Bank's capital consisted of bank notes issued up to the amount of the state loan. As the Bank made further loans to the government, its note issue increased correspondingly. These notes circulated among the government's creditors and could be exchanged for coin on demand at the Bank. This circulation long remained confined to the immediate vicinity of London.

The Bank of England managed to secure many other financial privileges in the course of its dealings with the government. It held temporary cash reserves, handled precious metals destined for the Mint, and engaged in foreign currency dealings necessary to finance British military forces fighting on the Continent. More than that, the Bank directors engaged in private banking, discounting bills of exchange and making short-term loans to the joint-stock trading companies.[17]

Other banks arose with similar intentions, most notably in

Scotland and Paris. The French *Banque Royale,* established
by John Law, issued its bank notes with the backing of
nothing but the "demand for money" - a scheme that could
have succeeded. However, accurately gauging this demand
proved to exceed the capacities of the Bank's directors and
like similar banks in Copenhagen and Stockholm, the *Banque
Royale* succumbed to the temptation of issuing too many
bank notes. In time, loss of confidence and speculative
assaults ruined these banks. The Bank of England succeeded
where so many others failed, because of the sagacity and
prudence of its directors. In successive eighteenth-century
crises the Bank always proved able to honor its obligations
when noteholders rushed to its windows demanding coin.
Consequently, it became the first important bank to make a
success not only of accepting deposits and effecting transfers
between accounts, but also of issuing bank notes, advancing
loans to businesses and the government, and discounting bills
of exchange.

The bourgeoisie: rising or ossifying?

In a multitude of ways, a capital market was taking
shape in northwestern Europe. The chronic problem of misinvestment - particularly overinvestment in land - was amelio-
rated by the expanding range of investment opportunities.
It would be another century before the capital market was
capable of regularly channeling capital to industrial enterprise. But trade and to a lesser extent agriculture benefitted
from an abundant source of credit, while employment in all
sectors benefitted from a money supply augmented by bank
credit creation. If Europe was underdeveloped, it is hard to
understand how this could have been because of capital scarcity.

The impact of these progressive developments did not reach
every corner of Europe. On the contrary, the full impact was
restricted to Amsterdam, London, and port cities, such as

Hamburg and Bordeaux, that were connected via the growing Atlantic-centered trading economy. As a consequence, one can identify a growing economic dualism that separated a relatively small number of growth poles and their hinterlands from vast regions of stagnant trade and institutional inertia. This condition is mirrored in the condition of the European bourgeoisie - it cannot, in fact, be comprehended as a single "class" with a common destiny.

In countless cities commerce and industry was mired in lethargy, protected from every innovation by urban trade privileges and guild regulations. It is sometimes thought that the bourgeoisie is intolerant of such fetters on individual initiative, but this is not so. Accommodation is the most frequent reaction. As these economically stagnant places were challenged by the superior financial and commercial institutions of the major ports and the unregulated industrial production of rural areas, strong tendencies arose among their middle classes to invest in real property, annuities, and government bonds. This undermined urban employment at the same time that it lent an aristocratic aura to middle class families, who became increasingly dependent for their incomes on rents and interest payments.

In the growing capital cities a different more energetic bourgeois group can be identified. Tax farms, state loans, and the exploitation of monopoly privileges created a kind of court capitalism. Particularly in France and Germany it attracted bankers and speculators from commercial enterprise who sought their fortunes through the cultivation of royal patronage. The wealth of the greatest of these court capitalists far exceeded that of the known wealth of the richest Dutch or English merchants and manufacturers, but one must not infer that they were therefore directly instrumental in securing the triumph of a truly capitalist economy. On the contrary, their positions were those of intermediaries between the capitalist and noncapitalist sectors of the economy. Their prosperity required the preservation of backward financial systems and imperfectly monetized rural economies.[18]

We can note here the existence in many European societies of a form of social convergence. Not only did important sectors of the bourgeoisie assume aristocratic characteristics and depend on a seigneurial economy for their profits, but many noble families became heavily involved in the bourgeois activity of capital investment. One obvious reason for this is, of course, the recent bourgeois origins of many eighteenth-century nobles. But this behavior was by no means confined to the new nobilities.

We must be careful not to accept uncritically aristocracies' definitions and descriptions of themselves. Behind the theoretical scaffolding of a legally privileged order graded by antiquity of lineage and behind aristocratic myth-making and posturing, there existed the social reality that the noble orders were, just as were the clerical and bourgeois orders, divided fundamentally by wealth. The power of money clearly exceeded the power of birth. The upper reaches of both nobility and bourgeoisie were severed from their respective lesser comrades and bound together by their administration of large pools of capital, their involvement in crown finance, and sometimes even their participation in such activities as mining, ironmaking, and canal building. The classic juxtaposition of a feudal nobility and a capitalist bourgeoisie, each representative of distinct socioeconomic worlds, obscures the fact that the class in control of capital in most of eighteenth-century Europe cut across these two orders.[19]

This fact notwithstanding, it remains possible to identify a sector of the third estate that was changing the face of the European economy. The bourgeoisie, which we might most appropriately claim was rising, consisted of those commission merchants, putting-out merchants, colonial traders, and others who exploited the new opportunities created by growing government demand, an increasingly efficient commercial network connecting the Atlantic ports, and the cost-reducing potential of rural industry. Particularly notable, and still particularly obscure, were the industrial entrepreneurs: men in the textile, mining, and metallurgical industries, brewing, paper- and glassmaking, who were able to exploit the new market opportunities by a willingness to invest capital in the production process and to introduce cost-reducing procedures. The true industrialists were still - with the notable exceptions of some aristocratic mine owners - among the humblest and least wealthy bourgeois. Large-scale industry was still something of a curiosity in the early eighteenth century. But among the masters in the Birmingham brass trade, the Liège iron masters, Wuppertal linen bleachers, and many others, often of peasant and artisan background, there existed a novel energy.

8
Mercantilism, absolutism, and economic growth

The state

Near the beginning of this volume we warned that no single obvious unifying theme renders the economic history of seventeenth- and eighteenth-century Europe intelligible. Indeed, the most important economic developments were those that impelled divergence in the institutions and endowments of the various European states. But the mind yearns for order and perhaps for this reason several generations of economic historians have struggled to fit the evolution of economic life in the sixteenth through eighteenth centuries under the umbrella of mercantilism. The conflicting definitions of the term and the numerous exceptions that must be noted no matter what definition one uses have persuaded us to avoid using mercantilism as an organizing concept in this volume. But it cannot be, and has not been, altogether ignored. By assuming more activist postures, seventeenth-century absolutist and constitutional states alike became more effective in their attempts to channel economic life to their ends.

Tariff legislation, industrial regulation, trade wars, tax laws, and currency manipulations were the methods used by most governments to influence their economies. Few measures were novel to this period, but gradually there arose a more coherent body of thought about how to use government power to achieve economic ends, and conversely, how to use economic power to achieve political ends.

One interpretation of economic policy in this period identifies as its outstanding characteristic the tendency toward the economic unification of the nation-state.[1] Medieval economic policy had been in the hands of various and overlapping authorities - municipal, religious, and royal. These agencies characteristically fragmented economic life by enforcing special privileges and by competing amongst each other for exclusive competences. With the rise of nation-states, so this theory of mercantilism goes, economic policy was held to be in the province of the central government, with the other authorities subordinate. Economic policy was intended to create a national economy which could be directed to enrich the nation as a whole. Such a unifying vision was thought to alter the emphasis of economic policy. Medieval economics was obsessed with questions of distribution and of maximizing the goods available for consumption: mercantilist economics redirected attention to the encouragement of production and exportation. The English Navigation Acts stand as a classic example of this interpretation of mercantilism. These acts, which took their definitive form in 1660, restricted the importation of most goods to either English vessels or the ships of the country from which the goods originated, and required English vessels to be built and manned domestically. The Acts aimed to encourage English shipping in the face of powerful Dutch competition. They went on to establish a framework for England's colonial economy: colonial exports - that is, the "enumerated" goods - as well as colonial imports henceforth had to pass through English ports on their way to or from other nations and had to be transported in English or colonial ships. These measures expressed the intention of endowing London with an entrepôt function.

The Navigation Acts and their later elaborations and amendments certainly exhibit a clear perception of the path of national economic development. The same cannot be said for all mercantilist measures. Government policies in the German states seemed more intent on cultivating the revenue potential of state-owned properties, and in both Germany and France, the revenue raising potential of tariffs, industrial regulations, and monopoly privileges often provided the chief motive for economic legislation.[2]

The history of La Rochelle, an important French Atlantic port, is illustrative of this dimension of mercantilism. After Henry IV brought peace to France with the proclamation of the Edict of Nantes, the Huguenots made this city, which prospered from the wine and salt trades, a bastion of their Calvinist "state within a state." Cardinal Richelieu's energetically pursued policy of suppressing the political autonomy of the Huguenots culminated in the Siege of La Rochelle, and the capitulation of the city to royal authority in 1629.

If mercantilism was a program of state-building and economic unification, an examination of royal economic policy in La Rochelle after the capitulation should demonstrate that fact. The new administration's first acts were to introduce central government taxes and bring under royal regulation the salt marshes that surrounded the city. The new regulations generated disputes, and in short order a vast array of judicial offices arose to handle the resultant litigation. Royal control of the city had eliminated the office of mayor, but in 1695 it was revived - so that it might be sold. The city's guilds, which pursued the venerable medieval policy of suppressing competition and enforcing limitations on the size of firms, gained support from the crown, which chartered them in return for yearly payments. In short, the government drew income from every privilege it created and protected, although a large part of this income flow was diverted to descendants of Richelieu and other well-connected nobles who won the judgeships and other offices created to administer these policies.[3]

This brings us to yet another dimension of mercantilist policy: the endless stream of regulations that emanated from government bureaus created impressive opportunities for corruption. Cynical observers note that prohibitions and regulations were often promulgated so fortunes could be made in granting exceptions.

The activism of governments in the economic life of this period can be understood only when placed in its context. That context was not theoretical (there did not yet exist a priesthood of economists); it was practical. The frequent disruptions of important foreign markets, the long-term changes in the structure of foreign trade, and the new internal problems created by violent short-term fluctuations demanded some form of response. Moreover, governments, perhaps because they were placing increasingly larger demands on their economies, were more sensitive than before to the need for stability and control. The *ad hoc* character of the resulting economic policies is clearly expressed by the timing of most enactments and "theoretical" publications: they were disproportionately bunched in economic downswings.[4]

The policies enacted to control the movement of precious metals demonstrate the practical orientation of mercantilist measures. At first glance, it is precisely here that economic policy exhibited its blindly dogmatic dimension. It is argued, that the mercantilists confused gold and silver with wealth and that they sought to amass precious metals as an end in itself - irrespective of the economic consequences on real economic factors. From the modern perspective the attention devoted to the in- and outflow of precious metals does seem suspicious. The precious metals were, after all, only commodities of trade, not the embodiment of wealth. Only the Dutch Republic, conspicuous for so many other reasons, seemed to have liberated itself from the Midas Complex. The Dutch placed no controls on the import and export of gold and silver; indeed, Amsterdam became the center of international speculation in precious metals. But, as we have seen, the Republic functioned as an entrepôt; gold and silver flowed through the central marketplace along with all other commodities. Where trade was bilateral rather than multi-lateral, the role of the precious metals was bound to be different. A nation that exported a domestically produced commodity and imported goods for final use was bound to find that its various bilateral trade connections did not each balance out. In the absence of a widespread payments network, the precious metals were necessary to the functioning of such trades. It was wrong of mercantilist writers to insist that each bilateral trading connection had to be positive to be useful, but it was not wrong that observers should have stressed the importance of an adequate supply of gold and silver to "finance" foreign trade.

The growing sophistication of the payments system using bills of exchange loosened the link between trade and precious metals, but the link remained until the last few decades of the seventeenth century. Then the payments system of the Amsterdam entrepôt and the bills business of the private bankers of London developed rapidly to blanket Europe and the chief New World trade zones with a durable financial network which featured permanent currency exchange quotations between Amsterdam or London and virtually all important commercial centers. Specie still flowed between these two cities to settle accounts but long-distance transfers were now generally confined to the trades with Russia, Asia, and sometimes the Levant.[5]

The gradual undermining of the validity of mercantilist concern about the stock of precious metals as it affected foreign trade balances did not do away with the issue altogether. Another problem arose in this period to direct attention to the supply of precious metals: unemployment. Economic fluctuations based on harvest results and such exogenous shocks as epidemics and wars were characteristic of all preindustrial economies. But when an agrarian, peasant society gave way to a more stratified structure with a large wage labor force, the number of factors causing fluctuations increased and their consequences became more severe.

Foreign devaluations, changes in the relative value of gold and silver, tariffs, gold and silver production, and the balance of trade all influenced the domestic money supply, and when the money supplies declined, for whatever reason, the ability and willingness of merchants to finance the putting-out industries with circulating capital declined. Through the multiplier effect, such a decline in investment diminished the overall level of employment. These monetary uncertainties, when added to the other causes of violent fluctuations, could, in the words of Thomas Mun, "suddenly cause much poverty and dangerous uproars, specially by our poor people."[6]

In this context we can better understand the intense interest of European governments in workhouses and other schemes to absorb unemployment in times of distress, in controls on the international flow of precious metals, and in industrial protection and import substitution measures. All aimed to protect the economy from the overwhelming and dangerous consequences of unemployment. This social dimension of mercantilism, consisting chiefly of defensive measures to preserve the social fabric, is not highly theoretical. Revolutionary visions of a new economic order cannot be ascribed to many mercantilist writers. But, most successfully in England, a rough and ready set of national controls was instituted which influenced the major variables in economic life. And in a fumbling, round-about way, some important advances in economic understanding were achieved. The early perception of the importance of precious metals led, under the stimulus of Thomas Mun's work culminating in *England's Treasure by Foreign Trade* (1664), to an increased understanding of the role of overall trade balances in the prosperity of the national economy. From this understanding stemmed the prohibitions of raw material exports and the protectionist measures (such as Colbert's 1664 tariff) designed to encourage import substitution.

If the mercantilist state's aim was to increase the nation's wealth, did the means exist to achieve this end outside of aggressive foreign trade policies? The corollary to the view that foreign trade could grow only at the expense of rival nations was the view that, domestically, the state's tax revenue gain was necessarily the people's loss. But this negative view of the impact of taxation gave way in mercantilist literature to the belief that it was possible to increase tax revenues (a foremost aim, as we have seen, of every seventeenth-century government), by expanding the tax base, and that fiscal policy itself could influence the growth of the economy. Colbert expressed this approach quite clearly in his 1670 *mémoire* on finances. Summarizing Colbert's view, Martin Wolfe notes that: "the object of economic statesmanship is to provide the monarch with the funds he needs for order and glory; to a large extent any increase in these funds must come from increases in the volume and circulation of cash, the only way to improve the tax-paying capacity of the population . . . the heart of fiscal policy is the effort to increase royal revenues indirectly, through economic improvements."[7] No government, least of all the French, can be said to have refashioned its fiscal system to stimulate the national economy. But a new awareness developed of the interrelation between the state and its gargantuan needs, on the one hand, and the economy's ability to support those needs on the other.

Looking back, one cannot help but be struck by the seemingly symbiotic relationship existing between the state, military power, and the private economy's efficiency in the age of absolutism. Behind every successful dynasty stood an array of opulent banking families. Access to such bourgeois resources proved crucial to the princes' state-building and centralizing policies. Princes also needed direct access to agricultural resources, which could be mobilized only when agricultural productivity grew *and* an effective administrative and military power existed to enforce the princes' claims. But the lines of causation also ran in the opposite direction. Success-ful state-building and empire-building activities plus the asso-ciated tendency toward concentration of urban population and government expenditure, offered the private economy unique and invaluable opportunities to capture economies of scale. These economies of scale occasionally affected industri-al production but were most significant in the development of trade and finance. In addition, the sheer pressure of cen-tral government taxation did as much as any other economic force to channel peasant production into the market and thereby augment the opportunities for trade creation and economic specialization. The state, the military, and the pri-vate economy could each stimulate the growth of the others; they could, that is, where institutions and social structure were effective in transmitting their varied impulses to each other.

As we investigate mercantilism, the state reveals itself as unifying agent, unethical fiscalist, and catalyst of economic development. It is, however, most convincing in its role as the agent of economic stability. It is true that government policy could easily be rendered ineffectual or appear contradictory given the imperfect control that the best of administrators held over their agents and the imperfect knowledge and in-effectual tools with which they had to work. Still, the irony remains that policies inspired by a desire for order and stabil-ity so often acted to unbind the fetters of the local peasant economy and thereby encourage the social stratification and market orientation that was, in time, to destroy much of what absolutism had wished to preserve.

Conclusion

Around the middle of the eighteenth century (and a bit earlier in the Mediterranean basin), the European econ-omy entered a new phase. Nearly everywhere a forceful de-mographic expansion replaced the stability or decline of the previous era. Prices began to rise once again; agricultural prices and rents, in particular, recovered sharply from the doldrums of the 1730s. Europe had not yet seen the last of the short-term mortality crises and years of food scarcity, but the violent fluctuations that had so long buffeted the European economy dampened noticeably after 1750. These shocks ceased playing such an important role in setting the tempo of economic life. Most notably of all, the post-1750 era witnessed the unprecedented growth of the English economy.

Because this new upswing ushered in the Industrial Revolution the period preceding it is cast in a new light. That period was, in retrospect, the last epoch of traditional Europe. A collection of societies composed of princes, aristocrats, peasants, and corporate towns, having access to productive factors not essentially different from earlier centuries, was about to enter onto a new economic path. What had prepared the ground for such a departure? How did the European economy of Louis XV and George II differ from that of Henry IV and James I?

In several important respects little had changed. The overall level of population had grown little; there had been a minor net increase in urbanization; the technological developments of the period were quite isolated and did not affect economic life on a broad front; few new long-distance trade contacts had been established; price levels had fluctuated around stationary or gently declining trends; the medieval legacy of seigneurial institutions, much bastardized to be sure, continued nonetheless to exert its perverse influence on rural life. There did not exist among the periwigged dandies of the mid-eighteenth century any more of an expectation of long-term sustained growth in their economy than had existed among their early seventeenth-century ancestors, encased in their ruff collars and doublets.

In short, many of the building blocks of economic life remained quantitatively the same as they had been at the beginning of our period. However, in this volume we have tried to uncover and understand the long-term process by which, to stay with our metaphor, the building blocks were being reassembled, behind a placid exterior façade, to erect an essentially new structure of economic life. It is in this *qualitative* dimension of Europe's economy that the manifestations of change are indeed numerous and significant.

In the first place, the economic geography of many areas was altered to exhibit a more strongly marked differentiation in land use. European populations, too, exhibited stronger spatial differentiation and social stratification. Most notable were two developments: the thickening of population in forest areas and on infertile soils as a consequence of the spread of rural industry, and the elaboration of a more clearly defined hierarchy of cities. While many smaller cities languished, there arose at the pinnacle of the hierarchy a new class of metropolises of unprecedented size and economic impact.

Another major field of development was in the organization - in contrast to the technology - of production. The principle of division of labor did not have to await the rise of the factory system to be made operative. In our period many regions felt the impact of agricultural specialization or witnessed the elaboration of a putting-out system in rural industry. These organizational changes can be seen as the result of two interacting pressures. Relative price changes and demographic movements created opportunities which were seized upon by merchants, industrial producers, landlords, and portions of the peasantry wherever the legal and institutional environment gave sufficient rein to their profit motives. Under these combined pressures an elaborate stratification of commercial farmers, cotters, wage-dependent laborers, plus a variety of artisan and service-sector workers came to populate the countryside.

Two points are worth emphasizing about these organizational changes: this social restructuring occurred much more in the countryside than in the cities, and many of the people pushing for these changes were located quite far down the social ladder. The most visible and powerful sectors of the bourgeoisie, for all their accumulated capital, appear to have remained dependent on precapitalist sectors of the economy and were ensconced in the institutions of the absolutist states. The new men who were attracted to the profit possibilities of production over those of exchange rarely came from the established bourgeois families. Even peasants played a role; not all of them were victims of the new economic forces.

Finally we come to the new power of markets. Markets had, of course, long influenced European economic organization, but in our period regional and international markets moved decisively to center stage. The more complete commercialization of rural economies was powerfully advanced by two forces: central governments, working to acquire a firmer hold on village-level economic resources, and commercial enterprise, seeking lower-cost sources of production. In the urban sector new commercial practices succeeded in greatly reducing transaction costs. This lowering of business costs was a key achievement of a trading system that could no longer depend solely on the exploitation of vast price differences among markets. Two sources of this achievement can be traced: the Dutch trading system, with its early specialization in bulk trades, and the competitive empire-building policies of the major states. The logistical and financial needs of these states, large-scale and concentrated, offered important economies of scale to merchants and bankers that carried over to the rest of the economy.

A measure of the degree to which integrated market systems took shape is illustrated by the behavior of wheat prices in the various market towns. The major achievement of the sixteenth century was to bring the low prices of eastern Europe somewhat closer to the price levels prevailing in western and southern Europe. Between 1600 and 1750 the price gap separating the areas of highest prices from those of

the lowest prices narrowed by half, and many regions participated in this convergence trend. In addition, the year-to-year
price changes of many markets displayed gradually fewer
divergent movements. This high correlation between markets
was most apparent in England, northwestern Europe, and the
Baltic ports.[8]

These improvements in commodity markets were overshadowed, at least in novelty, by the development of factor
markets - that is, markets for the factors of production (land,
capital, and labor). A characteristic of feudal economies is
the immobility of the factors of production; such economies
might have commodity markets but not factor markets, a
fact that obviously limits the available forms of productive
organization.

To what extent did real factor markets come into being in
the seventeenth and eighteenth centuries? The least progress
had been achieved in constructing a free market in land. The
residue of feudal land law and the hold of aristocratic landowners, buttressed now more than ever by entails, combined
to keep the land market very imperfect. But where feudal
ambiguities had been shorn from the concept of landownership and where a mortgage market arose to which all classes
of land purchasers had access, the market acquired a degree
of liquidity that stimulated more efficient land use. By 1750
these characteristics were far more pronounced in England
and the Netherlands than anywhere else in Europe.

Capital markets of a sort developed around the financial
centers of Amsterdam and London after the late seventeenth
century. They served governments, the great trading companies, and the mercantile sector of the economy; producers,
certainly industrial producers, had no direct access to this
market. But to the extent that circulating capital could be
conserved through the use of credit, it became possible to
invest more in productive activities.[9] This market, like the
land market, confined its development to a handful of regions.

The greatest amount of progress came in the elaboration of labor markets. Could a free labor market exist where the great bulk of the population was rural and where a stultifying paternalism continued to govern the relations between master and worker? The small size of most production units and the tendency for an employee to be regarded as a sort of fictive child of the employer unquestionably lent a unique character to labor markets. But the powerful and widespread process of social stratification we have identified in Chapters 2 and 3 should put to rest any question of the importance of labor markets by the eighteenth century. The substantial geographical mobility of the population in some regions tends further to support this view. Migrants seeking economic advantage generally confined their moves to quite short distances, it is true, but the large volume of these moves aided in the creation of a "competitive and acquisitive society."[10]

The European economies in 1750 were still far from having achieved efficient, widely-diffused factor markets. But by then a sufficient mobility in the factors of production had been achieved in the most advanced regions to allow innovations in the organization of production that could not have occurred in earlier centuries.

A highly visible characteristic of the changes we have been discussing in general terms is the motley pattern of growth and stagnation, of institutional suppleness and rigidity, that, despite the efforts of government policies, was much more apparent on a regional than on a national level.

What can account for the yawning gaps that opened up between regions and for the noteworthy lack of continuity displayed in the unfolding patterns of economic leadership between 1600 and 1750? One way to tie together some of the developments of this long epoch is to draw an analogy from the study of business cycles in the modern economy. In the downswing of the business cycles that seem to recur every few years, firms face weakening markets and reduced prices that put a downward pressure on profits. In response, firms seek ways to rationalize their operations, cut costs, and maneuver for position among their competitors in anticipation of the next business cycle upswing. Such a period typically is witness to a concentration of economic activity as weak firms fail to see the crisis through.

On a gigantic scale this sort of behavior can be identified after the onset of the seventeenth-century crisis. The economy that wished to cushion the blows sought to shift its emphasis from declining to expanding industries; in the seventeenth century this meant emphasizing livestock over arable farming, the new over the old draperies, and, in the following century, cotton over both linen and woolen cloth. An economy could seek to protect itself from the under-utilization of resources by protecting and subsidizing key industries. When market conditions improved, economies successful in these defensive measures would be well-placed to participate in the renewed expansion.

A third response was to reduce costs, the main opportunities for which came in the form of organizational and locational changes. The cost-reducing impact of, for example, the putting-out system, entrepôt commerce, or convertible husbandry certainly seem modest when compared to the technological breakthroughs of later decades, but in a context of static markets even small cost differentials could, in a cumulative process, open up vast chasms between competitors. What cost advantages could not achieve diplomatic and military policy might; the Anglo-Dutch, Dutch-French, and French-English wars that crowd the century after 1650 testify to the power of this belief. Because mercantilist literature so often stresses this point we need only mention here that it was not the only force behind the shifts in economic leadership.

The economies of Spain and her client economic centers in Genoa, southern Germany, and Flanders failed most completely to adapt to the new economic environment. The political failure of Habsburg imperial policy played a role in this, to be sure, but the inability of an imperial economic system to pursue the adaptive strategies outlined above also contributed. The Spaniards were not the first to discover that world empires are costly to maintain and can be given coherence only through administrative structures that sacrifice competition and economic flexibility. The empires that succeeded Spain - the English, Dutch, and French - were all much leaner operations. In this period commercial empires were designed for competitive exploitation of economic opportunities rather than territorial and administrative empires.

In the collapse of Italian industry and commerce we have another example of the consequences of inflexibility in the face of the new requirements of the seventeenth-century economy and one more difficult to explain. The decline of the Iberian empires had a severe impact on Italy, but more important were the internal rigidities of a mature industrial economy. Urban industry's commitment to products and markets that were in relative decline together with its high-production costs drove capital and labor into other sectors of the economy. This reaction, in the social context of seventeenth-century Italy, only exacerbated the structural problem of the economy.

The French economy also displays signs of being a victim of the crisis. However, the complexity of this largest of European states is demonstrated by the simultaneous evidence that exists supporting the opposite conclusion. France, despite being the home of classic, centralizing absolutism, possessed a national economy only in the most superficial sense. In fact, three separate economies can be distinguished, each governed by quite distinct factors. The economy of the southern region, facing the Mediterranean, existed until the 1670s in what has been identified as a precarious condition of Malthusian overpopulation. Then it suffered a sharp decline only partially relieved by state-subsidized industrial growth. In the north, particularly around the industrial cities, the 1620s and 30s brought on the sharpest contraction, and it was here that the economy was most frequently and severely jolted by subsistence crises. In both these vast zones the bourgeoisie depended heavily on crown policy and the continued existence of precapitalist organization in the rural economy.

The third French economy focused on the Atlantic port cities. These cities often had firmer contacts with other countries than with the rest of France, and they resisted more successfully than other cities in having their economic policies dictated from Versailles. They prospered with the expansion of the Atlantic economy; the 1660s ushered in a century of rapid growth for these cities and their hinterlands, a growth that accelerated remarkably after 1715. Although the Seven Years' War dealt a severe blow to the growth of French foreign trade, of greater importance to the future of the French economy was the fact that the impact of her foreign trade remained confined to limited sectors of the economy. The constituent parts of a vigorous economy existed in eighteenth-century France - commerce, colonial trade, rural industry, highly-skilled artisan industry - but they were not well connected with one another; their growth during the periodic commodity booms of the eighteenth century could not be transmitted to the other sectors and ramify through the economy.[11]

The Dutch Republic offers the clearest example of an economy that rose quickly to a position of economic leadership on the strength of cost-reducing measures in some sectors of agriculture and industry and, most notably, in commerce. But the Dutch economy is also a good example of another characteristic of this period, what we might call "high-level traditionalism." By the eighteenth century Dutch society was, by the standards of the time, well-off, educated, urban, mobile, and, if not secular, then at least tolerant. It had in these key respects moved a great distance toward social modernity. The economy featured a productive, commercial agriculture, an efficient trading system, and a diversified industrial sector. And yet, this vast achievement, which so impressed contemporaries, did not prevent the Dutch economy from sinking away into a complacent stagnation. The English, who feared their rivalry in the seventeenth century, could sing in the eighteenth century that

> in matters of commerce the fault of the Dutch is offering too little and asking too much.

To explain this decisive brake to the expansion of the Dutch economy the rivalry of larger, mercantilist states is often invoked, but there were also more fundamental causes. A thoroughly commercialized economy that had pushed preindustrial technology and organization to its limits did not necessarily clear a smooth path toward industrialization. A large bourgeoisie, even a bourgeoisie state, could accommodate to life within the larger nonbourgeois social framework; great accumulations of capital did not necessarily trigger industrialization - they may even have made it unnecessary; far-flung trade routes did not necessarily supply the home economy with forced draughts to fan the flames of industry - trade, after all, can substitute for industry. In this same vein, clearly-defined private property rights may very well have given capitalists the ability to capture the full benefits accruing from their investments, but such an institutional endowment could not assure that domestic industrial expansion would be the most profitable among investment opportunities; a prosperous, literate, commercially-oriented population did not necessarily crave - may indeed have abhorred - the satanic mills of an industrial society. In short, a high-level traditionalism may well have been the expected, normal product of the kind of economic achievement sought by Europeans in this period. At any rate, the Dutch Republic stands as an example of an economy whose intense specialization in one direction effectively closed the door to the kinds of social structure and economic policies required for industrial growth. Not every growth path led to the Industrial Revolution.

This brings us to England. It was here, of course, that technological and organizational changes sufficient to constitute a new economic system unfolded beginning in the second half of the eighteenth century. An explanation of this Industrial Revolution is beyond the scope of this book, but we cannot conclude an assessment of European economic history in the century and a half preceding 1750 without considering what England had achieved by 1750 that set her apart from her continental rivals.

Preindustrial industry, an infelicitous phrase for which we can substitute the term proto-industry, had spread over England. The textile industry and other relatively simple industrial processes had effectively attached themselves to low-cost rural labor organized in the putting-out system; mining, metallurgy, and the ironware trades had taken root wherever resources permitted; artisan industries remained attached to sources of skilled labor, still usually found in cities. But in this regard Britain was not alone: rural industry had spread over much of the Continent in search of low-cost labor; heavy industry, whose location by its nature is tied to resource availability, had many effective competitors in such places as Liège, the Rhineland, Saxony, Silesia, and Sweden. Moreover, around 1750 Russia emerged as a formidable iron exporter. The artisan industries, dependent on traditional upper-class markets, were probably more entrenched in the urban economies of France and Italy than in Britain.

What did distinguish Britain from her competitors already in the early eighteenth century were low-cost access to some raw materials, notably wool and coal, the ability to shift productive resources toward industries with relatively expanding markets, and, most important, the firm linkage of her industrial sectors with each other and with a highly efficient commercial and foreign trade sector.

Only toward the end of the seventeenth century, after decades of determined imitation, government protection, and military aggression, did British shipping and commercial facilities become competitive with the Dutch. And, in the eighteenth century, British colonial trade did not grow more rapidly than did that of France. But in Britain more than elsewhere lowered transactions costs and access to foreign markets stimulated domestic industry. And domestic industry's response was robust in part because agricultural developments lowered food prices at the same time as they released labor and provided raw materials to industry.

The industrial elements needed for future growth, present in many regions of Europe, were in England embedded in an economic structure that made merchants and industrialists sensitive to the opportunities of the mass market. Consequently, England's was the economy best poised for rapid growth in the next century.

Notes

The following abbreviations have been used in the notes:

A. H. R.	American Historical Review
Ag. H. R.	Agricultural History Review
Annales	Annales (Economies, Sociétés, Civilisations)
C. S. S. H.	Comparative Studies in Society and History
Ec. H. R.	Economic History Review
J. Ec. H.	Journal of Economic History
P. & P.	Past and Present
Scan. Ec. H. R.	Scandinavian Economic History Review
V. S. W. G.	Vierteljahrschrift für Sozial- und Wirtschaftgeschichte.

Notes to Chapter 1

1 Günther Franz, *Der Dreissigjährige Krieg und das Deutsche Volk* (Stuttgart, 1961); Irena Gieysztorowa, "Guerre et Regression en Masovia," *Annales* 12 (1957), 660-65; Aksel Lassen, "The Population of Denmark in 1660," *Scan. Ec. H. R.* 13 (1965), 29.

2 Karl Julius Beloch, *Bevölkerungsgeschichte Italiens,* vol. 3 (Berlin, 1961), pp. 352-54; Jorge Nadal, *Historia de la población española (siglos XVI à XX)* (Barcelona, 1966).

3 Roger Mols, "De Bevölkerungsgeschichte Belgiens im Lichte des Heutigen Forschung," *V. S. W. G.* 46 (1959), 491-511; J. A. Faber, et al., "Population Changes and Economic Developments in the Netherlands: A historical survey," *A. A. G. Bijdragen* 12 (1965), 47-113; G. S. L. Tucker, "English Pre-industrial Population Trends," *Ec. H. R.* 16 (1963), 205-18.

4 An enormous literature treats the phenomenon of famine crises. For a summary of recent findings see Pierre Goubert, "Historical Demography and the Reinterpretation of Early Modern French History: A research review," *Journal of Interdisciplinary History* 1 (1970), 37-48. For England see J. D. Chambers, *Population, Economy, and Society in Pre-industrial England* (Oxford, 1972), p. 96; for central Europe see Wilhelm Abel, *Massenarmut und Hungerkrisen im vorindustriellen*

Europa (Hamburg, 1974); for France see Jean Meuvret, "Demographic Crisis in France from the Sixteenth to the Eighteenth Century," in D. V. Glass and D. E. C. Eversley, eds., *Population in History* (London, 1965), pp. 507-22. An eloquent proponent of Malthusian crisis is Fernand Braudel, *The Mediterranean and the Mediterranean World in the Age of Philip II* (New York, 1972), pp. 427, 599-605. For a detailed account of Malthusian forces at work see E. Le Roy Ladurie, *Les Paysans de Languedoc* (Paris, 1966); an abridged version in English is *The Peasants of Languedoc* (Urbana, Ill., 1974).

5   Not because they did not try. For an analysis of plague epidemics and public health measures to combat them see Carlo Cipolla, *Christofano and the Plague* (Berkeley, 1973); Charles Carrière, et al., *Marseille, ville morte. La peste de 1720* (Marseilles, 1968).

6   Etienne Gautier and Louis Henry, "The Population of Crulai, a Norman Parish," and E. A. Wrigley, "Family Limitation in Pre-industrial England," in Orest and Patricia Ranum, eds., *Popular Attitudes toward Birth Control in Pre-industrial France and England* (New York, 1972); A. Chamoux and C. Dauphin, "La contraception avant la Révolution française. L'exemple de Châtillon-sur-Seine," *Annales* 24 (1969), 662-84.

7   Jean Ganiage, *Trois Villages de l' Ile-de-France au XVIIIe siècle* (Paris, 1963), p. 69; H. Charbonneaux, *Touvre-au-Perche aux XVIe et XVIIIe siècles* (Paris, 1970); J. Hajnal, "European Marriage Patterns in Perspective," in Glass and Eversley, *Population in History*, pp. 101-43.

8   Lawrence Stone, "Social Mobility in England, 1500-1700," *P. & P.* 33 (1966), 16-55; T. H. Hollingsworth, "A Demographic Study of the British Ducal Families," *Population Studies* 11 (1957), 4-26 and "The Demography of the British Peerage," *Population Studies* 18 (1964), supplement; Louis Henry, *Anciennes familles genevoises* (Paris, 1956); James C. Davis, *The Decline of the Venetian Nobility as a Ruling Class* (Baltimore, 1962), chap. III; J. A. Faber, *Drie eeuwen Friesland* (Wageningen, 1972), pp. 346-48.

9   Ronald Lee, "Population in Preindustrial England: An Econometric Analysis," *Quarterly Journal of Economics* 87 (1973), 581-607; J. T. Krause, "Some Neglected Factors in the English Industrial Revolution," *J. Ec. H.* 19 (1959), 528-40.

10   The best introductions to this subject are Gustav Utterström, "Climatic Fluctuations and Population Problems in Early Modern History," *Scan. Ec. H. R.* 3 (1955), 3-47; E. Le Roy Ladurie, "History and Climate," in Peter Burke, ed., *Economy and Society in Early Modern Europe* (New York, 1972); E. Le Roy Ladurie, *Times of Feast, Times of Famine: A History of Climate since the Year 1000* (Garden City, N.Y., 1971).

11   Earl J. Hamilton, *American Treasure and the Price Revolution in Spain 1501-1650* (Cambridge, Mass., 1934), pp. 34-35; Huguette and Pierre Chaunu, *Séville et l' Atlantique (1504-1650)*, 11 vols. (Paris, 1955-60). For a summary of their views see "The Atlantic Economy and the

World Economy," in Peter Earle, ed., *Essays in European Economic History* (Oxford, 1974), pp. 113-26.

12   Niels Steengaard, "European Shipping to Asia, 1497-1700," *Scan. Ec. H. R.* 18 (1970), 9; Nina Z. Bang, *Tabeller over Skibsfart og Varetransport gennem Øresund, 1497-1660,* 3 vols. (Copenhagen, 1906-22); see also P. Jeannin, "Les comptes du Sund comme source pour la construction d'indices généraux de l'activité économique en Europe (XVIe- XVIIIe siècles)," *Revue Historique* 231 (1964), 55-102, 307-40; H. Wiese and J. Bölts, *Rinderhandel und Rinderhaltung im nordwesteuropäischen Küstengebiet vom 15. bis zum 19. Jahrhundert* (Stuttgart, 1966), pp. 61-62. The yearly exportation of oxen from Denmark, Schleswig, and Schonen averaged 55-60,000 in the peak period, 1600-1620; by the mid-seventeenth century yearly cattle exports had fallen to 20,000 head.

13   Ruggiero Romano, "Tra XVI e XVII secolo. Una crisi economica: 1619-1622," *Rivista Storica Italiana* 74 (1964), 480-531 and "Encore la crise de 1619-22," *Annales* 19 (1964), 31-37; Barry Supple, *Commercial Crisis and Change in England, 1600-1642* (Cambridge, 1959), pp. 58, 75.

14   The literature on the quantity theory of money and its application to the sixteenth-century "price revolution" is endless. Fundamental are Hamilton, *American Treasure;* Frank C. Spooner, *The International Economy and Monetary Movements in France, 1493-1725* (Cambridge, Mass., 1972); F. Simiand, *Recherches anciennes et nouvelles sur le mouvement général des prix de XVIe au XIXe siècle* (Paris, 1932). A modern survey is Fernand Braudel and F. C. Spooner, "Prices in Europe from 1450 to 1750," in *Cambridge Economic History of Europe*, vol. 4 (Cambridge, 1967), pp. 374-486. For specific criticisms see M. Morineau, "D' Amsterdam à Séville: de quelle réalité l'histoire des prix est-elle le miroir?" *Annales* 23 (1968), 178-205; Ingrid Hammerström, "The Price Revolution of the Sixteenth Century: Some Swedish Evidence," *Scan. Ec. H. R.* 5 (1957), 118-54; Y. S. Brenner, "The Inflation of Prices in Sixteenth Century England," *Ec. H. R.* 14 (1961), 225-39.

15   E. H. Hobsbawm, "The General Crisis of the European Economy in the Seventeenth Century," *P. & P.* 5 (1954), 33-53, 6 (1954) 44-65; also in Trevor Aston, ed., *Crisis in Europe, 1560-1660* (London, 1965), pp. 5-62. For a critique of his argument see A. D. Lublinskaya, *French Absolutism: The Crucial Phase, 1620-1629* (Cambridge, 1968) chap. I. See also Roland Mousnier, *Le XVIe et le XVIIe siècles* (Paris, 1954).

16   Domenico Sella, "Crisis and Transformation in Venetian Trade," and "The Rise and Fall of the Venetian Woollen Industry," in Brian Pullan, ed., *Crisis and Change in the Venetian Economy* (London, 1968), pp. 88-105, 106-26; Brian Pullan, "Wage-Earners and the Venetian Economy, 1550-1630," in Pullan, *Crisis and Change*, pp. 146-74; James C. Davis, *Decline of the Venetian Nobility*, pp. 15-129.

17   The quotation is from Domenico Sella, "Industrial Production in Seven-

teenth Century Italy: A Reappraisal," *Explorations in Entrepreneurial History* 6 (1969), 247; Carlo Cipolla, "The Economic Decline of Italy," in Pullan, *Crisis and Change,* pp. 127-45.

18 The quote is from Jaime Vicens Vives, *An Economic History of Spain* (Princeton, 1969), p. 418; J. H. Elliott, "The Decline of Spain," *P. & P.* 20 (1961), 52-75; Earl J. Hamilton, "The Decline of Spain," in E. M. Carus-Wilson, *Essays in Economic History,* vol. I (New York, 1966), pp. 215-26; Pierre Vilar, "The Age of Don Quixote," in Earle, *Essays,* pp. 100-12.

Notes to Chapter 2

1 Studies that emphasize these interrelationships include Barrington Moore, Jr., *Social Origins of Dictatorship and Democracy* (Boston, 1966); Immanuel Wallerstein, *The Modern World-System, Capitalist Agriculture and the Origins of the European World-Economy in the Sixteenth Century* (New York, 1974); Otto Brunner, *Neue Wege der Verfassungs-und Sozialgeschichte* (Göttingen, 1968), chap. X.

2 An excellent introduction to the spatial patterns of European agriculture is available in C. T. Smith, *An Historical Geography of Western Europe before 1800* (London, 1967), pp. 191-342, 479-542. See also Fernand Braudel, *The Mediterranean, and the Mediterranean World in the Age of Philip II* (New York, 1972), pp. 25-102.

3 This discussion is based on the procedures employed in B. H. Slicher van Bath, "De oogstopbrengsten van verschillende gewassen, voornamelijk granen, in verhouding tot het saaizaad, ca. 810-1820," *A. A. G. Bijdragen* 9 (1963), 29-126, substantially translated as "The Yields of Different Crops (mainly cereals) in Relation to the Seed, ca. 810-1820," *Acta Historiae Neerlandica* 2 (1967), 26-106. F. B. McArdle, "Altopascio, 1587-1784: A Study in Tuscan Rural Society," Ph.D. diss., University of Virginia, 1974, pp. 98-99; E. Le Roy Ladurie, *Les Paysans de Languedoc* (Paris, 1966), p. 640; M. Morineau, "Was There an Agricultural Revolution in 18th Century France," in Rondo Cameron, ed., *Essays in French Economic History* (Homewood, Ill., 1970), pp. 170-82.

4 Smith, *Historical Geography,* pp. 506-18; P. Wagret, *Les Polders* (Paris, 1959); H. C. Darby, *The Draining of the Fens* (Cambridge, 1940); A. M. van der Woude, *Het Noorderkwartier,* vol. I (Wageningen, 1972), pp. 46-60.

5 For more detailed descriptions of agricultural techniques see B. H. Slicher van Bath, *The Agrarian History of Western Europe, 500-1850* (London, 1963), part III; and Eric Kerridge, *The Agricultural Revolution* (London, 1967), pp. 181-325.

6 The literature on the common fields and enclosures, particularly in England, is enormous. Some recent works include Joan Thirsk, "The Common Fields," *P. & P.* 29 (1964), 3-25; M. A. Havinden, "Agricul-

tural Progress in Open-field Oxfordshire," *Ag. H. R.* 9 (1961), 73-83; Donald N. McCloskey, "The Enclosure of Open Fields: Preface to a study of its impact on the efficiency of English agriculture in the eighteenth century," *J. Ec. H.* 32 (1972), 15-35; Charles Parain, "The Evolution of Agricultural Techniques," in *The Cambridge Economic History of Europe,* 2nd ed., vol. I (Cambridge, 1966), p. 138.

7　The anthropologist Eric R. Wolf defines peasants as "rural cultivators whose surpluses are transferred to a dominant group of rulers that uses the surplus both to underwrite its own standard of living and to distribute the remainder to [non-agricultural] groups . . ." Later he emphasizes that "it is only . . . when the cultivator becomes subject to the demands and sanctions of powerholders outside his social stratum that we can appropriately speak of peasantry." Eric R. Wolf, *Peasants* (Englewood Cliffs, N. J., 1966), pp. 3-4, 11.

8　A clear review of peasant obligations in France is available in Pierre Goubert, *The Ancien Regime,* vol. I (New York, 1973), pp. 122-34. For Germany and eastern Europe, where labor services were of great importance, see F.-W. Henning, *Dienste und Abgaben der Bauern im 18. Jahrhundert* (Stuttgart, 1969). The level of tithes, rent, and seigneurial dues could vary for many reasons, but Henning shows that a broadly consistent pattern of total payments existed: the total burden *per acre* fell as one moved east from the Low Countries while the burden expressed as a percentage of *output* per acre rose.

9　Eric R. Wolf, *Peasant Wars in the Twentieth Century* (New York, 1969), p. xiv; George M. Foster, "What Is a Peasant," in Jack M. Potter et al., *Peasant Society, a reader* (Boston, 1967), pp. 2-14; Moore, *Social Origins,* chap. VII.

10　David R. Ringrose, "The Government and the Carters in Spain, 1476-1700," *Ec. H. R.* 22 (1969), 45-57; Julius Klein, *The Mesta* (Cambridge, Mass., 1920); Jaime Vicens Vives, *An Economic History of Spain* (Princeton, 1969), pp., 422-27.

11　James Casey, "Moriscos and the Depopulation of Valencia," *P. & P.* 50 (1971), 19-40; Pierre Vilar, *La Catalogne dans l'Espagne modern,* 3 vols. (Paris, 1962), vol. I, part III; Smith, *Historical Geography,* pp. 528-39. For a review of the reform efforts of the Bourbon monarchy in the eighteenth century see Richard Herr, *The Eighteenth Century Revolution in Spain* (Princeton, 1958), pp. 86-119.

12　Denis Mack Smith, *A History of Sicily; Medieval Sicily, 800-1715* (London, 1968); Rosario Villari, *La revolta antispagnola a Napoli: le origini (1581-1647)* (Bari, 1967), pp. 61-2.

13　Braudel, *Mediterranean,* p. 427; Daniele Beltrami, *La penetrazione economica dei veneziani in Terraferma* (Venice, 1961); S. J. Woolf, "Venice and the Terraferma: Problems of the Change from Commercial to Landed Activities," in Brian Pullan, ed., *Crisis and Change in the Venetian Economy* (London, 1968), pp. 175-203.

14　J. M. Roberts, "Lombardy," in Albert Goodwin, ed., *The European*

Nobility in the Eighteenth Century (New York, 1967), pp. 83-101; Domenico Sella, "The Two Faces of the Lombard Economy in the Seventeenth Century," in Frederick Krantz and Paul M. Hohenberg, eds., *Failed Transitions to Modern Industrial Society* (Montreal, 1975), pp. 11-15; A. De Maddalena, "Il mondo rurale italiano nel Cinque e nel Seicento," *Rivista Storica Italiana* 76 (1964), 349-426.

15 Jerzy Topolski, "Economic Decline in Poland from the Sixteenth to the Eighteenth Centuries," in Peter Earle, ed., *Essays in European Economic History* (Oxford, 1974), pp. 127-42; M. Malowist, "Poland, Russia and Western Trade in the Fifteenth to the Seventeenth Centuries," *P. & P.* 13 (1958), 26-41; M. Malowist, *Croissance et Regression en Europe, XIVe-XVIIIe Siècles* (Paris, 1972); Anton Maczak, "Export of Grain and the Problem of Distribution of National Income in the Years 1550-1650," *Acta Poloniae Historica* 18 (1968), 75-98; Anton Maczak, "The Social Distribution of Landed Property in Poland from the 16th to the 18th Century," *Third International Conference of Economic History*, vol. I (Paris, 1968), pp. 455-69; F. L. Carsten, *The Origins of Prussia* (Oxford, 1954); Hans Rosenburg, "The Rise of the Junkers in Brandenburg-Prussia, 1410-1653," *A. H. R.* 49 (1943-44), 1-22, 228-242.

16 A. Nielsen, *Dänische Wirtschaftsgeschichte* (Jena, 1933); Aksel Lassen, "The Population of Denmark in 1660," *Scan. Ec. H. R.* 13 (1965), 1-30; E. Ladewig Petersen, "The Crisis of the Danish Nobility, 1580-1660," in Marc Ferro, ed., *Social Historians in Contemporary France, Essays from Annales* (New York, 1972), pp. 157-79.

17 Diedrich Saalfeld, *Bauernwirtschaft und Gutsbetrieb in der vorindustriellen Zeit* (Stuttgart, 1960), p. 132; Walter Achilles, *Vermögensverhältnisse braunschweigischer Bauerhöfe im 17. und 18. Jahrhundert* (Stuttgart, 1965); Friedrich Lütge, *Geschichte der deutschen Agrarverfassung vom frühen Mittelalter bis zum 19. Jahrhundert* (Stuttgart, 1963), pp. 134-54; Wilhelm Abel, *Geschichte der deutschen Landwirtschaft vom frühen Mittelalter bis zum 19. Jahrhundert* (Stuttgart, 1962); Klaus Winkler, *Landwirtschaft und Agrarverfassung im Fürstentum Osnabrück nach dem Dreissigjahrigen Kriege* (Stuttgart, 1959); Eberhard Weis, "Ergebnisse eines Vergleichs de grundherrschaftlichen Strukturen Deutschlands und Frankreiches vom 13. bis zum Ausgang des 18. Jahrhunderts," *V. S. W. G.* 57 (1970), 1-14. Weis estimates that as much as 90 percent of the land was owned or held in hereditary leases by the west German peasants in the seventeenth century. This figure is far higher than can be found in any other society.

18 Karlheinz Blaschke, *Bevölkerungsgeschichte von Sachsen bis zur Industriellen Revolution* (Weimar, 1967), pp. 181-91; Martin Kuhlmann, "Bevölkerungsgeographie des Landes Lippe," *Forschungen zur deutschen Landeskunde* 76 (1954); G. Hanke, "Zur Sozialstruktur der ländlichen Siedlung Altbeyern im 17. und 18. Jahrhundert," in *Gessellschaft und Herrschaft* (Munich, 1969), pp. 219-69; F.-W. Henning,

"Die Betriebsgrössenstruktur der mitteleuropäischen Landwirtschaft im 18. Jahrhundert und ihr Einfluss auf die Ländlichen Einkommensverhältnisse," *Zeitschrift für Agrargeschichte und Agrarsoziologie* 17 (1969), 171-93.

19 Roland Mousnier, *Peasant Uprisings in Seventeenth Century France, Russia, and China* (New York, 1970), pp. 38-39. On the level of taxation and the supply of money see Frank C. Spooner, *The International Economy and Monetary Movements in France, 1493-1725* (Cambridge, Mass., 1972) and Jean Meuvret, "Monetary Circulation and the use of Coinage in Sixteenth and Seventeenth Century France," in Peter Earle, ed., *Essays,* pp. 89-99, and Boris Porchnev, *Les Soulèvements Populaires en France de 1623 à 1648* (Paris, 1963).

20 Morineau, "Was there an Agricultural Revolution"; Le Roy Ladurie, *Paysans,* especially final chapter; Jean Jacquart, "French Agriculture in the Seventeenth Century," in Earle, *Essays,* pp. 165-84.

21 Marc Bloch, *French Rural History, An Essay on its Basic Characteristics* (Berkeley, 1970), pp. 112-49. For case studies see Robert Forster, *The Nobility of Toulouse in the Eighteenth Century* (Baltimore, 1960) and *The House of Saulx-Tavanes; Versailles and Burgundy, 1700-1830* (Baltimore, 1971); Pierre Deyon, "A Propos des Rapports entre la Noblesse Française et la Monarchie Absolute Pendant la Première Moité du XVIIe siècle," *Revue Historique* 231 (1964), 341-56; Pierre de Saint Jacob, *Les Paysans de la Bourgogne du Nord* (Paris, 1960); Pierre Goubert, "Le Paysan et la Terre: Seigneurie, Tenure, Exploitation," in Ernest Labrousse, et al., eds., *Histoire Economique et Sociale de la France,* vol. II, *1660-1789* (Paris, 1970), pp. 119-58.

22 Moore, *Social Origins,* p. 47. For an account of the growth of this sector see R. Dion, *Histoire de la vigne et du vin en France des origines au 19e siècle* (Paris, 1959).

23 Pierre Goubert, "The French Peasantry of the Seventeenth Century: A Regional Example," *P. & P.* 10 (1956) and in Trevor Aston, ed., *Crisis in Europe, 1560-1660* (London, 1965), pp. 155-64; Bloch, *French Rural History,* pp. 193-96; A. Soboul, "The French Rural Community in the Eighteenth and Nineteenth Century," *P. & P.* 10 (1956), 283-307 and "A propos d'une thèse recente sur le mouvement paysan dans la Révolution Française," *Annales Historique de la Révolution Française* 45 (1973), 85-101; Robert Forster, "Obstacles to Agricultural Growth in Eighteenth Century France," *A. H. R.* 75 (1970), 1600-15.

24 Jan de Vries, *The Dutch Rural Economy in the Golden Age* (New Haven, 1974), pp. 119-74, 224-35. For a review of the medieval heritage see Jan de Vries, "On the Modernity of the Dutch Republic," *J. Ec. H.* 33 (1973), 191-202.

25 B. H. Slicher van Bath, "The Rise of Intensive Husbandry in the Low Countries," in J. S. Bromley and E. H. Kossmann, ed., *Britain and the Netherlands* (London, 1960). Tobacco cultivation, it should be noted, was not confined to the New World. Competing with the land-intensive

cultivation of Virginia and the West Indies were small, labor-intensive farms that relied on access to plentiful manure supplies to grow successfully this soil-depleting crop. The Rhine valley of the Dutch Republic and Germany, Flanders, and several enclaves in France (where production was generally forbidden for the protection of the State Tobacco Monopoly) produced many millions of pounds and flourished particularly in the first half of the eighteenth century. Jacob Price, *France and the Chesapeake,* 2 vols. (Ann Arbor, Mich., 1973).

26 This is a central assertion of Wallerstein, *Modern World-System,* pp. 87-97.

27 Malowist, *Croissance et Regression,* pp. 131-36; Carsten, *Origins of Prussia,* pp. 111-16, 149-64. For an analysis of British grain exports see David Ormrod, "Anglo-Dutch Commerce, 1700-1760," pp. 204-45, Ph.D. diss., Cambridge University, 1973 and "Dutch Commercial Decline and British Growth in the Late Seventeenth and Early Eighteenth Centuries," in Krantz and Hohenberg, *Failed Transitions,* pp. 36-43.

28 J. A. Faber, *Drie eeuwen Friesland* (Wageningen, 1972), pp. 126-223; A. M. van der Woude, *Het Noorderkwartier* (Wageningen, 1972), pp. 593-601; C. Baars, *De geschiedenis van de landbouw in de Beijerlanden* (Wageningen, 1973), pp. 203-04.

29 That is, their wage was the output of the family farm divided by the number of family members, rather than the portion of total output attributable to the labor of an additional (marginal) worker. Franklin Mendels, "Agriculture and Peasant Industry in Eighteenth Century Flanders," in W. N. Parker and E. L. Jones, eds., *European Peasants and their Markets* (Princeton, 1975).

30 Paul Lindemans, *Geschiedenis van de landbouw in België,* 2 vols. (Antwerp, 1952); Chr. Vanderbroeke, "De graanpolitiek in de Oostenrijkse Nederlanden," *Revue belge de philologie et d'histoire* 45 (1967), 369-87.

31 R. H. Tawney, *The Agrarian Problem in the Sixteenth Century* (London, 1912); Lawrence Stone, *The Crisis of the Aristocracy, 1558-1641* (Oxford, 1965).

32 F. M. L. Thompson, "The Social Distribution of Landed Property in England since the Sixteenth Century," *Ec. H. R.* 19 (1966), 505-17; H. J. Habbakuk, "English Landownership: 1660-1740," *Ec. H. R.* 10 (1940), 2-17; Alan Everett, "Social Mobility in Early Modern England," *P. & P.* 33 (1966), 56-73; Lawrence Stone, "Social Mobility in England: 1500-1700," *P. & P.* 33 (1966), 16-55; Mary E. Finch, *The Wealth of Five Northamptonshire Families, 1540-1640* (Northamptonshire, 1956), preface; H. J. Habbakuk, "The Land Market in the Eighteenth Century," in Bromley and Kossmann, eds., *Britain and the Netherlands;* G. E. Mingay, "The Size of Farms in the Eighteenth Century," *Ec. H. R.* 16 (1962), 469-88; Joan Thirsk, "The Restoration Land Settlement," *Journal of Modern History* 26 (1954), 315-28.

33 E. L. Jones, "Agriculture and Economic Growth in England,

1660-1750: Agricultural Change," *J. Ec. H.* 25 (1965), 1-18, also in E. L. Jones, ed., *Agriculture and Economic Growth in England, 1650-1815* (London, 1967), pp. 152-71; G. E. Mingay, *English Landed Society in the Eighteenth Century* (London, 1962) and "The Agricultural Depression, 1730-1750," *Ec. H. R.* 8 (1956), 323-38.

34 Jones, "Agricultural and Economic Growth"; Joan Thirsk, *English Peasant Farming* (London, 1957); Kerridge, *Agricultural Revolution*, pp. 181-221, 295-310; J. D. Chambers, "The Vale of Trent, 1670-1800: A Regional Study of Economic Change," *Ec. H. R.*, supplement no. 3 (1957).

35 Joan Thirsk, "Industries in the Countryside," in F. J. Fisher, ed., *Essays in the Economic and Social History of Tudor and Stuart England* (London, 1961), pp. 70-88 and "Seventeenth Century Agriculture and Social Change," *Ag. H. R.* 18 (1970), 148-77.

36 Ormrod, "Anglo-Dutch Commerce," p. 406.

37 W. G. Hoskins, *The Midland Peasant* (New York, 1965), pp. 198-99.

Notes to Chapter 3

1 Barry Supple, *Commercial Crisis and Change in England, 1600-1642* (Cambridge, 1959), pp. 33-51; Astrid Friis, *Alderman Cockayne's Project and the Cloth Trade* (Copenhagen, 1927); Carlo Cipolla, "The Diffusion of Innovations in Early Modern Europe," *C. S. S. H.* 14 (1972), 46-52; W. C. Scoville, *The Persecution of the Huguenots and French Economic Development, 1680-1720* (Berkeley, 1960).

2 Gaston Zeller, "Industry in France before Colbert," in Rondo Cameron, *Essays in French Economic History* (Homewood, Ill., 1970), pp. 128-39; C. W. Cole, *Colbert and a Century of French Mercantilism*, 2nd ed. (London, 1964).

3 W. H. B. Court, *The Rise of the Midland Industries, 1600-1838* (Oxford, 1938), pp. 103-04; R. Patterson, "Spinning and Weaving," in C. Singer et al., eds., *History of Technology*, 3 vols. (Oxford, 1954-58); W. Endrei, *L'évolution des techniques du filage et du tissage du Moyen Age à la Révolution Industrielle* (Paris, 1968).

4 N. W. Posthumus, *De geschiedenis van de Leidsche lakenindustrie*, 3 vols. (The Hague, 1908-39); A. M. van der Woude, *Het Noorderkwartier*, vol. II (Wageningen, 1972), pp. 315-29, 457-507; J. G. van Dillen, *Van rijkdom en regenten* (The Hague, 1970), pp. 175-217.

5 Emile Coornaert, "French Guilds under the Old Regime," in Cameron, *Essays*, pp. 123-27; Herbert Kisch, "The Growth Deterrents of a Medieval Heritage; the Aachen Area Woollen Trades before 1790," *J. Ec. H.* 24 (1964), 513-37. For a classic analysis of industrial organization see George Unwin, *Industrial Organization in the Sixteenth and Seventeenth Centuries* (London, 1904); for a description of the persisting role of guilds in small cities see Mack Walker, *The German Home Towns, 1648-1871* (Ithaca, N. Y., 1971).

6 The classic description of the putting-out system and its growth in England remains Paul Mantoux, *The Industrial Revolution in the Eighteenth Century* (London, 1928), chap. I; for modern interpretations from the economic and sociological perspectives, respectively, see Franklin Mendels, "Proto-Industrialization, the First Stage of Industrialization," *J. Ec. H.* 32 (1972), 241-61; Rudolf Braun, *Industrialisierung und Volksleben: Die Veränderungen der Lebensformen in einem ländlichen Industriegebiet vor 1800* (Zurich, 1960). The special character of the household economy is analyzed in Jan de Vries, *The Dutch Rural Economy in the Golden Age* (New Haven, 1974), chap. I, and A. N. Chayanov, *The Theory of Peasant Economy* (Homewood, Ill., 1966).

7 S. C. Regtdoorzee Greup-Roldanus, *Geschiedenis der Haarlemer bleekerijen* (The Hague, 1936); Jan Craeybeckx, "Les industries d'exportation dans les villes Flamandes au XVIIe siècle, particulièrement à Gand et à Bruges," *Studi in Onore di Amintore Fanfani*, vol. IV (Milan, 1962), pp. 411-68; Herbert Kisch, "From Monopoly to Progress: The Early Growth of the Wupper Valley Textile Trades," (unpublished paper).

8 Hermann Kellenbenz, "Rural Industries in the West from the End of the Middle Ages to the Eighteenth Century," in Peter Earle, ed., *Essays in European Economic History* (Oxford, 1974), p. 45-88; Max Barkhausen, "Government Control and Free Enterprise in Western Germany and the Low Countries during the Eighteenth Century," in Earle, *Essays,* pp. 212-73; Herve Hasquin, *Une mutation: le 'Pays de Charleroi' aux XVIIe et XVIIIe siècles* (Brussels, 1971); Court, *Midland Industries.*

9 Carlo Cipolla, "The Economic Decline of Italy," in Brian Pullan, ed., *Crisis and Change in the Venetian Economy* (London, 1968), pp. 127-45; Domenico Sella, "The Rise and Fall of the Venetian Woollen Industry," in Pullan, *Crisis and Change,* pp. 106-26, and "Industrial Production in Seventeenth Century Italy: A Reappraisal," *Explorations in Entrepreneurial History* 6 (1969), 235-53; Ruggiero Romano, "A Florence au XVIIe siècle; Industries textiles et conjoncture," *Annales* 7 (1952), 508-12.

10 Charles Wilson, "Cloth Production and International Competition in the Seventeenth Century," *Ec. H. R.* 13 (1960), 209-21; Supple, *Crisis and Change,* 135-62; Pierre Deyon, "Variations de la production textile au XVIe et XVIIe siècles," *Annales* 18 (1963), 39-55.

11 Franklin Mendels, "Agriculture and Peasant Industry in Eighteenth Century Flanders," in W. N. Parker and E. L. Jones, eds., *European Peasants and their Markets* (Princeton, 1975); Conrad Gill, *The Rise of the Irish Linen Industry* (London, 1926); Charles Wilson, *England's Apprenticeship, 1603-1763* (London, 1965), p. 306.

12 Phyllis Deane and W. A. Cole, *British Economic Growth, 1688-1959* (Cambridge, 1962), p. 51; Domenico Sella, "The Two Faces of the

Lombard Economy in the Seventeenth Century," in Frederick Krantz and Paul M. Hohenberg, eds., *Failed Transitions to Modern Industrial Society* (Montreal, 1975), pp. 11-15; J. Marczewski, "Some Aspects of the Economic Growth of France, 1660-1958," *Economic Development and Cultural Change* 9 (1961), 369-86.

13 P. W. Klein, *De Trippen in de 17e eeuw. Een studie over het ondernemergsgedrag op de Hollandse stapelmarkt* (Assen, 1965); E. W. Dahlgren, *Louis de Geer* (Uppsala, 1923); Carlo Cipolla, *Guns, Sails and Empires* (New York, 1965); B. Boëthius, "Swedish Iron and Steel, 1600-1955," *Scan. Ec. H. R.* 6 (1958), 144-75.

14 J. Everaert, *De Internationale en koloniale handel der Vlaamse firmas' te Cadiz, 1670-1700* (Ghent, 1973), pp. 433-40.

15 Boethius, "Iron and Steel," p. 149-51; Rolf Sprandel, "La production de fer au Moyen Age," *Annales* 24 (1969), 311-12; K. G. Hildebrand, "Foreign Markets for Swedish Iron in the 18th Century," *Scan. Ec. H. R.* 6 (1958), 3-52; Court, *Midland Industries,* p. 133.

16 Rudolf Braun, "Early Industrialization and Demographic Changes in the Canton of Zurich in Comparison with English and German Cases," (unpublished manuscript); Mendels, "Peasant Industry;" B. H. Slicher van Bath, *Een samenleving onder spanning; geschiedenis van het platteland in Overijssel* (Assen, 1957), chap. VI; Karlheinz Blaschke, *Bevölkerungsgeschichte von Sachsen bis zur Industriellen Revolution* (Weimar, 1967), pp. 190-91. Also see Wolfram Fischer, "Rural Industrialization and Population Change," *C. S. S. H.* 15 (1973), 158-70; E. L. Jones, "The Agricultural Origins of Industry," *P. & P.* 40 (1968), 58-71; Joan Thirsk, "Industries in the Countryside," in F. J. Fisher, ed., *Essays in the Economic and Social History of Tudor and Stuart England* (London, 1961), pp. 70-88.

17 David G. Hey, "A Dual Economy in South Yorkshire," *Ag. H. R.* 17 (1969), 118; J. D. Chambers, "The Vale of Trent, 1670-1800: A Regional Study of Economic Change," *Ec. H. R.,* supplement no. 3 (1957), pp. 53-55. Hasquin, *Le Pays de Charleroi,* pp. 290-91; Paul Duprez, "The Demographic Development of Flanders in the Eighteenth Century," in D. V. Glass and D. E. C. Eversley, eds., *Population in History* (London, 1965), pp. 608-30.

Notes to Chapter 4

1 For an interesting if overstated argument on the importance of the sixteenth century "world-system" see I. Wallerstein, *The Modern World-System* (New York, 1974).

2 Huguette and Pierre Chaunu, *Séville et l'Atlantique (1504-1650),* 11 vols. (Paris, 1955-60); Woodrow Borah, *New Spain's Century of Depression* (Berkeley, 1951); Engel Sluiter, "Dutch-Spanish Rivalry in the Caribbean Area, 1594-1609," *Hispanic-American Historical Review* 28 (1948), 165-96.

3 Violet Barbour, "Dutch and English Merchant Shipping in the 17th Century," *Ec. H. R.* 2 (1930), 261-90; Gary Walton, "Sources of Productivity Change in American Colonial Shipping, 1675-1775," *Ec. H. R.* 20 (1967), 67-68 for a confirmation of the unassailed low-cost position of Dutch shipping in the seventeenth century.

4 W. Vogel, *Forschungen und Verusche zur geschichte des Mittelalters und der Neuzeit* (Jena, 1915), p. 319; Ralph Davis, *The Rise of the English Shipping Industry in the 17th and 18th Centuries* (London, 1962).

5 For reviews of Dutch commerce at its peak see Violet Barbour, *Capitalism in Amsterdam in the Seventeenth Century* (Ann Arbor, 1963); Charles R. Boxer, *The Dutch Seaborne Empire, 1600-1800* (New York, 1965); J. G. van Dillen, *Van rijkdom en regenten* (The Hague, 1970), pp. 15-174; A. E. Christiansen, *Dutch Trade to the Baltic about 1600* (Copenhagen, 1941); Pierre Jeannin, *L'europe du Nord-Ouest et du Nord aux XVIIe et XVIIIe siècles* (Paris, 1969).

6 For accounts of these trade wars and their economic impact see Charles Wilson, *Profit and Power, A Study of England and the Dutch Wars* (London, 1957); J. E. Farrell, "The Navigation Acts of 1651, the First Anglo-Dutch War, and the London Merchant Community," *Ec. H. R.* 16 (1964), 439-54; G. N. Clark, *War and Society in the Seventeenth Century* (Cambridge, 1958).

7 Frederick C. Lane, "National Wealth and Protection Costs," in J. D. Clarkson and T. C. Cochran, eds., *War as a Social Institution* (New York, 1941); P. Boissonnade and P. Charliat, *Colbert et la Compagnie de Commerce du Nord, 1661-1689* (Paris, 1930); Pierre Goubert, *Louis XIV and Twenty Million Frenchmen* (New York, 1970), pp. 131-41.

8 Barry Supple, *Commercial Crisis and Change in England, 1600-1642* (Cambridge, 1959), pp. 225-53; F. J. Fisher, "London's Export Trade in the Early Seventeenth Century," *Ec. H. R.* 3 (1950), 151-61; Richard T. Rapp, "The Unmaking of the Mediterranean Trade Hegemony: International Trade Rivalry and the Commercial Revolution," *J. Ec. H.* 35 (1975), 499-525.

9 Ralph Davis, "English Foreign Trade, 1660-1700," *Ec. H. R.* 7 (1954), 150-66; Charles Wilson, *England's Apprenticeship, 1603-1763* (London, 1965), pp. 160-84.

10 See for instance E. H. Hobsbawm, "The General Crisis of the European Economy in the Seventeenth Century," in Trevor Aston, ed., *Crisis in Europe, 1560-1660* (London, 1965), p. 47, where he speaks of colonial trade as a "forced draught" fanning the flames of English industry.

11 For an overview of these organizations see E. L. J. Coornaert, "European Economic Institutions in the New World; the Chartered Companies," in *Cambridge Economic History of Europe*, vol. IV (Cambridge, 1967), pp. 220-74. For a comparison of Portuguese and Dutch practices, see Niels Steengaard, *Carracks, Caravans, and Companies: The Structural Crisis in the European-Asian Trade in the Early 17th Century* (Copenhagen, 1973).

12 Niels Steengaard, "European Shipping to Asia, 1497-1700," *Scan. Ec. H. R.* 18 (1970), 1-10; C. R. Boxer, *The Portuguese Seaborne Empire, 1415-1820* (New York, 1969), appendix I; I. J. Brugmans, "De Oostindische Compagnie en de welvaart in de Republiek," *Tijdschrift voor Geschiedenis* 61 (1948), 18; Bal Krishna, *Commercial Relations between India and England (1601-1757)* (London, 1924). The tonnage figures are calculated under the assumption that East India vessels averaged 450 tons, except for Portuguese vessels, which were some 50 percent larger. The calculation of VOC manpower is a product of a computerized study of the VOC being carried out by J. R. Bruijn of Leiden University.

13 Theodore K. Rabb, *Enterprise and Empire: Merchants and Gentry in the Expansion of England, 1575-1630* (Cambridge, Mass., 1967).

14 Kristof Glamann, *Dutch-Asiatic Trade, 1620-1740* (Copenhagen, 1958); R. N. Chaudhuri, *The English East India Company, Study of an Early Joint-Stock Company, 1600-1640* (London, 1965) and "Treasure and Trade Balances: The East India Company's Export Trade, 1660-1720," *Ec. H. R.* 21 (1968), 480-502.

15 C. R. Boxer, *The Dutch in Brazil, 1624-1654* (Oxford, 1957); J. G. van Dillen, "De West-Indische Compagnie, het Calvinisme en de politiek," *Tijdschrift voor Geschiedenis* 74 (1961), 145-71; H. Terpstra, "Nederlands gouden tijd aan de Goudkust," *Tijdschrift voor Geschiedenis* 73 (1960); J. A. Williamson, *The Caribbee Islands Under the Proprietary Patents* (London, 1926).

16 Pieter Emmer, "The History of the Dutch Slave Trade, A Bibliographical Survey," *J. Ec. H.* 32 (1972), 728-47; Johannes Postma, "The Dutch Participation in the African Slave Trade," Ph.D. diss., Michigan State University, 1970; Cornelis Ch. Goslinga, *The Dutch in the Caribbean and on the Wild Coast, 1580-1680* (Assen, 1971); W. S. Unger, "Bijdragen tot de geschiedenis van de Nederlandse slavenhandel, II," *Economisch-Historisch Jaarboek* 28 (1958-59), 3-148.

17 Van Dillen, *Rijkdom en regenten,* pp. 379-80; K. G. Davies, *The Royal African Company* (London, 1957); John Carswell, *The South Sea Bubble* (Stanford, 1960), pp. 65-66; Unger, "Nederlandse slavenhandel," pp. 86-91. See also Roger Anstey, *The Atlantic Slave Trade and British Abolition 1760-1810* (London, 1974).

18 Robert P. Thomas, "The Sugar Colonies of the Old Empire: Profit or Loss for Great Britain?" *Ec. H. R.* 21 (1968), 30-45; Robert P. Thomas and Richard N. Bean, "The Fishers of Men: The Profits of the Slave Trade," *J. Ec. H.* 34 (1974), 885-914; Richard S. Dunn, *Sugar and Slaves: The Rise of the Planter Class in the English West Indies, 1624-1713* (Chapel Hill, N.C., 1972); Richard B. Sheridan, *Sugar and Slavery: An Economic History of the British West Indies, 1623-1775* (Baltimore, 1974). Sheridan calculates the rate of return on the very best sugar land in the mid-eighteenth century at up to 8.5 percent. See also Michael Craton and James Walvin, *A Jamaican Plantation: The History of Worthy Park, 1670-1970* (Toronto, 1970). Only the first

generation of this plantation's history enjoyed great profits. These profits were plowed into the expansion of the estate, which soon "staggered under the weight of mortgages."

19 Glamann, *Dutch-Asiatic Trade,* pp. 11, 244-65.

20 H. E. S. Fisher, "Anglo-Portuguese Trade, 1700-1770," *Ec. H. R.* 16 (1963), 219-33; V. Magalhaes Godinho, "Flottes de sucre et flottes de l'or (1670-1770)," *Annales* 5 (1950), 184-97; C. R. Boxer, *The Golden Age of Brazil, 1695-1750* (Berkeley, 1962), and *Portuguese Seaborne Empire.*

21 A. H. John, "Aspects of English Economic Growth in the First Half of the Eighteenth Century," *Economica* 28 (1961), 176-90; Paul Bairoch, "Commerce et Révolution Industrielle," *Annales* 28 (1973), 557.

Notes to Chapter 5

1 Karlheinz Blaschke, *Bevölkerungsgeschichte von Sachsen bis zur Industriellen Revolution* (Weimar, 1967); Martin Kuhlmann, "Bevölkeringsgeographie des Landes Lippe," *Forschungen zur Deutschen Landeskunde* 76 (1954); Julius Beloch, *Bevölkerungsgeschichte Italiens,* 3 vols. (Berlin, 1937-1961); Jorge Nadal, *Historia de la población española (siglos XVI à XX)* (Barcelona, 1966).

2 Aksel Lassen, "The Population of Denmark, 1660-1960," *Scan. Ec. H. R.* 14 (1966), 134-57; Reinholt Dorwart, *The Prussian Welfare State before 1740* (Cambridge, Mass., 1971), pp. 231-35; J. G. Simms, "Dublin in 1685," *Irish Historical Studies* 14 (1964-65), 212-26; Jacques Levron, *Versailles, Ville Royal* (Paris, 1964), pp. 94-5.

3 Colonial urban growth was apparently concentrated in two periods - one ending in the third quarter of the seventeenth century (probably earlier in South America), another beginning around 1750. The demand for European goods emanating from colonial urban growth has yet to be given careful attention. See, however, Ronald Hoffman and Carville Earle, "Urban Systems in Colonial America: A Perspective," (unpublished paper) and Richard M. Morse, "Trends and Patterns of Latin American Urbanization, 1750-1920," *C. S. S. H* 16 (1974), 416-47.

4 These figures are a product of research now being carried out by the author. "Europe" refers to the area east of Russia and the Ottoman Empire; "northern Europe" designates Europe minus Portugal, Spain, and Italy.

5 Jan de Vries, *The Dutch Rural Economy in the Golden Age* (New Haven, 1974), pp. 100-01; E. A. Wrigley, "A Simple Model of London's Importance in Changing English Society and Economy, 1650-1750," *P. & P.* 37 (1967), 44-70; Roger Mols, *Introduction à la démographie historique des villes d'Europe du 14ᵉ au 18ᵉ siècle,* vol. II (Louvain, 1955), p. 513; M. Reinhard and A. Armengand, *Histoire générale de la population mondiale* (Paris, 1961), pp. 244, 297.

6 Johann Peter Süssmilch, *Die göttliche Ordnung in den veränderungen*

des menschlichen Geschlechtes. . . , 3 vols., (Berlin, 1775), vol. I, pp. 73-80; Gregory King, *Essay upon the Probable Methods of Making a People Gainers in the Balance of Trade* (London, 1699), p. 8. See also Eli Hecksher, "Swedish Population Trends before the Industrial Revolution," *Ec. H. R.* 2 (1950), 266-77; de Vries, *Dutch Rural Economy,* pp. 115-17.

7 Louis Henry, "The Population of France in the Eighteenth Century," in D. V. Glass and D. E. C. Eversley, *Population in History* (London, 1965), pp. 443-44; C. De Tournon, *Etudes statistiques sur Rome et la partie occidentale des Etats Romains* (Paris, 1831), p. 244; Dorothy George, *London Life in the Eighteenth Century* (London and New York, 1925), p. 118; Leon Bernard, *The Emerging City: Paris in the Age of Louis XIV* (Durham, N. C., 1970), p. 286.

8 Wrigley, "A Simple Model."

9 For further discussions of urban provisionment see A. B. Hibbert, "The Economic Policies of Towns," in *Cambridge Economic History of Europe,* vol. III (Cambridge, 1965); and Charles Tilly, "Food Supply and Public Order in Modern Europe," in Charles Tilly, ed., *The Formation of National States in Western Europe* (Princeton, 1975).

10 Fernand Braudel, *The Mediterranean and the Mediterranean World in the Age of Philip II,* vol. I (New York, 1972), pp. 570-606; Denis Mack Smith, *A History of Sicily, Medieval Sicily, 800-1715* (London, 1968).

11 Lucien Febvre, "Preface," to Huguette and Pierre Chaunu, *Séville et l'Atlantique (1504-1650)* (Paris, 1955), vol. I, p. xiii.

12 Abbot Payson Usher, *The History of the Grain Trade in France, 1400-1710* (Cambridge, Mass., 1913), p. 60.

13 Alan Everitt, "The Marketing of Agricultural Produce," in Joan Thirsk, ed., *The Agrarian History of England and Wales,* vol. IV, *1500-1640* (Cambridge, 1967), pp. 466-592 and "The Food Market of the English Town, 1660-1760," *Third International Conference of Economic History,* Munich, 1965 (Paris, 1968), pp. 57-71; N. S. B. Gras, *The Evolution of the English Corn Market* (Cambridge, Mass., 1915).

14 David Ringrose, *Transportation and Economic Stagnation in Spain, 1750-1850* (Durham, N. C., 1970), pp. 22, 39-56.

15 De Vries, *Dutch Rural Economy,* pp. 202-04; *Tegenwoordige Staat van Friesland* (Leeuwarden, 1763), pp. 58-59; B. H. Slicher van Bath, *Een samenleving onder spanning* (Assen, 1957), p. 220.

16 The basic studies on the rise of coal and coal-using industries in this period remain John U. Nef, *The Rise of the British Coal Industry* (London, 1932) and *Industry and Government in France and England, 1540-1640* (Ithaca, N. Y., 1957).

17 From "Upon the Coal Pits about Newcastle upon Tine," (1651), quoted in Charles Wilson, *England's Apprenticeship, 1603-1763* (London, 1965), p. 80.

18 The subject of Castilian trade and transportation has recently attracted attention. See David Ringrose, "The Government and the Carters in

Spain, 1476-1700," *Ec. H. R.* 22 (1969), 45-57; *Transportation and Economic Stagnation;* and "The Impact of a New Capital City: Madrid, Toledo, and New Castile, 1560-1660," *J. Ec. H.* 33 (1973), 761-91. See also J. H. Elliott, *Imperial Spain, 1469-1716* (New York, 1963), pp. 292-93.

19 Franklin Ford, *Strasbourg in Transition, 1648-1789* (Cambridge, Mass., 1958), pp. 132-33.

20 William Albert, *The Turnpike Road System in England, 1663-1840* (Cambridge, 1972); T. S. Willen, *River Navigation in England, 1600-1750* (Oxford, 1936) and *The English Coasting Trade, 1600-1750* (Manchester, 1938); W. T. Jackman, *The Development of Transportation in Modern England* (London, 1962).

Notes to Chapter 6

1 Quote from Adam Smith, *Wealth of Nations,* Cannon ed., vol. I, p. 299; D. C. Coleman, "Labour in the English Economy of the Seventeenth Century," *Ec. H. R.* 8 (1956), 280-95. Herman Freudenberger, "Das Arbeitsjahr," in Ingomar Bog, et al., eds., *Wirtschaftliche und sociale Strukturen im saekularen Wandel* (Hannover, 1974), vol. III, pp. 307-320.

2 Charles Davenant, "Discourses on the Public Revenues and the Trade of England," in *The Political and Commercial Works of Charles Davenant,* vol. III (London, 1771).

3 Wilhelm Abel, *Agrarkrisen und Agrarkonjunktur,* 2nd ed. (Hamburg-Berlin, 1966), pp. 61-62; Sir William Petty, *Political Arithmetic* (London, 1690); "Considerations on Taxes," (1764), quoted in Paul Mantoux, *The Industrial Revolution in the Eighteenth Century* (London, 1928; reprinted, New York, 1961), p. 62. For a review of mercantilist wage theory see Richard C. Wiles, "The Theory of Wages in Later English Mercantilism," *Ec. H. R.* 21 (1968), 113-26.

4 Pierre Goubert, "The French Peasantry of the Seventeenth Century: A Regional Example," in Trevor Aston, ed., *Crisis in Europe, 1560-1660* (London, 1965), pp. 173-75 and *Beauvais et le Beauvaisis de 1600 à 1730,* 2 vols. (Paris, 1960).

5 For a classic description of these cycles see E. Le Roy Ladurie, "Grand cycle agraire," *Les Paysans de Languedoc,* vol. I, pp. 633-54.

6 See Harry Miskimin, *The Economy of Early Renaissance Europe, 1300-1460* (Englewood Cliffs, N. J., 1969), pp. 90-2, 105-12; R. S. Lopez and Harry Miskimin, "The Economic Depression of the Renaissance," *Ec. H. R.* 14 (1962), 408-26.

7 J. A. Faber, "The Decline of the Baltic Grain Trade in the Second Half of the Seventeenth Century," *Acta Historiae Neerlandica* 1 (1966), 108-31.

8 Jan ten Hoorn, *Naeuw-keurig reys-boek, bysonderlyk dienstig voor*

kooplieden en reysende persoonen (Amsterdam, 1679). A wide-ranging comparative account of material cultures is available in Fernand Braudel, *Capitalism and Material Life, 1400-1800* (New York, 1973).

9 Jan de Vries, "Peasant Demand Patterns in Friesland, 1550-1750," in W. N. Parker and E. L. Jones, eds., *European Peasants and their Markets* (Princeton, 1975).

10 Ruggiero Romano, "Per una valutazione della flotta mercantile europea alla fine del secolo XVIII," in *Studi in onore di Amintore Fanfani*, vol. IV (Milan, 1962); Braudel, *Mediterranean*, pp. 445-47; also see sources in Chapter 4, note 4.

11 De Vries, "Peasant Demand Patterns," Table 13; G. H. Kenyon, "Kirford Inventories, 1611 to 1776, with particular reference to the weald clay farming," *Sussex Archaeological Collections* 93 (1955), 93; Paul Biaroch, "Le rôle de l'agriculture dans la création de la sidérurgie moderne," *Revue d'Histoire Economique et Sociale* 44 (1966), 1-23.

12 W. G. Hoskins, "The Rebuilding of Rural England, 1570-1640," *P. & P.* 4 (1953), 44-59; M. W. Barley, "Farmhouses and Cottages, 1550-1725," *Ec. H. R.* 7 (1955), 291-306; Jan de Vries, *The Dutch Rural Economy in the Golden Age* (New Haven, 1974), pp. 200-02.

13 Concerning university education see Lawrence Stone, "The Educational Revolution in England, 1560-1640," *P. & P.* 28 (1964), 57; Henry Kamen, *The Iron Century* (London, 1971), pp. 284-97. Concerning basic literacy see Carlo Cipolla, *Literacy and Development in the West* (London, 1969); Lawrence Stone, "Literacy and Education in England, 1640-1900," *P. & P.* 42 (1969), 69-139; M. Fleury and A. Valmary, "Les progrès de l'instruction élémentaire de Louis XIV à Napoléon III d'après l'enquête de Louis Maggiolo (1877-1879)," *Population* 12 (1957), 71-92.

14 For descriptions of the French fiscal system see Pierre Goubert, *L'Ancien Régime*, vol. II (Paris, 1973); Martin Wolfe, *The Fiscal System of Renaissance France* (New Haven, 1972); Gabriel Ardant, *Théorie sociologique de l'impôt*, 2 vols. (Paris, 1965).

15 Geoffry Parker, *The Army in Flanders and the Spanish Road* (Cambridge, 1971), pp. 265, 271-72.

16 David G. Chandler, "Armies and Navies," *New Cambridge Modern History*, vol. VI (Cambridge, 1970); D. C. Coleman, "Naval Dockyards under the Later Stuarts," *Ec. H. R.* 6 (1953), 134-55; J. R. Bruijn, *De Admiraliteit van Amsterdam in rustige jaren* (Amsterdam, 1970), pp. 77-78.

17 A. H. John, "War and the English Economy, 1700-63," *Ec. H. R.* 7 (1955), 329-44; for military recruiting see A. Corvisier, *L'Armée française de la fin du XVIIIᵉ siècle au ministère Choiseul*, 2 vols. (Paris, 1968).

18 Quoted in Jaime Vicens Vives, *An Economic History of Spain* (Princeton, 1969), p. 416.

Notes to Chapter 7

1   See W. W. Rostow, "The Take-off into Self-sustained Growth," *Economic Journal* 66 (1956) 25-48, and *The Stages of Economic Growth* (Cambridge, 1960); R. E. Baldwin and G. M. Meier, *Economic Development: theory, history, policy* (New York, 1957), pp. 319-24.

2   Simon Kuznets, "Underdeveloped Countries and the Pre-Industrial Phase in the Advanced Countries," in United Nations, *Proceedings of the World Population Conference, 1954* (New York, 1955) vol. v, pp. 947-68; Phyllis Deane, "Capital Formation in Britain before the Railway Age," *Economic Development and Cultural Change* 9 (1961), 352-68 and *The First Industrial Revolution* (Cambridge, 1965), pp. 5-11; *Two Tracts by Gregory King*, George E. Barnett, ed. (Baltimore, 1936).

3   For a review of interest rates see S. Homer, *A History of Interest Rates* (New Brunswick, N. J., 1963). See also Carlo Cipolla, "Note sulla storia del tasso di interesse," *Economia Internazionale* 5 (1952), 255-74.

4   For the classic statement in support of this view see Karl Marx, *Capital*, vol. I, part 8, "The So-Called Primitive Accumulation," (Foreign Languages Publishing House, Moscow, 1961), 713-74; quote on p. 754.

5   E. Le Roy Ladurie, "Montpellier et sa campagne," *Annales* 13 (1958); G. Roupnel, *La ville et la campagne au XVIIe siècle*, 2nd ed. (Paris, 1955).

6   Robert Forster, *The Nobility of Toulouse in the Eighteenth Century, A Social and Economic Study* (Baltimore, 1960); Jean Sentou, *Fortunes et groupes sociaux à Toulouse sous la Révolution (1789-99); Essai d'histoire statistique* (Toulouse, 1969).

7   Pierre Deyon, *Amiens, capitale provinciale* (Paris, 1967), pp. 294-95, 333-36; Pierre Goubert, *Familles marchandes sous l'Ancien Régime: Les Danse et les Motte, de Beauvais* (Paris, 1959); Franklin Ford, *Robe and Sword, The Regrouping of the French Aristocracy after Louis XIV* (Cambridge, Mass., 1953), pp. 147-70.

8   Henri See, *Economic and Social Conditions in France During the Eighteenth Century* (New York, 1927), pp. 202-03; S. J. Woolf, "Economic Problems of the Nobility in the Early Modern Period: The Example of Piedmont," *Ec. H. R.* 16 (1964), 267-83; J. M. Roberts, "Lombardy," in Albert Goodwin, ed., *The European Nobility in the Eighteenth Century* (New York, 1967), pp. 60-82. For further examples of this phenomenon see Ruth Pike, *Aristocrats and Traders: Sevillian Society in the Sixteenth Century* (Ithaca, N. Y., 1972); George Taylor, "Non-capitalist Wealth and the Origins of the French Revolution," *A. H. R.* 72 (1967), 469-96.

9   B. Bennassar, *Valladolid au siècle d'or* (Paris, 1967) pp. 215-19; John Stoye, *Europe Unfolding, 1648-1688* (New York, 1969), pp. 117-18.

10 Max Weber, *The Protestant Ethic and the Spirit of Capitalism* (New York, 1958) p. 17.

11 On the development of public debt see R. Ashton, *The Crown and the Money Market, 1603-1640* (Oxford, 1960); P. G. M. Dickson, *The Financial Revolution in England: A Study in the Development of Public Credit, 1688-1756* (London, 1967); Alvaro Castillo Pintado, "Dans la monarchie espagnole du XVIIe siècles: Les banquers Portugaise et le circuit d'Amsterdam," *Annales* 19 (1964), 311-15 and "Los juros de Castilla. Apogeo y fin de un instrumento de crédito," *Hispania, Revista española de historia* 23 (1963), 43-70; Earl J. Hamilton, "Public Debt: History, Origin, and Growth of the National Debt in Western Europe," *American Economic Review* 37 (1947), 118-30. On mortgage market development see H. J. Habakkuk, "English Landownership: 1660-1740," *Ec. H. R.* 10 (1940), 2-17 and "introduction" to Mary E. Finch, *The Wealth of Five Northamptonshire Families, 1540-1640* (Northampton, 1956); Charles Jago, "The Influence of Debt on the Relations between Crown and Aristocracy in Seventeenth-Century Castile," *Ec. H. R.* 26 (1973), 218-36.

12 K. G. Davis, "Joint Stock Investment in the Later Seventeenth Century," *Ec. H. R.* 4 (1952), 300.

13 H. Luethy, *La banque protestante en France de la Révocation de l'Edit de Nantes à la Révolution* (Paris, 1959); Jacob M. Price, *France and the Chesapeake* (Ann Arbor, Mich., 1973); pp. 196-267.

14 N. W. Posthumus, "The Tulip Mania in Holland in the Years 1636 and 1637," *Journal of Economic and Business History* 1 (1929), 434-66; E. H. Krelage, *Bloemenspeculatie in Nederland* (Amsterdam, 1942); Charles Wilson, *Anglo-Dutch Commerce and Finance in the Eighteenth Century* (Cambridge, 1941).

15 R. de Roover, *L'évolution de la lettre de change du XIVe au XVIIIe siècle* (Paris, 1953); Joseph Sperling, "The International Payments Mechanism in the Seventeenth and Eighteenth Centuries," *Ec. H. R.* 14 (1962), 446-68; Jose Gentil da Silva, *Banque et credit en Italie au XVIIe siècle*, 2 vols. (Paris, 1969).

16 J. G. van Dillen, *History of the Principal Public Banks* (The Hague, 1934) and *Van rijkdom en regenten* (The Hague, 1970), pp. 256-69, 439-60; Violet Barbour, *Capitalism in Amsterdam in the 17th Century* (Baltimore, 1950), pp. 43-59.

17 J. H. Clapham, *The Bank of England: a history*, 2 vols. (Cambridge, 1944); Rondo Cameron, *Banking in the Early Stages of Industrialization; a study in comparative economic history*, (New York, 1967), pp. 15-59.

18 See Jacob Price, *France and the Chesapeake*, 2 vols. (Ann Arbor, Mich., 1973) for a detailed description of the workings of court capitalism. See also George V. Taylor, "Non capitalist Wealth and the Origins of the French Revolution," *A. H. R.* 72 (1967), 469-96; R. B. Grassby, "Social Status and Commercial Enterprise under Louis XIV," *Ec. H. R.* 13 (1960), 19-38, Heinrich Schnee, *Die Hoffinanz und der moderne Staat*, 5 vols. (Berlin, 1953-65).

19 A detailed defense of this argument for France is available in Pierre Goubert, *The Ancien Regime,* vol. I (New York, 1973), particularly pp. 135-38, 188-92.

Notes to Chapter 8

1 This interpretation is identified with Eli Heckscher, *Mercantilism,* 2 vols. (London, 1935). It dates from a much earlier time, however. See Gustav Schmoller, *The Mercantile System and Its Historical Significance* (London, 1895).

2 Jacob van Klaveren, "Fiscalism, Mercantilism and Corruption," originally published in *V. S. W. G.* 47 (1960), reprinted in the excellent introduction to the debate on mercantilism: D. C. Coleman, ed., *Revisions in Mercantilism* (London, 1969), pp. 140-61. See also Herbert Heaton, "Heckscher on Mercantilism," *Journal of Political Economy* 45 (1937), 370-93, partially reprinted in another useful collection on the subject, W. E. Minchinton, ed., *Mercantilism, System or Expedient* (Lexington, Mass., 1969), pp. 46-50.

3 David Parker, "The Social Foundation of French Absolutism, 1610-1630," *P. & P.* 53 (1971), 67-85.

4 Barry Supple, *Commercial Crisis and Change in England, 1600-1642* (Cambridge, 1959), pp. 226-27.

5 This matter has inspired a lengthy debate. See Joseph Sperling, "The International Payments Mechanism in the Seventeenth and Eighteenth Centuries," *Ec. H. R.* 14 (1962), 446-68; Charles Wilson, "Treasure and the Trade Balance: The Mercantilist Problem," *Ec. H. R.* 2 (1949), 152-61; Jacob Price, "Multilateralism and/or Bilateralism," *Ec. H. R.* 14 (1961), 254-74.

6 The clearest affirmation of this view is found in Supple, *Crisis and Change.* See also Charles Wilson, "The Other Face of Mercantilism," *Transactions of the Royal Historical Society* 9 (1959), 81-101.

7 Martin Wolfe, "French Views on Wealth and Taxes from the Middle Ages to the Old Regime," *J. Ec. H.* 26 (1966), 476.

8 Fernand Braudel and Frank Spooner, "Prices in Europe from 1450 to 1750," in *Cambridge Economic History of Europe,* vol. IV (Cambridge, 1967), pp. 395-400; C. W. J. Granger and C. M. Elliott, "A Fresh Look at Wheat Prices and Markets in the Eighteenth Century," *Ec. H. R.* 20 (1969), 257-65; Walter Achilles, "Getreidepreise und Getreidehandelsbeziehungen europäischer Räume im 16. und 17. Jahrhundert," *Zeitschrift für Agrargeschichte und Agrarsoziologie* 7 (1959), 32-55. In the seventeenth century, while northwestern European markets were becoming better connected to one another, markets within Poland and Italy demonstrated weaker correlations. See Achilles, p. 54 and E. Sereni, *Capitalismo e mercato nazionale in Italia* (Rome, 1966), p. 61.

9 Phyllis Deane, "Capital Formation in Britain before the Railway Age," *Economic Development and Cultural Change* 9 (1961), 352-68; François Crouzet, "La formation du capital en Grande Bretagne

pendant la révolution industrielle," *Second International Conference of Economic History,* 1962, vol. 2 (Paris, 1965), pp. 589-642.

10 The phrase is that of J. D. Chambers, *Population, Economy, and Society in Pre-Industrial England* (Oxford, 1972), p. 50.

11 Edward Whiting Fox, *History in Geographic Perspective* (New York, 1971); Ralph Davis, *The Rise of the Atlantic Economies* (Ithaca, N. Y., 1973), p. 227.

Index